I0080235

FISHING FOR THE VILLAGE

CREATING A DISCIPLE-MAKING COMMUNITY THAT BRINGS HEAVEN TO EARTH

CASSIE CARSTENS & GEORGE KELLERMAN

Fishing for the Village
© 2020 Cassie Carstens & George Kellerman

All rights reserved. No part of this publication may be reproduced, stored in a retrieval system or transmitted in any form or by any means, including electronically, mechanically, by photocopying or recording, without the prior written permission of George Kellerman and Cassie Carstens. No responsibility for any loss incurred by any person acting or refraining from action as a result of the material in this publication will be accepted by the authors or anyone involved in the production of this book.

While we have tried our best to avoid copyright infringement on any level, we would like to apologise if there are any unintentional infringements, and request that any legitimately aggrieved party contact the authors to rectify the matter. We would like to acknowledge and thank everyone who has contributed to this work on any level.

Editor: David Liprini
Cover Design: Paula Dubois
Cover Illustration: Paula Dubois
Design: Paula Dubois
Contributors: GK: George Kellerman, CC: Cassie Carstens,
CW: Carel Wandrag, JY: John Yip

Printed by **novus print**, a division of Novus Holdings
First edition 2020

ISBN 978-0-6398382-0-5 (Print)
ISBN 978-0-6398388-1-6 (ebook)

CONTENTS

Unless otherwise specified, all Scripture references are taken from the NIV translation of the Bible.

ACKNOWLEDGEMENTS

The writing of this book has been a real team effort. We would like to acknowledge the following people and groups who have contributed in immense ways to the completion of this book.

Cassie

One of my greatest joys ever was to write this book with my son, George. Discussing God and Kingdom work together has always given our relationship deeper value! Working on this book gave me an opportunity to pin down some fundamentals in my theology and filled me with a deep gratitude for the people — starting with my mom and dad — who helped shape this understanding of the Gospel in my life.

I have become very intentional about discipleship over the last few years. Unsurprisingly, during these years I have also "felt the fellowship" of the body of Christ more than ever before. Nothing has enriched my life more than my disciples. As this book reflects our journey, I pray that your hearts will be filled with the joy of the Lord and delight in our precious journey together.

My wife, Jenny, has shaped more of my understanding of God and his Kingdom than she or I could ever realise. She is my closest spiritual partner, and all that I say flows from both of our hearts.

My family, as the "first church", has experienced Kingdom in a beautiful way. What a joy to see how God has dispersed himself in you!

George

Thank you, Dad, for venturing into this project of putting words on paper together. It has been one of the most rewarding and satisfying things I have ever done in my life.

To the Wille Manne (Frankie, Muller, Herman, Gerhard, Daniel, Ruan, Jurie, Johan and Attie): every chapter of this book was written with your disciple-making journey in mind. Thank you for pushing me closer to God.

George and Cassie

First and foremost, we want to give thanks to Jesus Christ, the Holy Spirit and God the Father: May this book bring you glory.

Our discipleship family: We wrote this book to help you in your disciple-making as a super useful tool to build the Kingdom.

Co-authors Carel Wandrag and John Yip: We know what it takes to put a chapter together. We appreciate your wisdom and contribution.

Our editor, David Liprini: In a way, it feels like you are the author of this book when we consider all the corrections and edits you made. Without you, we would have never finished this book. Your insights, passion and patience have made it possible for us to put this manuscript together.

Our designer, Paula Dubois: Thank you for taking our words and wrapping them in beauty.

The reviewing team: We really appreciate your patience, effort and attention to detail.

The prayer team: Thank you for standing in the gap in difficult times.

The interviewees who shared their amazing stories: Bassem Emad, Casper Steenkamp, Hammie van Zyl, Johan Horn, Stiaan & Stephanie Dippenaar, Dorette de Kock, Dumisani Madondile, Inge Wandrag, Ruan Cilliers, Hein Reyneke, Zirk & Charne Kay and Marko & Maxie Pretorius. This book is in large part a recollection of all your teachings and stories.

The authors of all the brilliant books we reference and quote: Your hard work, revelations and insights are the rich soil in which this book has grown.

Our disciplers, disciples, tables of support and faith communities: May this book be a reflection of our DNA.

INTRODUCTION

—•—

Cassie Carstens

A few years ago, the following questions started churning through our community of believers:

What did Jesus mean by "Go and make disciples..."
during his last recorded conversation on earth?
What is the significance of those words and are we
really making disciples?

These questions struck a nerve in me when my father stepped down from active preaching to dedicate most of his time to a small group of people.

"Why?" I asked him.

"Well, is that not similar to what Jesus did?"

His decision to dedicate his life to investing in a small group of people awoke an urgency in me. It was a clear shift in my understanding and pursuit of disciple-making. And so my journey began.

As our community wrestled with these questions, we experienced momentous life changes. Similar themes and principles were affirmed during conversations, both within the group and with others. This book is a collection of these themes. Our discipleship community has discovered treasures we wished we knew long ago — glimpses of heaven in our community, and echoes of heaven impacting the world.

The title "Fishing for the Village" is a phrase we use within our discipleship community which we borrowed from a Fijian friend of ours. You can find the whole story in chapter two but, in short, when we fish (do something), we fish for the village (for the benefit of the entire community). With this mindset, our community has experienced a taste of heaven on earth. The title of the book also refers to discipling (fishing). Our hope is that communities will impact the world by fishing villages.

One of the most passionate voices on discipleship I know is the co-author of this book, Cassie Carstens. I asked him to reflect on his journey with discipleship.

Was disciple-making always a high priority for you?

The best way to describe the first seasons of my pastoral ministry would be to say that my spiritual and emotional motivations did not match up.

Spiritually, I wanted people to be in awe of God, to have Jesus as their personal Saviour and King, and to live in obedience to the guidance of the Holy Spirit in a faith community that impacts the world. All good!

Emotionally — I have realised this in retrospect — I was trying to impress. I had the vice president and four cabinet ministers in my first church. I did not want to look like a fool! In the second church I pastored this trend continued — I was the pastor of my university professors! The emotional pressure mounted. Then I moved into full-time youth ministry. To keep their interest, you simply have to impress!

By most accounts the results of my first 20 years of ministry were good, but if you had asked me if my ministry created disciple-making Kingdom warriors, my answer would have been: "not enough!" We spent too much time trying to impress, to be the centre of activity, instead of empowering others to empower more! As a result, there were too many passive admirers of Jesus. A shift needed to take place.

What shifted you towards having disciple-making as such a high priority?

The first shift within me happened through founding two leadership training institutes. It forced a shift in my orientation; from me being the central leader to equipping others for their work. The shift from

ME to THEM was already helpful, but it was a visit to Moldova where I saw intentional disciple-making that helped me turn the corner. I met a young discipleship group where some of them would hike in the snow for 200 kilometres on a weekly basis to disciple people. They had to do push-ups along the road to keep themselves warm. I saw and felt something I had never seen before. Now my spirit was receptive to more disciple-making stimuli. Seeing real discipleship, where young disciple-makers demonstrated a total commitment towards making disciples, had the emotional impact I needed at that stage.

Then I read about the history of the life of the early church in Rodney Stark's writings. The way the early church grew so phenomenally in the first 300 years caught my attention. I saw how the church can impact the world — a desperate need of our time! At the same time my wife and I worked in a township and I saw the impotence of the church there. The church had minimal influence in a sex- and alcohol-besotted environment. While doing that work, I travelled around the world and trained leaders from at least 40 nations every year, many of whom were pastors. Extensive research amongst them exposed how improbable it was that the church could provide answers for the needs of the world if it carried on with the same attractional Sunday-centred ministry.

The results of my research convinced me that we had to move our attention back to the early church approach. We needed to experience their worship, their time together, their sharing of financial burdens, their passion to reach the world, their compassion for those in need, their transparency, their study of the Word, their discipline, and so on. I was convinced that true disciple-making is the only strategic answer for our world in need.

What does your discipleship community look like?

I am currently responsible for 28 disciples across three groups. The first group comprises couples whom my wife and I disciple, the second is a handful of pastors whom I disciple and the third is a group of men in ministry whom I disciple. I see them at least once a month in groups and once a month or once every second month individually. We also have two weekend camps a year where we focus on creating the "tribal fire" (ethos) and entrenching key principles of the movement. Between these gatherings there are various interactions. We encourage every disciple to make disciples of Jesus, who will in turn also make disciples. In some cases, we already have six generations of disciples. We represent all the race groups in South Africa and come from a variety of churches.

There are so many books on discipleship. Why did you help write this one?

Before answering that question, I need to share something important. In no way are we saying we are perfect and have achieved success that demands attention. We still fall short in so many areas. We are not writing from the viewpoint of a professor teaching the student. These pages are a passionate call for all followers of Jesus to earnestly seek to make disciples of Jesus.

Having said that, our main reason for writing this book is to formulate our tribal language. Like all languages it will grow and adapt, but we had to start somewhere! When this tribe (our discipleship movement) got going in 2012, we started by asking ourselves what Jesus meant by "the Kingdom of God on earth as it is in heaven." We were thrilled with what we read about it, but very disappointed by what we saw as a demonstration of this.

We were convinced that our lives were supposed to be all about the Kingdom of God, but who would train us to live this life? Obviously, it should have been parents first and parish — the culture at church — second. But sadly, we felt that both have, with some inspirational exceptions, lost the heartbeat of this life. It seems that parents and parish have succeeded in teaching us how to believe in Jesus, but not how to live Jesus. Salvation was clear, but Kingdom not. Now, we felt that the Spirit wanted to resuscitate both family and church again.

We were convinced that our disciple-making movement should be a response to the call of the Spirit: Live! Live! (Ezek 16:6). We were desperate and inspired to find a way to live the Kingdom of God on earth as it is in heaven. We desired Jesus' Kingdom DNA to dictate our life on earth. We simply had to find a way of having heaven on earth and of bringing heaven home! This book looks at the key Kingdom principles that we believe will usher in heaven on earth.

THIS BOOK IS OUR TRIBAL LANGUAGE FOR NOW, BUT WE WANT EVERYONE TO HELP US MAKE IT BETTER

This book is our tribal language for now, but we want everyone to help us make it better. We want the language to develop in homes and on the streets, not in academic laboratories. We want this language to have one origin: the Word of God!

We have also written this book to inspire others. If you want to learn how the Kingdom of God could be lived in our day and age, or what it means to live with a Kingdom DNA, this book may help. If you want disciple-making to be a priority in your life, you will find theoretical and practical stimulation in this book. Many good books have been written about discipleship lately, but too few present a good framework or show enough practical application of biblical truths.

What would this book "reaching its goal" look like to you?

This book summarises the key principles of disciple-making as we see it and talks about our ethos (the way we do things). Even if it only benefits our community of disciples, it will have been worth the effort. Additionally, many young leaders worldwide have expressed interest in whole life coaching (mentoring) and holistic discipling. This book is a beneficial pathway for a deeper understanding of both pursuits.

This book is a marvellous tool for anyone interested in discipleship. It is specifically useful for those seeking a framework for practical discipleship or for those trying to understand the heart of discipleship.

Ultimately, we want Jesus to be pleased that this book contributed to the purifying of the church and to the growth of the Kingdom.

What would you consider the goal of a discipleship movement in our context?

We want our discipleship community to be part of the recalibration of the church in South Africa towards Kingdom purposes. Not enough pastors in Africa are involved in disciple-making. It would be wonderful if our community could have a catalytic impact in advancing disciple-making interest in South Africa. For better local impact we want our movement not only to grow deeper, but also wider. We have seen how the movement has contributed to reconciliation in South Africa and lifting financial burdens of the poor. By growing the movement, we will enlarge its impact as well.

Have you discovered key reasons why some disciples leave church or disciple-making?

As a pastor, I found that most people left because church was not entertaining enough or because another church was more entertaining or convenient. In the discipleship movement, people leave when they do not want to be held accountable, when their work consumes too much energy or when disciple-making is not their primary purpose in life. When the fundamentals of selfless sacrificial life are not solid, all sorts of problems emerge. If they do not crucify the ego, their relationship with God is conditional and relationships with others are contractual.

The cross — in this case, our cross — stands as the essential starting block for this race of life. This implies a constant battle with inner pride and a regular confession and acknowledgement of our dependence on God and others. This is counterintuitive to the trends of our time, but essential as the entrance pass to the Kingdom. We keep coming back to this point of living a selfless, sacrificial life because we need to eat it, assimilate it, speak it and live it consistently. When something goes wrong or there is any complaint, we go back to the start and depart from this point of self-denial again.

This is a good place to end the interview with that reminder: to live a sacrificial life. And this is also a good opportunity for you to start this book at the right place: at the cross.

HOW TO READ THIS BOOK

We wrote this as a workbook for discipleship groups to discuss together. We identified key discipleship principles, but the principles are so deep we could turn each one into a book. Instead of that level of detail, we captured the core of each principle and fleshed it out with Scripture, stories and practical examples to help it come alive. If you want to dig deeper into the topics we discuss, the books we recommend at the end of each chapter go into more detail.

The goal is not to read this book in one sitting. We hope you will mull over it, one chapter at a time. There are reflection questions, suggested Scripture readings and suggested books to read at the end of each chapter. To get the best out of the book, we suggest you read a chapter, read the suggested Scriptures and discuss the reflection questions with your discipleship group (or group of friends). Instead of using it as a manual or reading a chapter at your discipleship group gatherings, rather use it as pre-reading to frame discussions.

In some chapters you will find a section titled "What we do." In these sections we give glimpses of how we have applied the principle of the chapter. Our application of the principles might change over time, but we shared some of our stories to make this book more practical and less theoretical. These principles have changed our lives; may they change your life as well. Enjoy!

1

WHY DISCIPLESHIP

Why we are convinced that true discipleship is essential, and what it is all about

If you want an easy, unopposed, persecution-free life,
then you should keep your faith to yourself
and not make disciples.
But if you want the world to change and Christ to rule
in and through everyone and everything,
disciple-making is the only way.
Disciple-making requires total attention and
devotion to becoming like Christ,
and helping others to become like Christ,
not only believing in Christ.
In the Gospels, following Jesus and making disciples
is seen as one thing.
We must ask ourselves: can we be called Christians
if we do not make disciples?

1.1 GAME CHANGERS

—•—

George Kellerman

I am sitting on the steps of an embankment overlooking the grass field where a soccer game is being played by children of all ages. Tents of the overnight campers form the boundary line of the makeshift soccer field. All major South African ethnic groups are represented — black, white, brown — but nobody notices. It is a beautiful picture: various cultures and age groups blending beautifully and seamlessly. Adults interact in the shade of the trees — a few in serious discussion, while others converse in a more relaxed manner. Some people are swimming, others are drinking coffee and the fit ones have gone for a run up the mountain. I take photos of the people from my vantage point, trying to capture the idyllic moment.

There are so many people I would love to talk to if only the sun could stand still. I have not seen some of them in a long time, and others are grandfather-like people who give the wisest advice. And there are so many people with miraculous stories of how God has used them to impact the world in a massive way — it would be great to catch up with them. Looking over this group of beautiful people, the thought which has been echoing throughout the weekend surfaces again: "Is this not heaven on earth?"

I am at the bi-annual weekend gathering of our discipleship family. (By "discipleship family" I mean the network of groups of people who have disciple-making as their main priority.) These camps are major occasions for us, marking the only time we get together as one big family. This weekend has been an inspiring and life-enriching time, discovering together what Jesus meant when he said, "Go and make disciples" during his final speech on earth. A break in our busy weekend schedule has allowed me to drink in and savour this moment.

My contemplative state does not last long though. Someone walks by and introduces himself. I discover that it is his first time joining our wider community at one of these camps. We strike up a good conversation and chat about what we have learned this weekend. He explains how deeply the atmosphere amongst this group of people has impacted him — an atmosphere he has not experienced before.

"I see a love for Jesus, a dedication towards disciple-making and a desire to impact the world in each person I talk to. How did this DNA form in a community as big as this?"

"Well…" I started, wondering how to answer him. The most wholesome response would probably be input from my discipleship family friends, so I pointed to a group of them.

"… Let's ask them!" We walked over and I introduced my newfound friend, then relayed his question, adjusting it slightly to make it more personal.

"What was the game-changer that captured your attention for disciple-making?"

CAREL *(an actuary working for a multinational company and his wife, Inge, a stay-at-home mom and community builder/connector)*

The game-changer: living completely transparently with a group of people.

The game-changer for us was when we discovered that total transparency with a group of trusted people is actually possible. We could ask a difficult direct question to anyone within the group with no judgement or rejection.

We discovered this truth when we committed to radical transparency on sensitive issues such as sexuality and how we spend our money. It was especially scary at the beginning because we shared deep things we had not told anyone else. And it wasn't always comfortable. The group helped us see our blind spots and gently exposed our

> **THE GAME-CHANGER FOR US WAS WHEN WE DISCOVERED THAT TOTAL TRANSPARENCY WITH A GROUP OF TRUSTED PEOPLE IS ACTUALLY POSSIBLE**

weaknesses. But as the discipleship friendships developed, the radical transparency fostered a freedom and safety in the group we had never experienced before. We could share major decisions in this community with ease, which led to security and a feeling of oneness which we had always dreamt of. It also helped many of us sort out family and marriage issues which had lingered for years. We didn't need to carry the load by ourselves anymore!

Radical transparency thus brought radical freedom. It served as an example of how the body of Christ can be a counter-cultural force bringing freedom to many. We can now see how followers of Jesus can really become the "people of the light" spoken of in the Bible.

The total transparency we practised made it possible to keep a close eye on the dark places in each other's lives. And instead of having to chase it, accountability became a natural result of the openness and realness in our community. The honest sharing and loving confrontation led us to many new discoveries about God and his Kingdom.

STIAAN *(a high school teacher)*
The game-changer: when strong spiritual authority exists in an organic movement.

In our discipleship movement relationship is the big driver, not structure. Because the structure is loose and flexible and there are no paid staff, members don't have to wait for structure to determine their involvement. The organic (though intentional) way relationships grow and motivate people towards Kingdom living and Kingdom purpose is refreshing in a "religious" culture where people wait for external impulses to motivate them. The lack of structure also helps those involved take initiative themselves.

Discipleship allows someone (or a team) to have spiritual authority over your life. This was a big game-changer for me. Now I freely allow trusted people the authority to speak boldly into my life and tell me where I am not thinking or acting like Jesus. I am under a healthy spiritual covering for the first time, which is only really possible if someone knows me well enough. Because discipleship pushes relationships to be more intimate, it allows for spiritual authority to exist in a healthy way.

Holistic discipleship also moves discipleship from a purely spiritual level to a whole life level. It is amazing to sit with a mentor and ask deeply personal questions about anything pertaining to my life, knowing that we will ask that Jesus leads us together.

Spiritual accountability in discipleship relationships results in a strong commitment and a sense of responsibility between Jesus-followers. When our group committed to practise following Jesus together, it created a sense of co-responsibility for each other's spiritual walks with God. It was no longer just I (or my wife and I) who walked with God together. It became an us (a community) walking with God together, which also meant I became responsible for my peers' disciples' walk with God. This was a game-changer for our group. It changed the way we pray, the way we interacted with each other, the way we practised our calling, the way we spent our time — it changed everything!

I love that the disciple-making movement is very much focused on building the Kingdom. That doesn't necessarily mean motivating others to join the movement. The focus is always on helping those growing the Kingdom to be effective Kingdom builders wherever God has called them. It is amazing to be part of a team that thinks and dreams about building the Kingdom first and foremost.

DORETTE *(medical doctor)*
The game-changer: when the discipleship group has a clear outward focus.

I started my disciple making journey with a group of fellow students in my second year of medical school. Second year is known for being the most taxing year for any med student, so it is a bit ironic that this was the year that things changed for me. As a student group of Jesus-followers, we changed things up that year and organised a camp for teenagers instead of having our usual getaway retreat as a student body. At the camp I mentored a small group of teenage girls, which was a new experience for me. My entire life at that stage consisted of being fully focused on campus life — my studies and the upkeep of my vibrant social life. But at that camp, all my focus and energy was on serving and impacting that small group of teenagers. Although the camp drained me mentally and physically, I had never felt more alive than during that weekend. That camp was a catalyst, and something huge shifted within me. I tasted what it meant to live a purpose-driven outward-focused life. My primary purpose shifted from passing my studies and becoming a good doctor towards discipling teenagers.

THE DYNAMIC SHIFTED FROM AN INWARD CONCERN TO AN OUTWARD-FOCUSED GROUP

That weekend camp was a game-changing event for our student group as well. The dynamic shifted from an inward concern to an outward-focused group. Since then we haven't been the same. We found our purpose in discipling teenagers, and God moved in mighty ways amongst us. In one weekend we shifted from complaining about class and praying for the next exam to being a group of Kingdom-minded disciplers. From a group trying to find our calling, we became a group living our calling of disciple-making every day.

Risking my academic performance was a simple sacrifice to disciple the teenagers. The incredible thing was that God made it possible for me to study two-thirds less than my peers, but still maintain my academic performance. I was able to spend those two-thirds in investing my life into the teenagers. Time was never an excuse for me. Actually, time seemed to multiply when I gave it away. Finding the time and energy to invest in others gets more and more difficult as a doctor, but it cannot take away my desire and urge to disciple people. It is my primary purpose after all!

DUMISANI *(soccer coach)*

The game-changer: when each team member is a disciple-maker.

I am a soccer coach from a big township in South Africa. I grew up in a traditional church which believes that discipleship is doing one program after another, and you achieve spiritual maturity by becoming a church leader. This was exhausting and it seemed out of my reach, so I didn't really bother trying.

My story only started when someone explained to me that disciple-making is a movement and something even I could start. It was a simple understanding of journeying with someone as they journey with others. As we invest in a few they are also teaching others, and by doing that we can reach the city.

There was a field notorious for gang activity in our community, so I went there to look for "the few". I saw a group of young men standing around looking mischievous, undoubtedly part of a local gang. I felt compassion for them and for my threatened community, so I approached them. Since I could coach soccer, I offered to coach them. They agreed. We started our soccer practice and for a few weeks we had a good time. Until the day an opposing gang member came to our practice and stabbed one of my players (not fatally, thankfully). I arrived late on the scene to see my team, each one with a knife in hand, ready to take revenge.

Then the moment that changed everything. I tried to calm them and explained that the best revenge they could take was to keep on playing soccer to show the other gang what it means to have joy, something they surely are jealous of. By some miracle my team obliged and carried on playing. That event bonded us. I could then share with them the joys of following Jesus, and the joyous life he gives. My team changed.

I taught them how to read the Bible and hear the voice of God for themselves. I taught them how to pray. Their lives changed dramatically, to the point where they were walking the streets with Bibles under their arms instead of knives in their pockets. I taught them how to disciple others and quickly they formed gangs of Jesus followers. They asked about church, but I realised that they would not fit into any local church, so we started meeting on Sundays. Other children joined, as well as a few adults. Ex-convicts and ex-gangsters felt comfortable coming.

I quickly realised that this small disciple-making movement could become a church program again if we were not careful. So I reminded them regularly that discipleship is about a disciple-making movement. I taught them that they are subjects of ministry, not objects of ministry. I would disciple them as they disciple others. We believe each follower of Jesus should be involved in intentional disciple-making.

Soon, these ex-convicts and ex-gangsters were discipling others. This was the big game-changer for our group. It changed the whole dynamic of the group when each person was discipling one or more others. Each time we gathered, they were not complaining about life and holding out their hands to beg for attention. No, most of our conversations were about how to equip and better disciple their disciples. When we gather, our focus isn't on rehabilitating each other. No, when we gather, we primarily aim to reach more people for Jesus. What a joy in seeing ex-druggies, ex-gangsters and ex-convicts reaching the city for Jesus.

Shifts

"Do you think your discipleship family is perfect?" my new friend asked the group.

No! What we have is a taste of the new... or rather, the taste of the old true discipleship in a new context. We have discovered so much about discipleship! Things like selfless, sacrificial life, jour-neying with an intimate community, immediate obedience, impact-ing spheres of society and much more. This will be a long journey guided by the Holy Spirit and the Word, but we believe we are head-ing in the right direction.

As you read in those stories, massive shifts came about in the dynamics of the teams they journeyed with. Note these shifts in the person and in the dynamics of each team. Then ask yourself if these shifts are possible within your group and community.

After hearing these stories, is there not an excitement bubbling within you at the idea that the early community of believers (as described in Acts) is more likely than you originally thought?

We are excited to see many more stories unfold in our movement as we discover deeper realities of discipleship. We wrote this book to capture the stories, key principles, key biblical truths and practical applications we have discovered during our journey of discipleship and disciple-making. Join us on this life-changing journey of discovery as we spur one another on to obey the words of Jesus to "Go and make disciples" (Matt 28:19)!

1.2 AM I QUALIFIED TO MAKE DISCIPLES?

—•—

George Kellerman

I was leading a cell group for university students a few years back. After a year, we were the size of a small church spread across four groups. It struck me that I was largely responsible for guiding them in their understanding of Christianity and discipleship. They asked difficult questions, many of which I didn't know how to answer. I felt very unqualified. In all honesty, I was unqualified! I tried to avoid the responsibility, but realised that even if I could ignore it, the gap would remain. They wouldn't go to anyone else to ask the difficult questions because there wasn't really anyone else. Maybe you feel the same: responsible to make disciples, but unsure if you are qualified.

During the time of Jesus, discipleship (training) was reserved for the elite scholars. Ray Vander Laan explains the stringent disciple qualification as follows:

> "Children began their study at age 4-5 in Beth Sefer (elementary school)… The teaching focused primarily on the Torah, emphasising both reading and writing Scripture. Large portions were memorised and it is likely that many students knew the entire Torah by memory by the time this level of education was finished. At this point most students (and certainly the girls) stayed at home to help with the family and in the case of boys to learn the family trade… The best students continued their study (while learning a trade) in Beth Midrash (secondary school)." [1]

Only elite students could dedicate their lives to learn from the revered rabbis of the time. Many (like Peter, John and James) simply didn't qualify. They had to pick up the family trade and carry on with life. There must have been a sense of inferiority for these guys, and many of us feel the same way nowadays — inferior, not quite good enough to make disciples. "Disciple-making is reserved for the mature guys, the leaders, the pastors, isn't it?"

"I have too much stuff to sort out in my life before I can disciple people."

"If I am so messed up, how can I disciple other people?"

"I am not ready. I am not qualified."

These are some of the reasons I have heard over the years for not starting the disciple-making journey. I generally respond as follows:

"Yes, you are unqualified, but fortunately discipleship is not about pointing people to you and your performance. It is about pointing people to Jesus."

In its simplest form, disciple-making is about pointing people to Jesus. Pointing people to Jesus requires (for integrity's sake) your life-example to be pointed to Jesus as well. Therefore, it does not permit you to compromise your pursuit to become like Jesus. The point here is to shift the focus and attention away from yourself, and to help fix people's eyes on Jesus.

You might be too scared to make mistakes, but doing nothing will not help the cause either. Your inaction will not fill the gaps. Whether you want the responsibility or not, there are people who need you to point them to Jesus. If you ignore the responsibility, the gap will remain unfilled, and others could suffer because of it.

One of those guys who didn't make the cut after the first discipleship interview was Peter. He tried and failed at discipleship and had to return to the family trade — fishing.

But then Jesus stepped into his life.

As per usual, Peter and his brothers and some friends went out to fish at night. This particular evening was very uneventful. The fish just didn't want to bite. They tried all night, but they were unsuccessful after hours of trying, and returned to shore. The next day they saw a popular rabbi come along, followed by a handful of people. Before long, so many had joined that the rabbi needed to use a boat as a vantage point to address the crowd gathered on the shore. Jesus (you saw that coming, didn't you?) asked to use Peter's boat. After teaching the crowd, Jesus had a chat with him. Peculiarly, he suggested Peter go out and fish again. Bemused, Peter responded, "Master, we've worked hard all night and haven't caught anything. But because you say so, I will let down the nets" (Luke 5:5). The story continued as follows:

"When they had done so, they caught such a large number of fish that their nets began to break. So they signalled their partners in the other boat to come and help them, and they came and filled both boats so full that they began to sink. When Simon Peter saw this, he fell at Jesus' knees and said, 'Go away from me, Lord; I am a sinful man!' For he and all his companions were astonished at the catch of fish they had taken, and so were James and John, the sons of Zebedee, Simon's partners. Then Jesus said to Simon, 'Don't be afraid; from now on you will fish for people.' So, they pulled their boats up on shore, left everything and followed him" (Luke 5:6-11).

Let's look at a few takeaways from this story.

When Jesus offered Peter the chance to become a disciple-maker, Peter replied, "Go away from me, Lord; I am a sinful man!" (Luke 5:8).

That wasn't a thanks-but-no-thanks response from Peter. It was more of a please-don't-waste-your-time-on-me response. However, Jesus wasn't perturbed. I imagine he looked Peter in the eye, the corners of his mouth lifting in a smile as he responded:

"Don't be afraid; from now on you will fish for people" (Luke 5:10).

Hey Peter / (insert your name here), I don't care if you weren't the best Sunday-school student, or if you still have issues to sort out, or if you don't think you are ready. If you are willing, drop your nets (your current concerns) and see how the Lord will work in and through you.

If you feel you are too sinful, too broken, unqualified or unprepared, look up at Jesus. When you catch his eye, you will realise he is looking directly at you with that same gentle, knowing smile at the corners of his mouth. "Don't be afraid; from now on, you will be a fisher of men and women." The invitation to share the Kingdom of heaven is not reserved for the perfect or the ready. It never was. If you want to be part of it, look to him and borrow the words of Samuel. "Speak, for your servant is listening" (1 Sam 3:10).

Peter had to learn an important lesson about disciple-making before he committed to do so a few hours later. There was a significant link between the "fish for people" promise of Jesus and the miracle of the big catch that day. Before understanding what Jesus meant by "fishing for people", Peter had to understand that this type of fishing would depend on God, not on Peter's own skill or understanding. Peter and his friends tried to catch fish the whole night, but relying on their own ability they were unsuccessful. They did not even catch one fish! The next morning Jesus challenged them to go and fish again, and out of respect for the rabbi they obeyed his command. This time they caught so many fish that their boat and the boat next to them started to sink.

This "fishing" referred to by Jesus is not based on qualification or ability. It is based on obedience.

Many Bible scholars agree that the terms "fishing for men" and "making disciples" are one and the same thing. When people say they do not have the ability to disciple people (fish for men/women), they either misunderstand what Jesus meant by making disciples, or they are just looking for an excuse to escape the challenge.

After Jesus' offer to Peter and his companions, Matthew's version of the story recalls that "at once they left their nets and followed him" (Matt 4:20). From this response it was clear that they left everything (their calling, trade, lifestyle, home, friends, family, concerns, etc.) to follow Jesus. It was a costly all-in commitment to follow Jesus. To follow Jesus you don't need to be super learned, but you do need to be super committed. Embarking on this mission demands an all-or-nothing attitude. (Jesus also said, "You cannot be my disciple, unless you love me more than you love your father and mother, your wife and children, and your brothers and sisters" (Luke 14:26 CEV).)

What Jesus said after his offer to Peter to follow him is also very significant. When Jesus asked Peter to follow him, what did he say next? Follow me… and I will make you a better person? Follow me… and I will make you more knowledgeable? Follow me… and I will make you a powerful leader? No, Jesus told Peter, "Follow me, and I will make you fishers of men" (Matt 4:19 ESV). The following and the fishing are linked. They go together. Following Jesus without making disciples was never an option for Peter. And it should not be an option for us. It is essential to understand that they go together!

"So far as the visible Christian institutions of our day are concerned, discipleship clearly is optional." [2] Sadly, it appears it has become an "honourable" choice to become a disciple-maker. This has resulted in a reality where we almost have to re-convert Christians to become disciple-makers. It is as though Christians have two big commitments in life — to commit to follow Jesus and to commit to make disciples (which often happen some time apart.) But for Peter, to follow Jesus and to make disciples was one commitment — one inseparable choice, not two. If a person commits to follow Jesus, but does not commit to make disciples, one should question whether they are committed to Jesus at all.

Following Jesus implies a mission. "Follow me, and I will make you fishers of men" (Matt 4:19 ESV). In Jesus' eyes the mission was not separate from the identity. We have dichotomised mission and identity, creating an impression that discipleship is an additional responsibility over and above being a Christian. This development in Christian culture must be addressed. Being a Christian implies that you are a disciple-maker. Not a Christian *and* a disciple-maker; both. The latter is a function of the former. When Jesus says "follow me", there is a person ("me") and a mission ("follow") in the calling. You cannot have the person without the mission. Accepting the person implies accepting the mission. Disciple-making is not additional to Christianity; it is a defining element of Christianity!

Nowadays, disciple-making is treated as a branch of Christianity. For many Christians, disciple-making gets attention as an important aspect of the Christian faith. But disciple-making is not a branch of the Christian life. Disciple-making is the trunk from which all activities should flow. For the Christian life, it should be the main thing.

> "Why is it that we see so little disciple-making taking place in the church today? Do we really believe that Jesus told His early followers to make disciples but wants the twenty-first century church to do something different?... The members of the early church took their responsibility to make disciples very seriously. To them, the church wasn't a corporation run by a CEO. Rather, they compared the church to a body that functions properly only when every member is doing its part." [3]

Is discipleship your main priority? Is it your main thing? If discipleship is not your main thing, it will never be your thing! Understanding this principle is the foundation for discussing what disciple-making should look like. If it is not understood, disciple-making will remain just another thing we do now and then.

What We Do

We use terminology such as "discipler" and "disciples" because it makes sense to us. However, there are many other ways to talk about the same thing. Paul referred to Timothy as a "spiritual son" rather than a disciple. Jesus talked about being a "shepherd" to the flock. Spiritual "overseers" is also used in the Bible. Some people use the terms "spiritual mentor" and "mentees". It doesn't matter what you use as long as it captures the responsibility that exists between the "discipler" and the "disciple". Be careful that these terms don't create distance between the discipler and the disciple. Remember, the discipleship relationship is a role, not a qualification. It should encourage regular proximity, a deeper intimacy, a dedication towards disciple-making and a sense of responsibility in each other's lives.

Discussion questions
1 Who is qualified to make disciples of Jesus?
2 Do you feel qualified to make disciples? Why or why not?
3 What does the statement: "Disciple-making is not additional to Christianity; it is a defining element of Christianity!" communicate to you?
4 Is disciple-making your main priority? Why or why not?

Scripture to study • Luke 5:1-11

Books to read • Growing True Disciples, *by George Barna* • T4T: A Discipleship Re-Revolution, *by Steve Smith* • Contagious Disciple Making, *by David Watson and Paul Watson*

1.3 THE COST OF DISCIPLE-MAKING

———•———

George Kellerman

The story we used in the last chapter of how Peter and Jesus met (Luke 5:1-11) is echoed in John 21. These stories are so similar; it is clear there is a link between the two, even though the second story takes place a few years later, after the resurrection of Jesus. The story goes like this:

> Simon Peter, Thomas (also known as Didymus), Nathanael from Cana in Galilee, the sons of Zebedee, and two other disciples were together. "I'm going out to fish," Simon Peter told them, and they said, "We'll go with you." So they went out and got into the boat, but that night they caught nothing.
>
> Early in the morning, Jesus stood on the shore, but the disciples did not realise that it was Jesus.
>
> He called out to them, "Friends, haven't you any fish?"
>
> "No," they answered.
>
> He said, "Throw your net on the right side of the boat and you will find some." When they did, they were unable to haul the net in because of the large number of fish.
>
> Then the disciple whom Jesus loved said to Peter, "It is the Lord!" As soon as Simon Peter heard him say, "It is the Lord," he wrapped his outer garment around him (for he had taken it off) and jumped into the water. The other disciples followed in the boat, towing the net full of fish, for they were not far from shore, about a hundred yards. When they landed, they saw a fire of burning coals there with fish on it, and some bread.
>
> Jesus said to them, "Bring some of the fish you have just caught." So Simon Peter climbed back into the boat and

dragged the net ashore. It was full of large fish, 153, but even with so many the net was not torn. Jesus said to them, "Come and have breakfast" (John 21:2-12).

As you can see, this story is very similar to the start of Peter's journey with Jesus (see the previous chapter or Luke 5:1-11): The disciples were fishing on the lake of Gennesaret but caught nothing all night; Jesus asked them to try one more time, and this time they caught more than the boats could handle. However, this time the conversation went as follows:

> "When they had finished eating, Jesus said to Simon Peter, 'Simon son of John, do you love me more than these?' 'Yes, Lord,' he said, 'you know that I love you.' Jesus said, 'Feed my lambs.' Again Jesus said, 'Simon son of John, do you love me?' He answered, 'Yes, Lord, you know that I love you.' Jesus said, 'Take care of my sheep.' The third time he said to him, 'Simon son of John, do you love me?' Peter was hurt because Jesus asked him the third time, 'Do you love me?' He said, 'Lord, you know all things; you know that I love you.' Jesus said, 'Feed my sheep.'" (John 21:15-17)

Note the references to disciple-making in the two stories: "Feed my sheep" and "Fishing for men". Both phrases have a similar meaning — making and training disciples — and could probably be used interchangeably. Also note the repeating of a question Jesus asks three times ("Peter, do you love me?") in this story. The NIV, through the heading it uses, translates this as a motion to reinstate Peter after he disowned Jesus three times a few days earlier.

I often wondered why Jesus used these terms: "Feed my lambs," "Take care of my sheep" and "Feed my sheep" as a response to Peter's answer that he loves Jesus. The reason became clear after reading a few verses on (John 21:19) and comparing this passage to Luke 5:1-11 and Matthew 4:18-22. Jesus closed the conversation by saying, "Follow me!" an obvious echo and reminder of the first conversation in Matthew 4:19 when Jesus said, "Follow me, and I will make you a fisher of men." When we compare these stories, both include the invitation to "Follow me!" and a call to make disciples ("fish for people", "feed my sheep"). The repetition of the adjacent terms "follow me" and "make disciples" in each story makes it clear for us to see: following Jesus and making disciples are inseparable. They were always meant to be read together. Following Jesus and making disciples ought to be one choice, one commitment.

After comparing the two stories, the latter appears to be Jesus' way of reminding Peter of the former. I believe Jesus wanted to emphasise the necessity of making disciples and remind Peter of the cost involved.

In the first story, Peter understood the cost was leaving his nets (his career, livelihood, family, etc.) behind. In the second story, the conversation about the cost of making disciples was more intense. With the backdrop of his own crucifixion, Jesus implies that disciple-making would cost Peter his life. He even reveals the kind of death by which he would glorify God (by also being crucified) (John 21:19). If the cost of making disciples was not clear in the "leave your nets and follow me" discussion, or through Jesus' crucifixion a few days earlier, it was clear now.

After Jesus described the cost of making disciples and the all-in commitment required, I imagine him looking at Peter in a similar way to their first encounter, and with the corners of his mouth lifting in a smile, saying again, "Follow me!" (John 21:19)

Dietrich Bonhoeffer wrote a famous book called *The Cost of Discipleship*. He explained how following Jesus is free, but it costs us everything.

"The cross means sharing the suffering of Christ to the last and to the fullest... The first Christ-suffering which every man must experience is the call to abandon the attachments of this world… When Christ calls a man, He bids him come and die." [4]

Two of the main questions he asked in the book were:
1   Have we considered the cost of following Jesus?
2   Have we counted the cost of discipleship?

Similarly, and with the same earnestness, I would ask if we have counted the cost of disciple-making. David Mathis puts it this way:

"We are indeed called to embrace the cost of discipleship — make no mistake about that — to following Jesus, denying self, taking up our cross, and walking in the steps of our Lord, with all the believing, praying, giving, loving, and serving that involves. This is the first and most basic aspect of Christian discipleship: being a disciple of Jesus.

But Jesus himself calls us to more than just following him. Better put, his call to discipleship includes the call to disciple-making… Paul wasn't in prison just for being a disciple of Jesus. If he would have just loved Jesus and kept it to himself, no one would have bothered to go to all the trouble to put Paul into prison. But what got him locked up was that he made disciples of Jesus." [5]

Christians are persecuted around the world, but not just because they follow Jesus or attend illegal church gatherings. They are persecuted because they make disciples and multiply the faith in doing so. When they keep their faith to themselves the authorities rarely bother them. It is when they are on the move, sharing their testimonies and making disciples, that they become dangerous. We can also argue that Jesus was not crucified because he said he was the Son of God. He was crucified because he led a "rebellion" of people changing the world. He was crucified because he made disciples.

If you want to coast through this Christian life, then keep your faith to yourself. If you want an easy, unopposed persecution-free life, don't make disciples. But if you want to join with Paul in making disciples, be ready to count the cost. "In fact, everyone who wants to live a godly life in Christ Jesus will be persecuted" (2 Tim 3:12).

By now you might be wondering why we talk about the cost of disciple-making in a book trying to encourage it. We do it for the same reason we encourage people to follow Jesus. The sacrifice and commitment it takes to follow Jesus does not compare to the richness of knowing Jesus. Similarly with disciple-making. It is a massive sacrifice and commitment, but it does not compare to the richness of seeing others getting to know Jesus.

There are few better examples of a disciple-maker than Paul, so to study his understanding of disciple-making is an obvious must. He gives us a glimpse of his approach in a letter addressed to his disciple, Timothy. Paul's instruction and encouragement to Timothy about disciple-making in particular is captured in 2 Timothy 2:1-14. Let's look at these verses in more detail.

First, one of the most quoted verses about disciple-making:

"And the things you have heard me say in the presence of many witnesses entrust to reliable people who will also be qualified to teach others" (2 Tim 2:2).

We will work through this verse in more detail later, but for now note Paul's intentional and generational understanding of disciple-making. He is encouraging Timothy to make disciples who make disciples who make disciples.

The preceding and follow-up verses to this brilliant summary of disciple-making also demand our attention. 2 Timothy 2:1 shouts out, "BE STRONG!" ("You then, my son, be strong in the grace that is in Christ Jesus.") There is no point using the words "be strong" when things are easy and comfortable. We say "be strong" to encourage people when things are tough. The verse following

2 Timothy 2:2 says, "Join with me in suffering, like a good soldier of Christ Jesus." That doesn't sound particularly safe or pleasant. Paul wants Timothy to understand that disciple-making is a challenging and costly commitment. However, Paul then gives Timothy three metaphors (in three short verses) to encourage him in his disciple-making task. He encourages Timothy to be like a soldier, an athlete and a farmer.

The Soldier

"No one serving as a soldier gets entangled in civilian affairs, but rather tries to please his commanding officer" (2 Tim 2:4).

Someone who has been in war will be better able to describe the mindset of a soldier. But from what I know, most soldiers are ready to lay their lives down for the mission and for their fellow soldiers. In the heat of battle, a soldier cannot afford to question or second guess commands given by the commanding officer. Losing focus can cost him his life and the lives of those around him. There is no time or point for civilian talk and pleasing others. There is a war to be won, and the soldier better stay true to his mission.

OPPOSITION, HARDSHIPS AND DIFFICULTIES ARE THE NORM FOR SOLDIERS; IT IS ALSO THE NORM IN DISCIPLE-MAKING

I see too many followers of Christ signing up for the discipleship battle, only to get preoccupied with their busy lives and the responsibilities which (to their minds) trump disciple-making. I see followers of Jesus trying to please others (friends, family, spouse, boss) rather than their Commanding Officer. Disciple-making necessitates saying "no" to many people so you can invest your time in a few people. It is not about saying "yes" to well-intentioned initiatives at the cost of your focus. It is about being single-minded in pursuit of the most important mission we are called to — that of making disciple-makers.

Opposition, hardships and difficulties are the norm for soldiers;

it is also the norm in disciple-making. The cost of having no comfort is the norm for soldiers; it is also the norm in disciple-making. Being constantly called to battle is the norm for soldiers; it is also the norm in disciple-making.

The Athlete

"Similarly, anyone who competes as an athlete does not receive the victor's crown except by competing according to the rules" (2 Tim 2:5 NIV).

In disciple-making, we need a mindset of dedication, perseverance and discipline. We cannot cut corners or try to cheat the race. (We should ask ourselves if preaching to the masses as a substitute to training disciple-makers is not an effort to cut corners.) Disciple-making entails persevering with a small group of people for a long time.

There is a cost in "competing according to the rules." There is pain in adjusting your fleshly, worldly preferences to align to a different set of rules — Kingdom principles. The disciple should be disciplined to the prescriptions of the Word of God. The Word contains the rules for the race. It is all about obeying God's Word consistently.

I recall many early morning workouts, disciplined routines and training schedules when I was an athlete. Disciple-making involves dedicated prayer times, late evening discussions and sacrificed "free" time. It is about routine preparations and diligently persevering with the group of people God has called you to.

The Farmer

"The hardworking farmer should be the first to receive a share of the crops" (2 Tim 2:6).

A common trait among the farmers I know is that they are not scared to work hard, and not shy to make things happen. Without recognition or reward, they keep the faith and do what they need to do, trusting the crops are in God's hands. They put in hours and hours of work, only to reap the harvest a season later. Their time-schedule is synchronised to the season of the land. If unexpected weather comes, they adjust and make sure things still happen.

The reward of the harvest is a farmer's motivation. The Bible frequently reminds us of the reward awaiting the faithful, of the Kingdom that will come on earth and the eternal reward that is worth the temporal effort. Likewise, we should keep our eyes on the Promised Land towards which we work persistently.

Disciple-making is rarely glamorous, fancy or sleek — it is more often than not plain hard work. It requires sacrificing recognition and quick results. You will have to adjust your priorities, life-style and time-spending habits to make time for your disciples. It is about diligently and obediently investing in the lives of others, not knowing what the harvest will produce.

Disciple-making is about taking initiative. It is about starting conversations, making plans and arranging gathering times. It is about initiating the difficult conversations with your disciples and cultivating the right soil for others to grow.

There is so much more to discuss on these three examples, but to borrow the words of Paul: "Reflect on what I am saying, for the Lord will give you insight into all this" (2 Tim 2:7).

To borrow from Paul in closing:

"Remember Jesus Christ, raised from the dead, descended from David. This is my gospel, for which I am suffering even to the point of being chained like a criminal. But God's word is not chained. Therefore, I endure everything for the sake of the elect, that they too may obtain the salvation that is in Christ Jesus, with eternal glory" (2 Tim 2:8-10).

Discussion questions

1 What are the similarities in the stories between Luke 5:1-11 and John 21?
2 Does the commitment to follow Jesus differ from the commitment to make disciples? Why or why not?
3 What are the costs involved in disciple-making?
4 How are these costs applicable to your life?
5 What are the specific characteristics of a soldier/athlete/ farmer that we need in discipleship and which of these do you struggle most with in your discipling?

Scripture to study • Matthew 4:18-22 • Luke 14:25-35 • John 21:2 • Timothy 2:1-13

Books to read • Cost of Discipleship, *by Dietrich Bonhoeffer* • The Great Omission, *by Dallas Willard* • Follow Me, *by David Platt*

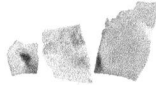

1.4 **LIKE CHRIST**

—•—

George Kellerman & Cassie Carstens

If you only had 10 seconds to describe discipleship, what would you say? We are convinced that the heart of discipleship is: "Practising Jesus Together!" If becoming like Christ is the destination, practising Jesus is the journey. The goal is to become like Christ. More comprehensively, the goal is that we become like Christ together (Eph 4:16). Discipleship is not an individualistic matter. It is a journey where we train, travel, sacrifice and battle together to become more like Christ. And in doing so, help others to become like Christ too.

Most pastors spend a great deal of time preaching about "finding life in Christ" (doctrine). Far fewer tackle "living like Christ" (duty) with the same regularity and clarity. The problem is that while doctrine satisfies the desire for knowledge, duty calls for action. Thus, the net effect of most preaching ends up being about "knowing", but not "doing". This leads to a church well versed in orthodoxy — right doctrine — but weak orthopraxy — right practice. The world needs more than knowledge of Christ; it needs Christ-like action! A discipleship community should focus on following the example of Jesus' life.

We believe it all starts with a trustful surrender of the whole being to the influence of Christ. Our discipling process then helps us stay in this condition of total surrender. Discipleship helps us practice surrender in all the dimensions of our lives to his rule and guidance. We inspire each other to remain in Jesus, the vine of life, and to trust him completely to infuse the spiritual power in us needed for victory.

We regard faith in Christ and conformity to his character as inseparable. Whoever does not rest in full faith of his salvation will not have the strength to follow his example; and whoever does not desire and stretch to follow Jesus' example will not feel the need to rest in his salvation. It is only through both practices that real followers of Jesus are produced.

Believing Jesus is our life (Col 3:4), we understand that we obtain life through Jesus. In the same way, we experience real life when we live like Jesus. Whoever claims to live in Christ, must live as Jesus did (1 John 2:6). In his book, *Like Christ*, Andrew Murray explains it well:

> "The fruit of a life in Christ is a life like Christ. He that seeks to abide in Christ must walk even as He walked. He that seeks to walk like Christ, must abide in Him. These two — abiding and walking — are inseparable. The abiding in Him always precedes the walking like Him. And yet the aim to walk like Him must equally precede any large measure of abiding." [6]

He goes on to say the following:

> To each one who knows that the Lord has washed away his sin the command comes with all the touching force of one of the last words of Him who is going out to die for us: 'Even as I have done to you, so do ye also.' Jesus Christ does indeed ask every one of us in everything to act just as we have seen Him do. What He has done to ourselves, and still does each day, we are to do over again to others. In His condescending, pardoning, saving love, He is our example; each of us is to be the copy and image of the Master." [7]

How should we follow the example of Christ? We are not like Christ in his mediation, in that we cannot die for the forgiveness of sins or resurrect to overcome the power of death. However, as followers (disciples) of Jesus, we should follow the example he set for us in the Gospels.

Here are some of the ways in which we can become like Christ:

- In serving and suffering for others
- In his self-denial/self-sacrifice/self-crucifixion
- In freedom from this world; enduring temptations and putting to death earthly desires
- In suffering wrong, enduring persecution
- In his admiration for, prayer to and total devotion to God
- In doing God's will as he lived in unity with God
- In being led by the Word and the Spirit
- In joining his heavenly mission, being totally set aside for God's work
- In his selfless sacrificial love
- In forgiving others
- Manifesting the fullness of God by living a life that bears the fruit of the Spirit
- In doing only what he saw his Father doing
- In generous and joyous giving.

We know our efforts to live like Christ are not to earn anything or replace anything Jesus has done for us. By becoming like Christ, we glorify God through the release of his Spirit.

God wants us to become like Jesus so we can become the people he intended us to be. As Paul describes it: "For God knew his people in advance, and he chose them to become like his Son, so that his Son would be the firstborn among many brothers and sisters" (Rom 8:29 NLT).

Jesus said that, "Whoever finds their life will lose it, and whoever loses their life for my sake will find it" (Matt 10:39). Because Jesus is "the perfect me", we move closer towards God's purpose for our lives as we grow towards Jesus. And as we grow together towards Jesus, we experience the beauty of entering the realm of God's design for the body of Christ. Through this, we become well-prepared for the day we will ultimately be with him and become like him.

Before we can *make* disciples of Jesus, we first need to *be* disciples of Jesus. Being a disciple of Jesus does not mean passively consuming his teachings. It implies a devotion to do what Jesus did. Biblical historian, Ray Vander Laan, explains it as follows:

"The Hebrew word for disciple is talmid. This word stresses the relationship between rabbi (teacher or master) and disciple (student). A talmid of Jesus' day would give up his entire life in order to be with his teacher. The disciple didn't only seek to know what the teacher knew, as is usually the case today. It was not enough just to know what the rabbi said, but the foremost goal of any talmid was to become like the rabbi and do what the rabbi did." [8]

The intensity of the pursuit to become like the rabbi is well expressed in this story told by Rob Bell:

"This system continues today to some extent in Israel. It's not uncommon for a Rabbi to go into the bathroom and be followed by his disciples. Coming out of the stall, the Rabbi might say, 'Blessed art thou O God, for giving us holes in our bodies.' And then the disciples would repeat what the Rabbi had said, because their entire purpose is to be exactly like their Rabbi, even down to bodily functions.

One of the Sages from the Mishna [ancient Jewish literature] is quoted as this, 'May you be covered in the dust of your rabbi.' Rabbis are passionate and animated. They would spend their days taking their disciples around teaching them, and as they traveled from place to place, they would literally kick up a cloud of dust. And because the disciples were following the Rabbi, at the end of the day, they would actually be covered in the dust their rabbi kicked up. May you be covered in the dust of your Rabbi." [9]

If a person is not willing to re-adjust and realign their entire focus in life, it is difficult to talk to them about discipleship. For this person, discipleship will remain an activity, a curriculum, or a program followed at church and cell groups. To become a disciple of Jesus is to give your whole life over to the process of transformation. As conversion expects of us to turn away from our own worldly desires, so the process of disciple-making demands a continuous setting of the mind away from earthly things, to the "things above" (Col 3:2).

Jesus said that one cannot be his disciple unless one lets go of one's dearest possessions and closest relationships — even one's own life. To be his disciple is to immediately heed the call to redirect all attention and focus on God. However, we are warned to consider the cost carefully (Luke 14:28) — discipleship is not only a heart-surrender, it is a life-surrender!

Let us look at some things Jesus said which describe the life-surrender needed to become a disciple of Jesus:

- "And whoever does not carry their cross and follow me cannot be my disciple... In the same way, those of you who do not give up everything you have cannot be my disciples" (Luke 14:27).
- "Then a teacher of the law came to him and said, 'Teacher, I will follow you wherever you go.' Jesus replied, 'Foxes have dens and birds have nests, but the Son of Man has no place to lay his head'" (Matt 8:19-20).
- "Enter through the narrow gate. For wide is the gate and broad is the road that leads to destruction, and many enter through it. But small is the gate and narrow the road that leads to life, and only a few find it" (Matt 7:13-14).

Disciple-making requires total attention and devotion to becoming and helping others to become like Christ. It can be as difficult to "promote" surrendering to Jesus as it is to "promote" discipleship. Both require total commitment, the sacrifice of time and comfort, and a pursuit of vulnerability and selflessness. Disciple-making demands both a redirection of life focus and a stepping up of commitment towards a new purpose in life. This is not something to step into expecting personal reward beyond experiencing the joy of seeing people growing in Christ and become more like Jesus. But what better reward could there possibly be?

Since the journey of surrendering our lives and becoming like Jesus is not easy, we need support. In our discipleship teams, we encourage each other constantly, affirming that we are here to become more like Christ. As iron sharpens iron, we are sharpening each other to become more selfless, to become more like Christ. Challenging one another to make disciples is an encouragement towards selflessness. As friction is needed for iron to be sharpened, so confronting each other is encouragement to become like Christ.

Asking tough questions is encouragement towards brokenness and becoming more like Christ. We aren't just encouraging each other towards becoming better people. We are helping one another to kill our egos and become more like Christ. The friction of challenging each other can turn sour if the motive (of becoming like Christ) is misunderstood. However, a lack of friction is equally unhealthy, because it dodges the shared pursuit of becoming like Jesus. If we agree that the journey is about killing the ego so that Christ can become more, we are free to challenge and sharpen one another. This frees us to practice Jesus together, and we are free to become like Christ.

Discussion questions

1   Do you want to be like Jesus? Why or why not?
2   How do you become like Jesus?
3   How can we help each other to be more like Jesus?
4   Earlier in the chapter, there is a list of different ways in which we can become like Jesus. Which of these will be most difficult for you?

Scripture to study • 1 John 2:3-11 • Mark 8:34-38

Books to read • Like Christ, *by Andrew Murray*

1.5 HOLISTIC DISCIPLING

—•—

George Kellerman

When I think back to the most significant discussions I have had with my disciples, they usually started with the question: "What can I do about this issue?" The application discussions after this popular question lead to more life-changing experiences than any fancy teachings or biblical exegesis. Discipling would be easy if it was limited to spiritual teaching and coaching; it could then be a finite and academic exercise. Many people — even church leaders! — see it as a spiritual exercise with no practical responsibility. But discipleship cannot stop there. It is so much more than that.

There are many ways to describe the dimensions of a person. The most common one is body, mind and soul (body, soul and spirit in some traditions). However, we refer to six dimensions — spiritual, emotional, intellectual, physical, environmental and social. (See image below.) This isn't about creating a perfect academic model. Rather, we want something that makes practical application easy to frame. We emphasise the importance of whole-life discipleship, because our goal is for their whole lives to be redeemed towards

The six dimensions that make up the human being

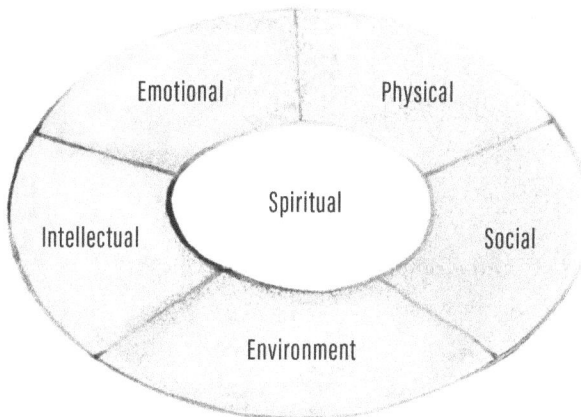

their original intent. To quote Mark Foreman, "Jesus comes not to serve one part of the person, but the whole person (mind, body and soul), and in so doing, bring redemption to culture." [10]

As beings with many dimensions, it is of little use to focus on one and neglect the rest of the person. For example, poor sleeping patterns (physical dimension) can negatively impact your emotional state, which has a bearing on your relationships, which may cause you to implode spiritually. Taking a holistic approach instead of just focusing on the spiritual makes discipleship more complex, but also far more effective.

We often limit salvation to meaning "filling the hole in my heart" instead of "making my whole life whole." As Mark Foreman describes it:

"The two terms, salvation and wholeness, help the other find its roots. Salvation is the act of restoring unto wholeness. Salvation is the action; wholeness is the product. Together, they represent the process of bringing about a wholly integrated human being. This was and still is Jesus' offer." [11]

Landa Cope helps us towards an even broader understanding of wholeness:

"God's plan for redemption is for individuals, but it is also a reconciliation plan for nations. We have the keys to the blessings of the nations… [but we fall short when we] reach the nations, but we leave them in injustice, disease, illiteracy, and poverty." [12]

We often see individual salvation and being filled by the Spirit as our ultimate destiny when it should actually be the holistic salvation of nations. In one of her sermons, Landa describes how we have shrunk Jesus into a "tiny Jesus who can save the soul, but not the world." All nations and all spheres of society need redemption, not only all spheres of the human being. This is the mandate of our discipleship movement: to disciple the nations!

We must guard ourselves from falling into the dualistic mindset of working hard to keep our spiritual life intact but allowing our daily life to erode.

We follow Jesus' example of discipleship. He did not allow people to limit things to the spiritual when the real problem was in other dimensions. For example, he did not allow the rich young man to focus on eternal life while his financial life was not according to God's will (Mark 10:17-23).

In the same vein, if a disciple struggles with pornography our initial focus is not spiritual discipline. We first address the devastating effects of pornography before talking about strengthening their spiritual life. (The great thing is that dealing with an issue like this typically improves their spiritual life in the process.) Some years ago, I was discipling a group of young men who wanted to delve into the topic of spiritual gifts. However, I discovered that some of them were still watching pornography, so I refused to spend time on spiritual gifts until we addressed the issue eroding our spiritual walk together.

Another example of this is the way we choose the speakers who address our disciples. We consider character and integrity before competence. Their holistic maturity should weigh much heavier than their spiritual giftedness. As Mark Foreman puts it: "This is why the words holy and whole are etymologically and conceptually connected. Holy Jesus is Wholly Jesus. Holiness is the manifestation of wholeness." [13] Spiritual maturity is dependent on maturity in all the dimensions of the wholeness spectrum.

For us, practical Christianity is essential.

To disciple people on life issues is challenging but critical, and there are no issues more pivotal than money, sex and power (terms made popular in Richard Foster's book, *The Challenge of the Disciplined Life: Christian Reflections on Money, Sex and Power* [14]). If you have never talked to your disciples about these topics, then it is questionable whether you are truly discipling them. That sounds harsh, but we stand by it because nothing ruins lives faster (or deeper) than struggles rooted in this age-old trifecta. And while they have been with us since the dawn of mankind, culture today idolises them on a grander scale than ever before. (See chapter 3.6 (Redeeming Culture) for more on the idols of money, sex and power.)

We often hear people saying things like "my pastor is discipling me", but when we go deeper, there isn't any substance outside of the spiritual realm. The pastor has no clue what is going on in the person's life when it comes to the idols of money, sex and power. There is nothing wrong with only receiving spiritual guidance from your pastor, but if that is the case please don't call it discipleship. Discipleship is holistic coaching.

We want our disciples to follow Christ, not just in theory, but in daily practice. Paul says that, "We all possess knowledge. But knowledge puffs up while love builds up" (1 Cor 8:1). We want to see our disciples translate their love for God into loving relationships with their family, neighbours and the people who challenge them

DISCIPLESHIP IS JOURNEYING THROUGH LIFE WITH YOUR DISCIPLES

the most. We hold to James 2:22 which says that our faith is only completed in action, and John's exhortation that to love God is to love your brother (1 John 3:16-18).

We also need to be careful not to focus on spiritual disciplines while love for our neighbour is dwindling. "If I have the gift of prophecy and can fathom all the mysteries and all knowledge, and if I have a faith that can move mountains, but do not love, I am nothing" (1 Cor 13:2). Discipleship amounts to nothing if we do not teach people how to love practically. I hesitate to train guys on topics such as prophecy and speaking in tongues if I have not thoroughly covered love, both practically and culturally.

For example, as a white privileged South African I cannot disciple other white South Africans without helping them address the pertinent issues of racism and economic inequality in South Africa. As a white South African, to love my neighbour means to love my all my neighbours, whether they look like me or are in the same economic class as me or not, by confronting racism and inequality. Similarly, as a citizen in a European country, to love my neighbour means to love the thousands of immigrating refugees by helping them rebuild their lives, and helping my fellow citizens respond to the challenges of cultural integration. Or as a Palestinian, to love my neighbour means to love my Israeli neighbours even though our nations might be officially or unofficially at war. Discipling someone holistically means to teach them how to love practically.

Discipleship is journeying through life with your disciples. Jesus did not remain in synagogues to provide endless teachings. Most of his recorded discipleship took place in simple, practical settings. He was constantly investing in his disciples while on the road, eating with people, and other mundane daily activities. When discipling people on life issues, there is no better way than to set a good example. Observing how I pray, treat my wife and children or interact with strangers points to Jesus much more than any teaching on those topics. Can I honestly repeat Paul's words to my disciples: "Follow my example, as I follow the example of Christ" (1 Cor 11:1)? If you want to disciple people in prayer, you have to pray with them. If you want to disciple people in parenting, invite them to stay in your home for a while. If you want to disciple people in serving people, go serve somewhere together.

What We Do

Holistic discipling means the love and life of Jesus integrated into everything we do. In its simplest form, it is doing life together by practising Jesus together with a group of people. How it looks practically, varies.

It could mean for families to move into the same house, or it could mean for a group to gather intentionally on a weekly basis. It could mean reaching out to people in need or it could be just chilling together. Many factors play a role in the manner and how much time we need to spend together.

We will explore practical applications of the life-on-life concept in more detail in chapter 2.1 (Fishing for the Village). For now, note that by simply spending time together there is a good chance all six holistic dimensions will be covered. We cannot limit discipling to teachings and meetings. We must challenge our personal bubbles to allow for more life-on-life experiences with others.

We also do "personal development" sessions with our disciples. This is a more structured meeting time than the life-on-life interactions. We plan these sessions intentionally to meet every dimension of the disciple's life. We work through each of the six dimensions one at a time to ensure they are healthy and growing in all areas of their lives. This helps highlight areas which need attention or where Satan can find a foothold in their lives

Discussion questions

1 How well are you able to integrate your spiritual growth into practical applications?
2 In which of the six dimensions of your life (spiritual, emotional, intellectual, physical, environmental and social) are you struggling the most?
3 Are you being discipled and discipling others in each of the six dimensions? If not, which are being neglected?

Scripture to study • James 2:14-26

Books to read • Wholly Jesus, *by Mark Foreman* • Like Jesus, *by Andrew Murray* • Just Like Jesus, *by Max Lucado* • The Challenge of the Disciplined Life, *by Richard Foster* • Celebration of Discipline, *by Richard Foster*

1.6 DISCIPLESHIP STATEMENTS THAT MAKE US NERVOUS

———•———

Cassie Carstens

Working with church leaders since the 1990s, I have encountered some strange interpretations of discipleship. This isn't only a local issue either. I have mentored and trained church leaders in over 100 nations since I started. And in all of them, I have seen misunderstanding and malpractice around disciple-making.

As church leaders, we have not done a great job teaching people about disciple-making. If we had, the entire world would be a different place. It is a bit embarrassing since discipleship should be one of the most (if not *the* most) important topics of every church's teaching. If I could go back in time, I would do things differently; in theory, in theology and in practice.

Along our journey, we have met people around the world who are leading the way in disciple-making. We are excited to see God changing the hearts of Christians to renew their passion to disciple others. But there are still major shortcomings in the global church's understanding of discipleship. As we visit churches, Christian conferences and train church leaders around the world, the language we hear people use when they talk about discipleship still makes us nervous.

The following statements are examples of what makes us nervous about the global church's understanding of discipleship.

1. "Everything we do in church is discipleship"
Yes, discipleship should permeate everything we do. Yes, whatever we do should impact people. But this statement is concerning on a few levels.

Firstly, there is little intentionality in a broad statement like this. The heart is good, but it lacks focus. Making disciples needs focus and intentionality!

Secondly, it sounds impersonal. True discipleship is an entirely personal process. Whenever we speak of church, it should be in the context of relationships, and shared journeys of growth. Making disciples is a life-on-life process, of developing and being developed by others.

Thirdly, it can disguise a program-based orientation. A focus on performance and a reliance on programs sucks the life right out of discipleship. Churches that do this centre on a few actors and leave most of the people as passive recipients of entertainment. This is the opposite of true discipleship. Everyone should be proactive in spiritual co-development.

2. "Cell/small/life groups are discipling groups"

It is marvellous when that statement is true but, unfortunately, that is rarely the case. The reality is that most cell groups are more or less static. They focus on spiritual growth instead of holistic development. They focus inward instead of outward, becoming spiritually obese by taking in the whole time and never giving out. They teach but do not empower, they comfort but do not challenge, and they maintain but do not multiply. It is rare that I hear of cell groups practising genuine transparency and accountability. Commitment to the group is a meeting once a week, and a chat over coffee on Sunday. That is a good place to start, but without committed Kingdom building between meetings, it misses the point. They talk about wanting to become more like Christ, but don't take the right steps to pursue it. Making disciples implies an active, intentional, nurturing community. The group shares responsibility for each other's lives, building the Kingdom together as they grow to become more like Jesus.

3. "We have a discipleship program at the church"

Programs are an issue when they are presented as complete solutions, instead of a step in a longer process. Marriage enrichment courses are great but will not ensure a good marriage without full commitment from both partners. Even the best youth programs won't lead to a good teenage life if the teenager is unwilling to do their part. In the same way, we know discipleship programs are limited. Anyone who says they have a complete understanding of discipleship because they did a program is ignorant. As if discipleship is something we can ever complete!

Furthermore, offering a discipleship program implies that it can be isolated to a specific event. As we said earlier, discipleship is a lifelong process. Events play a part but are no more the sum of discipleship than the Gospels are the sum of the Bible.

Offering a discipleship program also insinuates that it is not part of the DNA of the church, but an addition to something more important. Discipleship should be the vehicle upon which the church is built, not a nice tool to use when the leaders see fit.

Lastly, "having a discipleship program" suggests that discipleship can be seen as a passive study event. While there is theory to discipleship (hence us writing this book), it is primarily a dynamic process of transformation from human-like to Christ-like. Making disciples is a lifelong process where the Bible is the handbook.

4. "Some members at our church do discipleship"

This may seem obvious, but discipleship should be part of the DNA of any church. This statement makes it clear that it isn't. Even more misguided, it implies that discipleship is optional. It suggests that making disciples is something only an elite Christian club — those who "have a gift" in disciple-making — can do. Which, in case you were wondering, is not true in any way. This assumption is based on the lie that good works or spiritual "success" is a necessary qualification to make disciples. When church leaders approach discipleship this way, they are misrepresenting the Gospel. Making disciples should be an essential and fundamental responsibility of every follower of Jesus.

5. "I disciple my friends"

Discipling your friends is a great place to start, true. But we do get nervous when disciple-making stops at the people you are familiar with. The danger here is to focus inwards by discipling each other in the group. It is more challenging to turn outwards and be intentional about multiplying disciples.

Also, instead of being accountable to a group, people turn to a single accountability partner. We have found that something special happens when a group is transparent with each other. One-on-one accountability has its place, but it can't replace the group dynamic. Not only is there less emphasis on commitment, intentionality and multiplication, but depth is also sacrificed for comfort.

It makes sense; when your discipleship partner is a close friend, you don't want to risk ruining the friendship by being too confrontational — it feels safer to keep the level of discipleship shallow and avoid those deep, uncomfortable places where the real growth happens. Making disciples is an intentional and multiplying process and cannot be restricted by the limitations of comfort.

6. "I make disciples, but no one disciples me"

Discipleship should mostly happen through example. But how can you show someone a working model of accountability if you aren't being held accountable yourself? How can you model a discipleship relationship if you aren't in one yourself? The good and bad experiences you share with your discipler are a training ground that empowers you to become a good discipler. We believe disciple-making is only effective if there is a pull and a push dynamic. Your disciples push you, and your discipler pulls you. The questions and challenges you face with your disciples push you to ask them of your discipler. As they help you answer the questions, they pull you up. Your growth will always be limited if you don't have this double dynamic. True discipleship has the push and pull dynamic of discipling and being discipled.

7. "I do one-on-one discipleship"

The deeper we get into the 21st century, the more individualistic society seems to become. And discipleship is paying for this individualism-at-all-costs. When Jesus left the earth after three years of making disciples, he prepared them to develop interdependently. They had a shared mission that required a communal environment. Today, the treasure of that Christ-centred communal environment has been all but buried. The idea is still applauded, but in practice it is far less popular. When asked to share control of decisions about money, time or career by your discipler or discipleship group the tune quickly changes to, "you don't have the right to tell me what to do!" We are rarely challenged like that in individual discipleship, and even when we are, it lacks the impact of team input. Interdependence only grows when we trust a team, which is something one-on-one discipleship cannot offer.

Making disciples implies individual and team-based development.

8. "When I preach as a pastor, I do discipleship"

Many pastors are happy to preach, but are not nearly as comfortable in an emotionally intimate environment. Preaching allows them to add value without getting too close to people. It protects them from the demands of people. Proclamation is clearly a part of discipleship, but if it causes distance and exclusivity it is a problem. You can't make disciples if you aren't willing to be vulnerable.

Making disciples is a process of interacting in an emotionally intimate environment.

9. "My pastor disciples me"

We must understand the difference between spiritual coaching and holistic life coaching. Holistic life coaching includes spiritual coaching, but it rarely works the other way around. Jesus' discipling was holistic life coaching. He spoke to the rich man about money and to the woman at the well about sex. If your pastor does not speak to you on a practical level about money, sex, power and the other issues you face, he is not your discipler. He may be your spiritual coach, and may be brilliant at it, but discipling demands whole-life-coaching. Making disciples demands whole-life coaching.

Weaving through all of these limited or misguided statements forced us to consider how we should define discipleship. This will get refined along the way, but for now, our "current (loosely defined) definition" of making disciples is:

An intentional and multiplicative process
of holistic development in an intimate and active
nurturing community, practising to be like Jesus
on his Kingdom mission.

Making disciples is the active outward-focused process of discipleship. Discipleship is the broader concept which includes being a disciple of Jesus, practicing Jesus together with a group of people and making disciples of Jesus.

The rest of the book will expand on, colour in and hopefully make this definition come alive. Please journey with us in discovering together, asking together, searching together, challenging together and, most importantly, obeying the command of Jesus to make disciples together.

Discussion questions

1   In your own words, how would you define discipleship?
2   Which of the statements mentioned in this chapter are most applicable to your context? Which is the most worrisome in how discipleship is applied in your context?
3   What is the biggest change needed in your church towards a stronger application of discipleship?

Scripture to study • Matthew 28:16-20

Books to read • Letters to the Church, *by Francis Chan* • Follow Me, *by David Platt*

1.7 THE DISCIPLESHIP WHEEL

—•—

George Kellerman

When I train, I like to use illustrations to help others remember the basic principles of the Bible and of God's kingdom. This is one of (hopefully) many other things I share with Dawson Trotman. Dawson founded a ministry called The Navigators in 1933. The Navigators "is an international, interdenominational Christian ministry that helps people grow in Jesus as they navigate through life." [15] They worked with Billy Graham's ministry including assisting it in the follow-up work after his crusades. While teaching in the 1930s, Dawson developed one of the best illustrations I have seen to describe a balanced Christian life. Now known as the Navigators' Wheel, it is also an apt illustration to describe the balanced life of a disciple of Jesus. We have adopted and adapted it for our discipleship training. [16]

A common question we hear is, "what curriculum do you use in your discipleship gatherings?" It is understandable that churches want to offer a toolkit to people wanting to train others, but the last thing we want to do is limit the discipleship journey to a simple curriculum, especially due to the implication that completing it automatically "qualifies you" as a discipler. We want to provide tools for discipleship but have no desire to legitimise discipleship through them. The wheel illustration is one such tool. It should be used like a compass rather than a road map, guiding rather than directing people towards being disciples of Jesus.

The wheel explained

The *hub* is the source, the torque that rotates the wheel. Torque describes the tendency of a force to rotate an object from its centre. Christ is the centre of our lives, the hub. He is our driving force and source of power for life. His Spirit transforms us to become like him and leads our lives according to his perfect plan. Thus, at the centre, which is the main goal of becoming like Christ, we put: like Christ. Christ is not only the driving force as King of our lives, he is also the main attraction. God's intent is that we become like him to be perfect (Rom 8:29). He becomes our goal, the one we imitate.

The *rim* converts the internal torque and power of the hub into external action. It represents the external response to the internal source. Our external response to the torque should be Bible-based, Spirit-led obedience. Our obedient responses should be integrated into everything we do, flowing through our whole life (emotional, social, intellectual, environmental and physical). Dualistic discipleship disappears (and holistic discipleship appears) when we integrate the love and life of Jesus into every sphere of our lives.

The *spokes* help the hub and the outer rim stay in sync with each other. They deliver the power from the hub to the rim of the wheel and keep the outer rim from being crushed. For the outer rim to stay intact, the spokes also need to be in sync with each other. In our analogy, the spokes help our Bible-based, Spirit-led obedience-in-action stay in sync with the living Christ. The spokes deliver the power of Christ to the obedience-in-action. We have adapted the spokes slightly from the original Navigators' Wheel to integrate it with the balanced discipleship life that Jesus modelled. His life had three clear dimensions: upward, inward and outward disciplines.

Upward disciplines relate to our intimacy with God. It is an upward focus into who God is, how he loves us and desires fellowship with us, and how we can abide in him. When we abide in him, we find our belonging and our identity as children of God in him. It is about worship, prayer, and receiving and accepting his grace.

Inward relates to the inward transformation taking place in our surrendering to Christ. It is an inward focus on the heart transformation that we are undergoing while becoming more like Christ. It is about battling selfish desires, becoming more selfless through sacrificial love, brokenness, self-denial and self-emptying. At its core, it is about contentment with the goal of "becoming less so that God can be more"; about emptying ourselves of selfish desires so we can be filled by Christ's character.

Inward is about who we are (our identity), with two of the most essential values (love and humility) flowing from who we are as followers of Jesus.

Outward is how we relate to others, which we have split into two spokes. The one spoke is how we relate to our body/team of disciples, and the other how we relate to people outside our team of disciples. These are usually the people the Lord has called our discipleship team to serve.

The outward-body spoke is us practising Jesus together in teams. It relates to how we support one another, function, grow and fellowship together, and move in sync until we come to the full measure of maturity in Christ.

The outward-go spoke is the outward-focused mentality we should constantly be cultivating. It refers to where we go to the poor and the needy, where we go and witness and share the story of Jesus, and where we multiply and spread wider. Sometimes we serve a specific group of people as a discipleship team, but this spoke also refers to the people each member serves in their unique context, by being salt and light in the world.

Richard Foster applied a similar approach in his book, *Prayer*:

> "Without pressing the analogy too far, it is helpful to see that the three movements into prayer are trinitarian in character. The movement inward is prayer to God the Son, Jesus Christ, which corresponds to his roles as Saviour and Teacher among us. The movement upward is prayer to God the Father, which corresponds to his role as sovereign King and eternal Lover among us. The movement outward is prayer to God the Holy Spirit, which corresponds to his role as Empowerer and Evangelist among us." [17]

The following chapters will go deeper into the meaning of each aspect of the Discipleship Wheel, giving meat to the framework we have just provided.

What We Do

We use this wheel in many ways:
- We use it to explain discipleship in a simple way, and to explain the key principles of discipleship.
- We use it to assess areas in discipleship that are still lacking (or not well developed) within our discipleship groups and

within our discipleship movement. For example, when going through each aspect of the wheel, we might discover that our discipleship group is struggling to have intimacy with God (upward spoke), which will lead to more attention given to that aspect.

- We use it to identify which of these aspects need more attention within our gatherings. For example, when going through each aspect of the wheel, we might discover that our gatherings are neglecting the outward-go spoke, which might lead to more time being spent on witnessing, social justice initiatives, etc.

2

JOURNEYING TOGETHER (OUTWARD)

**Key essentials when you journey together
as the Body of Christ**

*Jesus' disciples and the early church knew
what Jesus meant when he said,
"I have come so that you can have life in abundance!"
In our search for that life,
we discovered a journey together that
brought us heaven on earth!
There are key essentials on this journey
— a restructuring of life —
that we want everyone to discover.*

2.1 FISHING FOR THE VILLAGE

—●—

George Kellerman

A Fijian friend visited our discipleship group and shared the following story, which made a big impact on our lives.

When a Fijian fisherman goes out to fish, the mothers from the village wish him well. He usually returns from his trip to find the mothers waiting on the shore. They take the fish he caught and distribute them throughout the village. It would be unthinkable for the fisherman to take the fish home for himself. When he goes out, he does not fish for his family; he fishes for his village. This story made us think. When we go to work, or get a big opportunity, or a big bonus, do we fish for our household alone, or do we fish for the village?

This story led to a huge shift in the way we approach and practice community. Instead of using our finances purely for our households, we gave to families in need within the community. We have provided large interest-free loans and built houses for one another. We also started considering our time as a communal resource, instead of a personal one. We broadened our connection and fellowship with a larger group of people. As we got more involved in one another's lives, our village expanded.

The next step in challenging our individualism was to explore communal living within our culture. Can village life be lived in suburban neighbourhoods? We heard amazing stories of close community when families moved into a house or an apartment block together. But living in the same space didn't always translate to communal experiences. We also heard stories of people living past each other while living in the same house. We discovered that while it may help, communal living is not only dependent on proximity. It depends on the level of life-on-life experiences.

For us, the life-on-life principle means shared experiences where personal space shrinks and lives become open books, resulting in the organic blending of individuals' lives. The deeper our life-on-life experiences, the more people rub off on each other. "Personal space" and "personal time" are often the enemies of life-on-life experiences. In individualistic Western settings, this is a big challenge.

We need to invite more and more people into our homes — figuratively and literally. As followers of Jesus, we are the light of the world. For people to see more of this light, they need to see more of us. Matthew 5:14-16 talks about this:

> "You are the light of the world. A town built on a hill cannot be hidden. Neither do people light a lamp and put it under a bowl. Instead they put it on its stand, and it gives light to everyone in the house. In the same way, let your light shine before others, that they may see your good deeds and glorify your Father in heaven."

As our understanding of the need for life-on-life discipleship grows, we have welcomed even deeper shared experiences, from sharing meals, weekends and holidays to sharing homes and even fostering and adopting children. Each of these experiences increases our likelihood of rubbing off on each other, growing our discipleship relationships in an organic way and experiencing deeper levels of fellowship.

As the size of your village grows, so does the challenge of keeping up with everyone. You will only ever have 24 hours in a day, and work and sleep take up between 14 and 20 of them. But even if you aren't able to spend a lot of time with your community, you can still experience close fellowship. We have found that the depth of your involvement in one another's lives is usually dependent on the following questions:

- Do you share your biggest life struggles?
- Do you help each other overcome your deepest insecurities?
- Do you help each other discover and live your life callings?
- Do you share big decisions with each other?
- Are you present during the important occasions in each other's lives?

Sharing the important things builds close community. You can spend days together, but if you don't go deep, you will never experience true intimacy.

Life struggles and insecurities usually occupy most of our mental capacity. Working through these issues together eases the burden and keeps you in touch with each other. Sometimes, it requires long conversations to draw out insecurities, but it is well worth it. Once we become conscious of our insecurities, we can deal with them. As we practice vulnerability, trust is developed and both parties grow in the process. In our group, the practice of being vulnerable and transparent has resulted in wonderful things. People have felt safe enough to share secrets and go to levels of relationship they weren't even able to reach with their own families.

Helping each other live our calling is deeply significant. Do you know each other's calling? Do you help each other make disciples? Do you help each other live out your unique assignments on earth? If you can answer yes to these questions, you are helping each other live out your God-intended purposes! It is amazing how a sense of "I am valued; I am supported; I am empowered" grows in a relationship like this.

As with our resources and time, our big decisions also belong to the village. By including the community, it is easier to share big life moments. Not only does this help prevent unwise decisions, it is also a way to practice accountability, co-responsibility and interdependence. These are key ingredients for a healthy community, but without intentional steps like the ones above, it is easier to not do them.

Big decisions we share with each other include:
- Life partners
- Family planning
- Job offers
- Living standards
- Where children should go to school
- Vocational calling.

You might not see each other often, but being present during the important moments can add more value than hours of casual chat. Times of distress, rites of passage, baptism and big celebrations are just some of the moments you should add to your calendars.

Our group uses the term "code red" to identify these important moments. When those events happen, we call a code red and make a point of sharing the event with each other. We do everything we can to be there for the person for whom the code red was called, even if it means travelling a long way in the early hours of the morning. In the rare instances we can't make it, we try to visit them as soon as possible. These moments don't come often, but if you share them, strong communal ties are usually the result.

Stephanie clearly understands shared life. She was close with a co-disciple who was about to give birth to her third child. Her friend's husband shared that he knew very little about the birth-giving process. Stephanie decided to help the medical staff and the husband as a birth-assistant (doula) during the birth. She drew from her own experience and did extra research in preparation. She made the environment as pleasant as possible and was responsive to the needs of the parents and the baby during the tense moments before birth. Afterwards, everyone shared how great her contribution was in the birth process. The mother felt comforted, her husband could step up in his role as encourager, and Stephanie felt a real, intimate connection with this family. The baby was received by the community as one "belonging to us"!

By sharing critical essentials, we have discovered new levels of communal living. The chapters that follow will give you deeper insight into these critical essentials. We hope you will be encouraged to become part of a close-knit community soon.

Discussion questions

1   How can we share deeper life experiences together?
2   How can we sacrifice our personal space to allow for more experiences together?
3   Practice bridging the gap of "keeping the distance" by asking each other one or more of the following questions:
    • What is your biggest life struggle at the moment?
    • What are your deepest insecurities?
    • What is your life calling?
    • What big decisions are you currently struggling with?

Scripture to study • Acts 2:42-47 • Matthew 5:14-16

Books to read • Radical Together, by *David Platt* • Life Together, *by Dietrich Bonhoeffer*

2.2 ETHOS: THE TRIBAL FIRE

—•—

Cassie Carstens

Establishing a New Culture: The Tribal Fire

All around the world we hear a cry for "redeeming the culture of the church". It is an unsettling truth that the church is not effective as a transformation agent of society in a world that is imploding morally. We need a new movement of God's grace to raise up a new Kingdom tribe that can take people to the promised land.

Phyllis Tickle says that around the year 2000 we entered what she calls "The Great Emergence." According to her, roughly every 500 years the empowered structures of institutionalised Christianity become an intolerable carapace that must be shattered for renewal and new growth to occur. This new era, called the era of the emerging church, is a time for principle-based and purposeful experimentation, as we try to carve out a new demonstration of God's church for our time on earth. [18]

The quest for an authentic Kingdom culture is therefore at the centre of our endeavour. What should a 21st-century Kingdom culture look like? What are the key values that should carry the culture? What would the DNA of that culture contain? What carries and promotes this culture?

Ethos: How We Feel Things

This book describes key values that have emerged in our discipleship movement. One of them is what Erwin McManus calls the "e-motion" of a culture. The "e-motion" of a culture refers to what we feel (emotion) when we spend time with a group of people. It also refers to the passion in action (motion) that drives the community.

Every person's preference for practicing spirituality should be enriched by the other forms. The ways people practice spirituality differ, their emotions differ, and the way people connect with God differ. Some people are mystical in their spirituality while others are more cognitive; some focus on doctrine while others are more concerned with social justice. None of these are right or wrong, but it is important not to neglect those not common to your own practice. Every person's preference for practicing spirituality should be enriched by the other forms.

Ethos: The Tribal Fire

Where do these preferences come from? According to Aristotle, people are motivated (persuaded) by three things: Ethos (credibility), Pathos (emotional appeal) and Logos (logic reasoning).

In *An Unstoppable Force*, Erwin McManus draws from all three motivations and re-frames "Ethos" for us.

> "If a worldview is the way a community sees reality, then an ethos is the way a community feels reality. Ethos is what happens when many individuals make autonomous choices that create a unified movement. Ethos moves us when nothing else will and like nothing else will. Ethos can be described as the tribal emotion. Like emotions fire us up, ethos is the tribal fire. Ethos is the fuel of our caring and the fire of our passions. Ethos is the e-motion of the community.
>
> Ethos (n.): The fundamental character or spirit of a culture; the underlying sentiment that informs the beliefs, customs and practices of a group or a society. The distinguishing character or disposition of a community, group or person."[19]

Ethos is the first thing we encounter at our meetings, and the social air-conditioning of our gatherings.

When we study the brain as the director of human behaviour,

it makes so much sense. The way our brain processes emotions and the consequent secretion (or not) of the "happy hormones" (dopamine, serotonin and oxytocin) directly determines how our life experiences make us feel. This impacts our decisions and behaviour.

The "love hormone" oxytocin is released upon physical contact (like a hug), stimulating feelings of love and trust. That is why considerate physical contact can be such a powerful remedy when someone is going through a tough time.

Dopamine is a "pleasure hormone", released when we strive towards a goal with specific rewards. It also stimulates creative thinking. Affirmation and celebrating achievements boost dopamine output in the brain.

Serotonin acts like a mood stabiliser, providing release from anxiety. Our brains produce it when we remember happy events in the past or focus on what we're grateful for in the present. Grateful reflection is a great practice to get into.

AND IF WE ARE INVITING OTHERS TO VISIT OUR GATHERINGS, WE SHOULD CREATE AN ENVIRONMENT WHERE OTHERS EXPERIENCE THE PRESENCE OF GOD

To create a happy hormone environment for our gatherings is essential, but it is also important to ask ourselves what the most dominant factor forming our ethos should be. What about the ethos that God wants? We want people to firstly have a sense of *"theo-motion"*, not emotion (*theo-* meaning "God"). The move of God amongst us must be prevalent. It is God's meeting that we step into. Our question should be: what about the ethos that God wants? His Spirit should be the director. And if we are inviting others to visit our gatherings, we should create an environment where others experience the presence of God. For us, it is not so much about being "seeker-sensitive". That emphasis can lead away from a focus on God towards a focus on our needs, which violates our essential value of selflessness.

We believe that Jesus created a joyous, liberating atmosphere, an inviting and life-changing space that communicated the Jubilee message (Luke 4:18-19): heaven on earth! This is the real e-motion we want all to experience: heaven on earth. God embracing us with his heavenly love.

On the horizontal inter-relational level, everyone in the fellowship should feel like they belong. This is one of the deepest needs for humanity, and should be easy for children of God, since we all belong intimately to our Father in heaven. He has moulded us into one family; we belong to the Father and as brothers and sisters to each other. We should communicate that belonging by:

- Appreciating the value of other people as saints through Christ
- Appreciating the significance of the calling of each person
- Celebrating the complementary contribution of each other as we make the function of the body of Christ complete
- Enjoying the fruit of the Spirit and the gifts of the Spirit in each other.

But the big pull of the meetings should come from God. He needs to pull us into his all-redeeming presence. The Word and Sprit should dominate our gatherings.

We Go First

"After suffering a stroke and on his deathbed, Robert the Bruce, the greatest of Scotland's kings, knew he would be unable to fulfil his solemn vow to go on a pilgrimage to the Holy Land. He asked his lifelong friend, Sir James Douglas, to carry his heart there instead. With the heart of the Bruce contained close to his own, Douglas, in the thick of the fighting and deserted by his Spanish allies, threw the heart of the Bruce deep into the melee, biding it 'Go first as thou hast always done.' Douglas himself was killed in the ensuing fighting." [20]

Mel Gibson made an epic movie about this in 1995 with the inspiring mantra: "Fight for the heart of your king! Forward brave heart!" This attitude is part and parcel of the DNA of our movement. We know we have to be courageous if we want to possess the Promised Land.

"A share in the heavenly kingdom is sought with most ardent zeal and intense exertion" (Matt 11:12, Classic Amplified translation).

We want all disciplers to instil this attitude in the hearts and minds of their disciples. We want everyone to be culture changers and trendsetters of a new culture. We do not follow culture, we make it!

In our movement we have various brave men and women; pioneers of ministries and initiators of many initiatives. Several of them have ministered in restricted countries; others have cabined with street sleepers to reach them for Christ; some have crossed mountains on foot to reach the unreached; others work at night to reach prostitutes for Jesus. We have brave men and women who fan the flame of the tribal fire, but we have to make sure that this DNA is transferred to the generations that will follow us.

We want everyone to be passionate to win territory for Christ. We go first!

DNA Carriers

Any movement needs "initiators" and "validators". The initiator, Jesus, had validators in Peter, John and James (and later Paul). Not only did they validate what he has lived and taught, but also ensured that Kingdom DNA would remain in the disciples and transfer to new disciples joining the movement.

Every discipleship group should do what Jesus did. Therefore, we work hard through counselling and discussions to help instil Kingdom DNA in every person we disciple. We train our disciples to be disciple-makers. Every person should focus on getting their disciples to be carriers and multipliers of the DNA.

Since the issue of Kingdom DNA is so central in the movement, we frequently hear these types of phrases in our movement:

- "Do they have Kingdom DNA?"
- "Does this sound like Kingdom thinking?"
- "Is this Kingdom language?"
- "How can we change this into Kingdom?"
- "How can the Kingdom come through this?"
- "Are we on a Kingdom mission with this?"

We have also borrowed the beautiful phrases that The World Needs A Father movement often uses: "How can we bring heaven to earth?" "How can we bring heaven home?" "Is this heaven-people thinking?"

What We Do

There are two specific activities we practice to flame the tribal fire. Twice a year we hold camps (retreats) for the whole discipleship family. This is where we work more intentionally on understanding our values and the ethos of our movement. The interaction over this longer period also builds relationships, is a good test for us to see if we are diverse enough, and an opportunity to celebrate our diversity (of age, race, culture and gender).

The second big activity to flame the tribal fire is the compassion outreaches we hold two or three times a year. Here we collectively help people in need, which reminds us what we are here for: to be changers of society. And as we engage with the pain and struggles of this world, we come close to the crisis of this world. We experience the passion that is created between the crisis and the vision. As the passion is ignited, the tribal fire flares high!

Discussion questions

1   How would you describe the atmosphere in your community/tribe from the perspective of a newcomer?
2   How can the atmosphere in your gathering change to be a joyous, liberating, inviting, gracious, life-changing atmosphere?
3   What needs to change in your community for people to say they experience heaven among you?
4   In what way can you fan the "tribal fire" as a group?

Scripture to study • Romans 12:9-21

Books to read • An Unstoppable Force, *by E.R. McManus*

2.3 JOURNEY TOGETHER AS A TEAM

George Kellerman & Cassie Carstens

If you are a follower of Jesus, you probably already have an idea of what it is like to journey — to get to know, listen, wrestle, and walk — with God. But have you experienced this journey as a team? Drawing closer to God and learning how to listen to him as a team? Enquiring about the sin within the team and going through the process of repentance and forgiveness as a team? Receiving guidance of what the collective role is in his Kingdom? It is a different experience, this communal journey, yet one that God often uses to move his people. When God spoke in the Old Testament, it was often to the nation of Israel, not to individuals. Jesus often addressed his bride, the church. Most of the New Testament letters were written to churches, not individuals.

Are we not much more likely to hear God's voice if we seek him as a team?

I BELIEVE GOD SPEAKS TO THE COLLECTIVE MORE OFTEN THAN TO INDIVIDUALS

There is a short, beautiful story of a team journeying together in Acts 13:1-3. It is one of those stories I wish the author had told in more detail, but even the three verses tell us quite a lot. It talks about a group of people (including Barnabas and Saul) who prayed and fasted together. During one of their meetings in Antioch, the Holy Spirit told them to set Barnabas and Saul aside for a particular work. The story records the Holy Spirit speaking to the whole team, not just Paul and Barnabas. They heard God together and responded by being obedient as a team, sending Paul and Barnabas to take the message to the island of Cyprus and beyond.

I believe God speaks to the collective more often than to individuals, which could be one reason we struggle to hear him. In individualistic cultures, we rarely approach him collectively. Acts 13 opened our eyes to this, so we approached God as the student ministry leadership group. As a team, we asked God the simple question, "What do you want us to do as a team in your Kingdom?"

After praying together, I asked each person to write the three things they felt the Lord was leading us to do as a team. We were amazed at the response. Every single person wrote something along the line of "teenagers", "leadership" and "training". The unity of our response made it clear what our calling was as a team. After some research, we found a school where we could do leadership training for teenagers. We doubled the size of our team and developed and organised a seven-week training for 100 teenagers. We mentored 500 students during the first four years, and up to the time of writing, these trainings are continuing. This all happened from seeking God as a team and being obedient to him as a team.

Group, Team… Body!

The success of most sports teams rises and falls with their ability to work as a team. It is quite strange then, that it is rare to find a church where teamwork is a priority. Most churches are satisfied to function in groups. In this sense, a group is a collection of individuals who interact around common interests. However, they don't have a shared purpose, and rarely depend on each other to achieve their shared or individual goals.

At the very least, we should function as a team. A team is a collection of individuals who depend on and support each other in the pursuit of a shared purpose. Far too many people share how their worst experience of fake teams was in a church. People described how the teams they were in showed no evidence of interdependence, and when they needed support, it was not there.

However, working as a team is just a stepping stone. The Bible calls us to be more than just a team. The image used is that of a body, which demands a much higher level of functioning together.

1 Corinthians 12 beautifully explains how the church body could work together:

1 One spirit (the Spirit, not different opinions) manages us *(11)*
   - As a result, the intention is to benefit everyone *(7)*
2 We are one body (Jew and Greek) *(13)*
   - For that to happen, our civil and family identity (and our loyalty towards our possessions *(1 Cor 7:30))* must be secondary to our Kingdom loyalty!
3 We appreciate our different functions: *(17-20, 28)*
   - without feeling inferior *(15-16)*
   - without feeling superior *(21-22)*
   - without trying to be self-sufficient *(21-22)*
4 We must appreciate diversity *(21-22, 28-30)*
5 We must humble ourselves by empowering the weak *(22-23)*
6 We must have equal concern for each other *(25)*
7 We should have solidarity with those that hurt and rejoice with those who are honoured *(26)*
8 Everyone should develop their own gifts, and practise love (the greatest gift) *(31)*

The Message translation describes our new identity as a body beautifully:

"We all said goodbye to our partial and piecemeal lives. We each used to independently call our own shots, but then we entered into a large and integrated life in which he has the final say in everything." (1 Cor 12:12-13 MSG)

When one part hurts, all parts should suffer together. But how much suffering in your church goes completely unnoticed? We are called to function as a body. A body is interdependent, interconnected members co-creating a shared experience and identity. We share heartache, brokenness, joy and achievement together. We share the same mission!

Breaking Through Resistance Barriers

Why would Jesus want us to become a body? Why would he want us to spend the time and effort required to develop intimacy? Why would he want us to battle through our differences together, to move from being a group to being a team to eventually becoming a body? This prayer gives us a taste of Jesus' passionate desire for his people to become one:

FOR A GROUP TO BECOME A TEAM IS A CHALLENGING PROCESS, AND TO GROW FROM A TEAM TO A BODY IS EVEN MORE INTENSIVE

"I have given them the glory that you gave me, that they may be one as we are one — I in them and you in me — so that they may be brought to complete unity. Then the world will know that you sent me and have loved them even as you have loved me" (John 17:22-23).

Another metaphor used to describe the church (the body of believers, not a building) is that of the bride (of Jesus) (Rev 19:7; 21:2, 9; 22:17). As a bride prepares extensively for her wedding day, so should we do all we can to make ourselves pure as a church. But we first need to learn how to move from group to team. Only then can we learn how to turn a team into a body.

All collections of individuals start off as a group. For a group to become a team is a challenging process, and to grow from a team to a body is even more intensive. Becoming a body takes an incredible amount of time and effort. We need to learn ways to accelerate the process. The next section shares some keys we have discovered.

On the journey to functioning as a body, we will encounter resistance barriers. Resistance barriers are present when growth has stagnated and reached the ceiling of the current level. However, breaching a resistance barrier puts the team on a new trajectory of growth. Focussing on breaking through these specific barriers allows a group (or dare I say team) to reach amazing new heights. The three major resistance barriers to breach are:

1. The barrier of individualism.

We cannot function as a body without allowing the team to trump the individual. We have to surrender our desire for self-reliance and show our allegiance to the body. If you struggle to trust the intentions of others, the 99% rule is a great place to start. Simply put, it assumes that 99% of the time the motives of others are good, and any hurt is unintentional. When we assume good intent, we are quicker to understand and less likely to blame.

The Zulu phrase, "Umuntu ngumuntu ngabantu" expands on this idea. Translated, it means "a person is only a person through other people." We will never reach our full potential without others. To do so, we must commit to unmasking personal issues and improving our self-knowledge.

2. The barrier of solidified convictions.

The more preconceived ideas we carry, the less we allow others to shape our thinking. One detrimental form of that is stereotyping. Once I throw away the key to things I have decided, I forfeit my ability to function as a team player.

On the other hand, I open myself up to being a team player by surrendering my preconceived ideas. To do this, start by assuming that the best answer is usually the third alternative. The third alternative isn't necessarily the literal third choice; rather, it is somewhere between my opinion and that of the other. Inviting the perspectives and insights of other genders, cultures, people groups and generations are key to breaking through the barrier. Always approach life with the intent to enrich your convictions.

3. The barrier of exclusion.

There is an advanced moment in team formation where "I thinking" turns into "we thinking". In close relationships, we share everything with the other person. Dr. James Hastings defines love as:

"… that principle which leads one mortal being to desire and delight in another, and reaches its highest form in that personal fellowship in which each lives in the life of the other, and finds [their] joy in imparting [themselves] to the other, and in receiving back the outflow of that other's affection unto [themselves]." [21]

When a group of individuals reach this state, the transition from "I" to "we" can take place. There is an exchange and integration of qualities, and a fusion of strengths where potential mushrooms. People step out of themselves and into the group, and allow others into their space. As the process gets deeper, co-discovery and co-development takes place. This closeness finds its ultimate expression in sincere intimacy. It is a way of life in which the distance between two people dissolves and new horizons appear. You know your team is reaching that point when a member can say, "We achieved the objective!" even if they didn't take part at all.

Trust: The Most Essential Ingredient For A Team

As the nature of successful teams varies according to context and goals, it is hard to pinpoint every single ingredient that makes them work. However, there is one element that is common to all successful teams — trust.

Many people acknowledge that they struggle to trust others. This mistrust has several roots, most of which fall into one of a few broad categories. (This is by no means a complete list, but can serve as a starting point.)

The first is the mother wound. Your mother was supposed to impart intimacy to you during the first five years of your life through frequent physical contact, affection and consistency. If she was unable to offer those things, a mother wound is often the result. One of the symptoms of a mother wound is an inability to trust, especially when there is no other obvious reason.

Alternatively, you may no longer trust people due to a series of bad experiences. Even one harsh betrayal can ruin your desire to trust for years to come. Some people stop trusting as they discover the vileness of humanity, and how willing people are to hurt others if they can get something from it. Still others have prideful hearts that look down on others in self-absorbed contempt. They are unwilling to trust a person's integrity or competence, because no one measures up to their standards.

Trust is essential if we are to build effective teams of disciples. But how can we accomplish it in the face of this mistrust?

In his book, *The 8th Habit*, Stephen Covey describes 10 trust deposits we must make to build "capital" in the trust bank. For every deposit we make, we have to sacrifice something of our own. It does not come without cost. It is our responsibility to pay the cost and not wait on other people to act first. [22]

Key Deposits Are:

1. Seeking first to understand the other person's frame of reference
2. Making and keeping promises
3. Honesty and integrity
4. Kindness and courtesies to acknowledge the feelings of others
5. Trying to find a win-win alternative (that benefits both parties) or no deal
6. Clarifying expectations on who should do what, and why
7. Being loyal to those not present (no gossiping!)
8. Sincere apologies (no justification)
9. Giving and receiving feedback to clarify our blind spots
10. True forgiveness from which you can move on.

Five More Vital Deposits That Build Trust:

1   Do not catch people off-balance by springing surprises on them.
2   Ensure your dealings with people are as unbiased as possible. Everyone must have an equal chance.
3   Live from an attitude of abundance (giving). An attitude of scarcity (getting) makes people nervous.
4   Moral behaviour creates trust.
5   Apply good discretion in decision-making.

The idea is to work on your own trustworthiness and create an environment of trust. The higher the level of performance needed, the higher the degree of trust should be.

If we manage to develop that trust and function as a body, the following great scenarios are likely to await us:

- We will hear the voice of God better.
- Everyone will be valued.
- Our deepest need is to belong. We will experience this in abundance.
- The synergy from combining our strengths will be astounding.
- We will radically reduce the weight of our pain and burdens as we share them.
- It will draw the interest of the world.

To journey with God as a team is a very special experience. We experience his guidance together. We hear his voice together. We recognise team obedience steps to take together. We experience him talking to us individually at the same time about the same things. Teams on the move, being guided by the Holy Spirit, are a powerful force indeed!

Discussion questions

1 Would you classify yourselves as a group, a team or a body? Why?
2 What will help you become a body?
3 How can you move from "I thinking" to "we thinking"?
4 What trust deposits do you want to give special attention to in the coming week?

Scripture to study • Acts 13:1-3 • 1 Corinthians 12

Books to read • The 8th Habit, *by Stephen R. Covey*

2.4 TRANSPARENCY: PEOPLE OF THE LIGHT

George Kellerman

I have come to learn that transparency brings liberation. And if transparency leads to freedom — one of the things people crave the most — why are we not craving transparency? I needed to put this theory — that transparency leads to freedom — to the test, and where better than one of the toughest contexts for transparency: finances. Why do people keep what they earn, owe and spend such a secret? Why do I keep it a secret? Not having a good answer to that question, I realised I needed to test the theory myself. I prepared a breakdown of my personal finances for a small panel of close friends and gave them carte blanche to be completely honest. I invited them to ask me tough questions, and decide how I should change my spending, saving and giving habits.

As the presentation approached, I couldn't help but wonder if I was in my right mind when I first had the idea. What will they think of me when they learn how much I earn and how I spend it? Suddenly, it didn't seem like such a good idea. When the presentation arrived, so did the tough questions and embarrassment I had been fearing. But to my surprise, an incredible sense of community and liberation from money completely overshadowed my discomfort. I felt liberated!

Transparency brings liberation, and more than that — it fosters fellowship and intimacy. This became the first of many such evenings, and it still amazes us how a simple transparency exercise can bring such closeness in community. We laid many of our other struggles on the table, and the transparency and trust has grown to a point where remarkable things are happening. We have helped each other build houses and lived with each other when it was necessary. We loan each other money, pool our funds and give to worthy causes, ask each other challenging questions and make big financial decisions together. We try to live like the church community described in Acts as far as possible.

As I was discovering the value of transparency in practice, something else happened. I started noticing how often transparency, usually referred to as "light", was discussed in Scripture. Jesus spoke about it from the start of his ministry, and in the first chapter of his epistle, John introduced Jesus as "the light". To John, light was exposing, revealing, the truth, openness, life-giving, and love-abounding. This light metaphor framed how he described Jesus and throws down a challenge for us: should those characteristics not be a fundamental description of a people who follow Jesus? Scripture refers to people who follow Jesus as "people of the light". Should his followers not be known as people who expose darkness, reveal truth, live open lives, bring life to situations, and abound in love? Are we people of the light?

> "But more than that, the effect of such sins is always to make us "walk in darkness" — that is, to cover it up and hide what we really are or what we are really feeling. That is always the meaning of "darkness" in Scripture, for while the light reveals, the darkness hides. The first effect of sin in us is always to make us hide; with the result that we are pretending, we are wearing a mask, we are not real with either God or man. And, of course, neither God nor man can fellowship with an unreal person." [23]

Are we real with one another? Are we really people of the light? True transparency happens when our lives are completely open towards each other. No masks, no pretension, no hidden corners. Old wounds are faced, bad memories recalled, and embarrassing sins revealed. It is a place that welcomes tough, honest questions, and doesn't shy away from necessary confrontation. Sins and blind spots are exposed, and lives become full of light. As people of the light, our lives should look different to the surrounding culture. We should be able to open the dark parts of our lives to each other, challenge each other on real issues, and make major life decisions together. However, it is not without risk. Making ourselves open to immature and untrustworthy people could lead to deep disappointment. Transparency is a difficult process, but is also the best opportunity for real, deep fellowship. So why do we rarely see it happening?

TRANSPARENCY MAY BE RISKY, BUT NOT BEING TRANSPARENT IS EVEN MORE SO

Transparency may be risky, but not being transparent is even more so. Satan prowls around like a roaring lion looking for someone to devour. If we do not bring things into the light, Satan can manipulate the dark places. However, a life that is open, real and vulnerable removes many of the dark strongholds Satan seeks to target. It prevents hidden sins, reveals weaknesses, and can offer relief for numbing fears and shameful hurts. A life exposed to trusted people helps prevent a life exposed to darkness! Although it can be uncomfortable, it is much safer to live exposed lives. Unfortunately, Western Christianity has embraced the idea that "my life is my business", despite Scripture's clear teachings to the contrary. Because of this trend, we rarely see exposed lives in small groups. But that begs the question: how deeply do we care for one another? If we ignore the dark places in our team members' lives, can we say we love one another? If we leave our friends to fight their battles all alone, can we call ourselves people of the light?

A lack of transparency also risks affecting our fellowship with God. We cannot separate fellowship with God from fellowship with others. They are codependent. Fellowship with people depends on our vulnerability and transparency with God, and our intimacy with God depends on our ability to be vulnerable and transparent with others. We will only have real fellowship with God if we have real fellowship with people.

"Now the work of the Lord Jesus Christ on the Cross was not only to bring men back into fellowship with God, but also into fellowship with their fellow men. Indeed it cannot do one without the other. As the spokes get nearer the centre of the wheel, they get nearer to one another. But if we have not been brought into vital fellowship with our brother, it is a proof that to that extent we have not been brought into vital fellowship with God. The first epistle of John (what a new light Revival sheds on this Scripture!) insists on testing the depth and reality of a person's fellowship with God by the depth and reality of his fellowship with fellow believers" [24] (1 John 2:9; 3:14-15; 4:20).

Transparency is a fantastic way to prevent loneliness. You might enjoy a degree of fellowship with people, but the secrets, major life issues and big decisions you keep to yourself will isolate you. How often do we see our friends making bad choices or struggling with major life issues, but are unable to speak into their lives because we were never given permission to do so? The lack of mutual openness paralyses our ability to deal with the real issues. They may invite us in for tea and small talk, but the inner rooms of their lives are out of bounds.

So how do we allow people to speak into our lives? How do we achieve an atmosphere of total transparency? This isn't an exhaustive list, but here are some practices we have found useful:

We commit to it. Our discipleship team decided from the start that our goal would be total transparency with each other. Even though it might take a while, we wanted to get to a place where we could ask any question at any time. We also realised that we needed to recommit to it regularly, since transparency remains a difficult thing. Because risks are inevitable on the road to vulnerability, a commitment to total transparency is critical to help the team to stay on course.

We challenge the toughest areas. Transparency requires a head-on approach for it to become a core value on your team. We identified the things we struggled with the most and asked each other unflinching questions about those areas on a regular basis. We made it our goal to not allow these areas to defeat us. We wanted to be real people, and to be real people we needed to be willing to deal with the real issues. For example, two of the things we dealt with as a group of young men were how we spent our time, and pornography. We would often ask each other questions such as, "Did you spend your time with purpose?" and "Did you sin in pornography?" These are hectic questions, and not easy to answer. But as we shared our issues, the questions became easier to answer, the dark areas shrank, and we struggled with them less. We experienced victory because we brought them into the light, before each other and before Jesus. The most difficult areas to expose are usually related to money, sex or power, so if you don't know where to start, start there!

We submit major life decisions to one another. Sharing decision-making responsibilities with each other has amplified our experience of community. By sharing personal matters, we experience the intimacy of community even though we live some distance apart. Inviting others into our big decisions also invites them into our lives. We give them the right to offer meaningful input on matters most dear to us. These big decisions could include who to marry, what career to pursue, where to live, and so on. If you aren't yet married, sharing responsibility for the decision of who you date is critical. We have seen too many lives going awry due to bad relationship choices made in isolation. A few years back I had to make a big career decision. I had many doubts and fears. After opening up the decision to the community at one of our gatherings, I felt assured in the decision I had to make. It was incredible to move from uncertainty, fear and loneliness to certainty, peace and fellowship in the space of only a few hours.

It is natural to feel uncomfortable at the idea of sharing decision-making responsibility on such a personal matter. However, practicing intentional transparency is exactly the thing that allows real community to exist. Sharing decision-making on intimate levels helps us understand how co-responsible we are for each other's spiritual growth.

We confess. When someone walks into a discipleship gathering and says, "Guys, before we start, I need to confess something...", you know that the transparency and trust level of the team is very high. We have a team member who has raised the level of transparency within the team by his willingness to be vulnerable. Confession should become a habit and norm within a discipleship team. So too should confrontation. If we really love one another and there is trust within the group, we shouldn't be afraid to confront each other where necessary. Risking the health of a friendship for your friend's well-being is tough, but it speaks to a deeper love and obedience. That said, it is important to handle both confession and confrontation with humility, respect and compassion. These are key elements of transparency, and when done right prove that light has triumphed. But done wrong, they can devastate relationships.

Discussion questions

1   What does it mean to live as children of the light?
2   Why is transparency a scary concept?
3   Why is transparency important?
4   What major life decisions should we submit to one another?

Scripture to study • John 1:1-9 • 1 John 1:5-10 • Ephesians 5:8-14 • John 3:19-21

Books to read • The Essentials of Theory U, *by Otto Scharmer* • Transparency, *by Warren Bennis, Daniel Goleman and James O'Toole*

2.5 RESPONSIBILITY & COMMITMENT

George Kellerman

A few years back, I was shepherding a student ministry and needed to build a core leadership team to disciple the student discipleship groups. Before long, I identified a handful of strong leaders who I felt would be able to shepherd the student groups. However, with more responsibility comes the need for greater accountability. As university students, sexual purity was a critical, often difficult aspect of moral authority we needed to deal with. I had regular discussions with them on this topic. One of the first questions I would ask was, "How are you doing with your sexual purity?" One week, after a long awkward silence, one of the leaders realised I wasn't going to just let the question slide.

"That is a hectic personal question, man. I need to improve in this area, but yeah, these things are personal."

Awkward silence ensued again, so I tried a different approach.

"Well, we need to talk about this if you are going to be discipling students. So let me ask you: are you staying within the physical boundaries you and your girlfriend set for your relationship?"

He gave me an uncomfortable look. "How can you ask these questions, man? Who gave you the right to ask these questions?"

"If I am not asking these questions, who will?"

Okay, so I didn't say that last bit out loud, but I did think it. Unfortunately, before long he withdrew from our team. The questions became too personal or offensive, I guess, but I felt responsible for him. I was supposed to shepherd him in a way that safeguarded and guided him and his team. Did I overstep the line? How far should my responsibility and accountability reach?

Paul and the Corinthian church struggled with a similar issue. The church in Corinth was complaining to Paul about the way he executed his authority over the church. They didn't like his rebukes and strong words. They complained that Paul's letters were "weighty and forceful" (2 Cor 10:10). In today's language, their message to Paul would probably have read, "Who gave you the right to speak to us like that? What reason do you have to come at us acting like you are our boss? What authority do you have over us to say what you say?"

In 2 Corinthians 10, Paul makes it clear he believes God assigned the church in Corinth to him as part of his mandate. The authority he has been given over them is part of his role and responsibility given by God, not for any other reason.

"We, however, will not boast beyond proper limits, but will confine our boasting to the field God has assigned to us, a field[A] that reaches even to you... For we do not want to boast about work already done in another man's territory" (2 Cor 10:13-16 NIV 1984).

Whether Paul and Timothy wanted it or not, God had given them the church of Corinth as a territory (sphere of influence) to actively develop. To accomplish this, they were given a sphere of influence (a role and responsibility) over a specific group of people. And when God assigns a role and responsibility, he assigns spiritual authority. They derived their authority from God's direction, not a sense of self-importance. Paul and Timothy did not assign it to themselves. Since the assignment was given by God, the spiritual authority was implied in the assignment — in the role that Paul and Timothy had to fulfil. By accepting responsibility, they acknowledged that they had to answer to God for what happened with the

---

A   The Greek word for "field" is "kanon", which means "a definitely bounded or fixed space within the limits of which one's power of influence is confined", "a measuring rod/rule" or "a principle or law of investigating, judging, living, acting." For more, see https://www. biblestudytools.com/lexicons/greek/kjv/kanon.html

Corinthian church, which was an incredible responsibility, if you think about it. Paul and Timothy were eager to reach the rest of the world, but they had to see to Corinth's growth first. Once Corinth was sufficiently mature, God opened other territories for Paul and Timothy to enrich.

Like with Paul and Timothy, God assigns to each of us a role and responsibility to build up a person or group. However, don't for a moment think it makes you more important than anyone else. If anything, it should humble you. God is trusting you with the development of a person or group for a time. And as you trust God's assignment and guidance, you will become a space to display godly authority in a beautiful way.

Unfortunately, it is all too easy to overstep the boundaries of the territory God gives us. When we lose sight of God, if we miss his guiding voice, we often end up leading people on our own mission. Some people overreach, and instead of giving the small group quality input, they try to grow the group as large and as fast as possible. Others abuse their responsibility for their own profit; be it emotional affirmation, financial gain or power. Too many people have experienced such manipulation by church leaders. But when done right, taking responsibility leads to the safe-keeping of people's hearts and the accountability of people's obedience.

Are only some people expected to be spiritually responsible for others? To answer "yes" is like saying: "Only some parents should take care of their children." To not take up responsibility is to leave a gap. Leaving a gap is to fail to safeguard, protect and develop the people assigned to you. This is what is meant by the watchman not sounding the alarm in the story in Ezekiel 33, or the shepherd not tending the sheep in the story in Ezekiel 34 and 1 Peter 5. To do nothing is to let the enemy destroy the people you should protect. Unfortunately, this is all too commonplace. Most people have little or no accountability structure in their lives and get into serious trouble while their friends look on in silence.

"So they were scattered because there was no shepherd, and when they scattered they became food for all the wild animals. My sheep wandered over all the mountains and on every high hill. They were scattered over the whole earth, and no one searched or looked for them" (Ezek 34:5-6).

Who will stand as watchmen? Who will take up their places as shepherds? These roles are not exclusive. Every Christian should partake.

Once you accept that you need to be a watchman or shepherd, the next question is, to whom?

Many Christians assume only pastors and deacons should be allowed to hold others accountable, but we forget Paul's encouragement to Timothy: "Pass on what you heard from me... to reliable leaders who are competent to teach others" (2 Tim 2:2 MSG). Spiritual authority is for people like Paul or Timothy, and other reliable men and women.

So who is reliable in this context, you ask? You could be. In discipleship, the first qualification is a willingness to be discipled, and to disciple.

We need to ask God where he has assigned us. Which person or people should we disciple? Is it one person, or five people, or thirty? What kind of relationship should we build with them? Similarly, who is responsible for the territory I am in? To whom do I need to submit? How can I honour and empower them?

So how do we foster healthy responsibility and commitment? One way is to encourage people to commit to be devoted to each other. Romans 12:10 pleads for us to, "be devoted to one another in brotherly love. Honour one another above yourselves." Devotion to one another goes beyond mere friendship. It is accepting responsibility for each other, holding each other accountable and being willing to challenge sin. We must honour one another, serving and caring as we strive to become more like Jesus. Journeying with many people is very challenging, so you need to pray about how many people you can serve well. Rather choose fewer people and go deeper, than many people to whom you won't be able to give your full attention. We have discovered that the best opportunity to experience this is within discipleship relationships, because of the high level of commitment between one another.

What We Do

Agreeing to disciple or to be discipled is a serious commitment. A sense of responsibility underpins the relationship, which builds devotion to each other. In our group, we formalise the relationship to a degree. This helps clarify the role you play in each other's lives, allows the discipler to speak with more freedom into the life of the disciple and allows the disciple to speak with more freedom into the life of the discipler.

Discussion questions

1   To whom should you be a watchman/shepherd/discipler? Who has God assigned to you to disciple?
2   What kind of relationship should you build with them?
3   Who is responsible for the territory you are in? Who needs to keep you responsible and committed?

Scripture to study • 2 Corinthians 10 • 1 Peter 5:1-5

Books to read • Building Up One Another, *by Gene A Getz*

2.6 OPEN DOORS: HOW FAR SHOULD WE GO?

—•—

George Kellerman

How far does my responsibility stretch? This question often pops up when talking about accountability within discipleship. Responsibility within discipleship is similar to the relationship between parent and child; Paul even refers to his disciples as spiritual sons and daughters in his letters. Or, as we call them, spiritual younger brothers and sisters.

Your responsibility for the person you disciple goes beyond giving pointers and good advice. Amongst other things, it should include safe-keeping, guiding and correcting. Safe-keeping and guiding have their challenges, but correcting is usually the most difficult part. You can also read "correcting" as "disciplining" or "rebuking"; words which appear often in the Bible, but in verses we prefer to glance over.

Just as it is awkward to discipline someone else's child, so correcting the people we disciple can be very uncomfortable. In this age of "everything goes", correcting a friend feels unnatural. And once you have settled with the idea of correcting someone else, you face even more questions. How far does my responsibility to this person stretch? How much should I correct them? And who am I to judge?

DO YOU CARE ENOUGH TO CONFRONT THE PEOPLE YOU DISCIPLE?

It is important to remember that you are not correcting someone to prove a point. Correction always needs to benefit the person being corrected. Whether they realise it or not, appreciate or despise you for it, correction should always help them grow. Confrontation is rarely easy or pleasant, but it is critical for growth. Just as healthy discipline benefits a child in the long run, so healthy correction adds value within discipleship. It is necessary and is a sign that you care enough about the person to confront them.

Do you care enough to confront the people you disciple?

If you care for someone, it doesn't help them at all if you ignore the wrongs they commit. To be nice is not always loving. And to be loving is not always to be nice. The Lord says he "disciplines those he loves" (Prov 3:12 and Heb 12:7-13). If you love someone, correction should become a natural part of your relationship. Regular correction of your disciples when required is not only proof of your love for them, but also a proof you have taken up responsibility for them.

Correction usually starts with tough questions and progresses from there. Sometimes stern words or direct condemnation of actions or thought patterns is needed. Other times an honest, direct conversation is all that is required. "As iron sharpens iron, so a friend sharpens a friend" (Prov 27:17 NLT). When iron sharpens iron, there is always friction. Friends need friction to sharpen one another.

But what if the person you are discipling is not open to correction? What if they feel it is not your place to correct or confront them? What if their door is closed to correction?

When I was a young boy, I remember watching my sister trying to escape discipline. When she knew punishment was coming, she would run to her room, slam the door and try stop my father from entering the room. When he got in, she would scream at the top of her lungs. This is not so different from adults today. People even run away, slam doors and throw tantrums. When it is someone we are responsible for, however, we must decide: should we barge open the door or let them be? Are we crossing a boundary by entering, or condoning their actions by our silence? Should we assume responsibility to open the door, or should we wait to be invited in? Should doors be open or should we "wipe the dust off our feet" (Luke 10:11) when the doors are closed and walk away? This is a difficult, situational question to answer.

There are many stories of bad experiences with the misapplication of spiritual authority. While some come from misunderstandings or unrealistic expectations, the fact remains: it is a touchy subject. Just mention the word accountability and many people get a bad taste in their mouth. If we want to redeem the principle of accountability, it will be an uphill battle. This is in no small part due to the fear that people will use the intimate things we share against us. For accountability to work, trust is essential.

"If we knew each other's secrets, what comfort we would find." [25]

Imagine a world where a group of people live totally open lives with one another. A community where doors are open, and people invite others to speak into their lives. A space where views can be challenged, and correction is accepted as a healthy part of growth. An environment free from fear, full of love and trust — full of light. In this kind of environment, rebuke and correction fit into the bigger picture of becoming like Christ and are both given and received with love. How amazing would that be!

You might be thinking, "amazing, sure, but also totally unrealistic." Actually, it is not as unrealistic as you think. But it takes hard work, commitment and vulnerability. The rest of this section will look into some of the ways we go about trying to build that kind of environment within our discipleship groups.

Opening Up My Door

There is always risk attached to transparency and accountability. Broken trust, manipulated vulnerability, emotional abuse; the list is long and painful. If you have been hurt like that, it is incredibly hard to risk trusting again. However, if we want to experience accountability as it was intended, we need to risk opening our doors. The best people to open up to are those to whom you have made a commitment. If you are married, your spouse should be at the top of the list. But you should also include others, such as the people around your table of support (see chapter 2.9), and your discipleship group.

Opening Up Others' Doors

I don't have a textbook answer for correction and accountability. To be honest, I don't think there is any one answer that works in every situation. But the Bible contains many principles that help us find our way around giving and receiving correction. Luke 17:3 and Matthew 18:15 are good places to start:

"So watch yourselves. If your brother or sister sins against you, rebuke them; and if they repent, forgive them."

"If your brother or sister sins, go and point out their fault, just between the two of you. If they listen to you, you have won them over."

When I am in a confrontational situation, I usually ask myself three questions. Firstly, do I care enough for this person, their spiritual growth and the people they will influence? Secondly, what should I do to fulfil the responsibility the Lord has given me to hold them accountable? And thirdly, is there enough trust between us for them to take this the right way?

The most common mistake I make when correcting my friends is assuming more trust than there actually is. Without trust, accountability and correction can be unpleasant. You need to take time to build trust before diving into correction. As the trust between you grows, so can the correction. *The 8th Habit*, **WE CANNOT WAIT FOR PERFECTION BEFORE BEING WILLING TO HELP OTHERS WITH THE SAME ISSUES** Stephen Covey talks about the trust deposits we must make in the trust account before people will trust us. There must be enough trust in the trust account to make withdrawals, otherwise the experience usually ends up being negative. (See chapter 2.3 for more on trust deposits.)

The most common excuse I hear for not correcting or rebuking friends/disciples is, "I am not perfect. How can I point out something in my friend when my life is a mess?" Some people even point to Matthew 7:4 — "How can you say to your brother, 'Let me take the speck out of your eye,' when all the time there is a plank in your own eye?" This feels like a powerful reason to avoid correction, but the reality is, we will never be perfect. We cannot wait for perfection before being willing to help others with the same issues. Sometimes, the fact that you are also struggling with the issue (provided you are open about it) increases the likelihood of the person listening to you. Also, remember that you are correcting people for their benefit, not yours! When you both understand that you are working together to become like Christ, correction is far more likely to be well received.

As you probably realised by now, correction is not easy. But if you do it sensitively and with the right motives, it can be the most loving thing you can do for a friend. As you let go of your own comfort and desire to please people, and put holiness before friendship, you will discover holy friendships.

I remember rebuking a close friend about his choice of girlfriend during our university days. He was furious and wouldn't speak to me for a month. I knew I was risking our friendship by rebuking him, but I wanted the best for him and knew I was the best person to confront him. A few months after he ended the relationship, he met another woman, who later became his wife. While they were dating, he thanked me for having the courage to rebuke him. We are still close friends today, and have great respect for each other.

If you practice discipleship with real love, you may need to risk a relationship for the sake of being obedient to God. If God tells you to warn, correct, or rebuke someone, you have the choice to obey him or to please your friend. Sometimes things will resolve nicely. Other times, they won't. Your challenge is to stay obedient to God, no matter what.

Creating an atmosphere where we can be transparent is not easy and does not come naturally. However, it is necessary if we want to be able to confront and correct each other in a gracious, loving manner. My discipleship team recognised this, so we built transparency into our team culture from the beginning. It was a process to become comfortable enough to confront each other. We needed to create a space for the team to feel safe to open up and let accountability happen. Here are a few tools we use to create that space.

We give permission. Regularly give one another permission to speak with freedom into each other's lives. One question we ask to stimulate this conversation is, "What are your biggest concerns for my life?" When you ask this question regularly, you train yourself to be open to others. When a contentious issue crops up, the closed door will be more likely to swing open.

We go on trust walks. A trust walk is something simple, but always has an impact when used. It is sometimes easier to talk about deep issues when you are moving and not directly facing the person you are talking to. The group members walk in pairs for a set time, then switch partners. Sometimes the conversation is deep and personal, other times it is confession, or even confrontation. The purpose is to share anything which is otherwise difficult to talk about in the day-to-day life.

We help each other to avoid crossing the line. When someone has overstepped the code of conduct, we call it "crossing the line". If someone is called out for "crossing the line", they need to speak to God about the issue in question. They should evaluate their actions and motives and compare them against what the Bible says. It is critical that they do this without defending themselves or trying to justify their transgression. The next day, the person who called them out needs to chat about what happened with them. If they get stuck on the issue, other people in the group are called on for counsel.

We bring specific areas of weakness into the light. Seeing as we rarely have enough time together, we commit to talking about the areas in our lives where we are the weakest. These are the areas that require intentional, focused transparency. We talk about them openly to make sure that Satan doesn't have space to build influence in that area. Sin breeds in the dark, and by talking about things we bring them into the light. However, intentional transparency or accountability does run the risk of becoming too selective. We cannot afford to focus so intently on one issue that we ignore others. To avoid that from happening, we use these intentional transparency times to probe and ask tougher questions.

We share our life timeline. A life timeline has many forms, but the simplest is to draw a timeline of your life, pointing out significant events. Each person has 10 minutes or so to share, then the others have 10 minutes to ask questions. Sharing in this manner allows the rest of the group to learn a lot more about the person in a short space of time.

We lower our masks and share our weaknesses. People connect in strength, but bond in weakness. We make a point of sharing with each other when our lives get tough. We try to remove our own masks and other team members' masks as often as possible. Asking "What were your highlights and lowlights this week?" is a good way to draw tough times out of people who prefer to act as though everything is okay.

Discussion questions

1   What were your highlights and lowlights this week?
2   How can we create an atmosphere where we can easily confront each other and easily confess to each other?
3   What areas should we intentionally expose and be transparent about in our group?
4   What are your biggest concerns for my life? (Ask this in groups of three.)

Scripture to study • Hebrews 12:4-13 • 2 Timothy 3:16-17 • Acts 5:1-10

Books to read • Authentic Christianity, *by Peter Watts*

2.7 SUBMISSION

——•——

Cassie Carstens

At a marriage enrichment seminar, we asked the young married people to answer the following question for us:

Which of the following situations would be the worst for you?
1   That you lose all your money and remain poor forever (poverty)
2   That you never have sex again (celibacy)
3   That you lose your power to decide and others have to decide for you (submission).

The majority by far picked losing the ability to make their own decisions. They clearly stated that submission is the most difficult choice of all.

Despite the centrality and beauty of the biblical concept of "submission", so many people rebel against it due to a society ravaged by misused power and abusive authority.

The pain of misused power has crippled our understanding of authority. Women being raped, babies being aborted, the force of military intrusion, mutilation of civilians in war and the brutality of corporal punishment when the anger of immature parents explodes have all maimed and disfigured the value of authority to such extent that "pure authority" is hard to find, and unthinkable in the minds of most.

But we simply cannot close our eyes to the significance of submission.

We find echoes of submission throughout the Bible. Sometimes it is directly addressed, while other times it is nestled in complementary concepts like dependence, following, self-sacrifice, honour, obedience and so on. We first see it when God asks Adam to submit to the rules of paradise: "You must not eat from the tree…" (Gen 2:17; 3:3). Satan was the first rebel, trying to direct Adam and Eve away from submission and make the rules for their own lives. He succeeded, and paradise was lost.

So, how does submission look in all its Kingdom beauty?

Let me explain by giving you an ugly picture of non-submission. A week ago, we could smell that our two-year-old grandson had relieved himself in his diaper. Grandma quickly showed willingness to help his mother get the mess cleaned up. But Sir Stinky threw a big tantrum and tried to resist the clean-up operations. Watching from a safe distance, I wondered if this wasn't the ultimate example of ungratefulness. Someone else is willing to clean up the mess you made, and you are stubbornly resisting it? The perfect picture of choosing rebellion over paradise. Submitting to their assistance would have ushered in comfort and a clean bottom, but by resisting, the baby preferred to stay in its mess.

Is this not amazing that we enter life in a state of dependence and submission and often exit life like that as well? Life itself often forces us into submission — submission to the assistance of others.

There are many beautiful examples of submission. The way a blind man trusts a guide dog; the submission of a mountain climber dangling from a cliff to the rope; the submission of a passenger to the driver of a car; the submission of a trapeze artist to the safety net; the submission of a child jumping into the arms of a father, and the submission of a sinner to the redemption of God.

Richard Foster writes about the liberation of submission. He says:
1 "Submission brings freedom from the bondage/obsession to have everything go your way.
2 It brings freedom to give in to others and loosens us from the stubborn grip of self-will.
3 It makes us see other people differently. We are free to genuinely value and respect them. Their plans and dreams

become important to us. We carry an inner attitude of mutual subordination. We share the sorrow of their failures and the joy of their successes.

4   You are free from your own rights or expectations and the seething anger and bitterness that comes when you think people do not treat you as you feel you deserve." [26]

We also have to understand the paradox of Jesus' invitation to deny ourselves to enable us to find ourselves (Matt 10:39). Denying ourselves does not necessarily mean we lose our identity. We often find our identity in submission to a higher cause. Jesus teaches that the way to self-fulfilment is through self-denial (Mark 8:34-35) — he even modelled it for us. He denied himself and through that he was given a name above all names (Phil 2:6-9).

The Bible encourages us to have the same attitude as Jesus by looking to the interests of others (Phil 2:4); by considering others better than ourselves (Phil 2:3); by being like-minded with others (Phil 2:2). (Refer to chapter 4.4 (Descending into Greatness) for an elaboration on this point.) As we walk in these Jesus-modelled attitudes, we discover a rich new identity. We become a Kingdom people, a selfless nation who pride themselves in serving others. We become cross-bearing-followers as we follow the Cross-Bearer who did not come to be served, but to serve (Mark 10:45).

When our eyes open to this truth, we see that "revolutionary subordination" is the key to understanding and living the Gospel. Dying to self is the way to abundant spiritual life and to restoring social life. With this policy, Jesus undermined all attitudes based on "power over others" and self-interest.

Understanding this gives us insight into why Paul and Peter emphasised submission (revolutionary subordination) so much. Paul first calls for an attitude of submission in those who were already subordinate because of their culture:

"Wives, be subject to your husbands… children, obey your parents… slaves, obey in everything those who are your earthly masters…" (Col 3:18-22).

He then turns to the culturally dominant and calls them into the submission-life:

"Husbands, love your wives… fathers, do not provoke your children… masters, treat your slaves justly and fairly…" (Col 3:19-4:1 and parallels.) And he encouraged everyone to be submissive to governing authorities (Rom 13:1-8). These exhortations reveal to us that in submission, we learn a concrete way how to be subordinate to the Lord! That is why we hear the theme over and over: "… As you do to the Lord!" (Eph 5:21; 6:7). Each of these situations become an opportunity to learn and practice the virtue of submission.

Through this new lens we see how the principle of submission, obedience, and honouring God and his Word permeates through the Bible.

In the Old Testament we see multiple calls to submission: to the law of paradise (Gen 2:17), to the law of the promised land (Deut 6 and 30),and to the law of a prosperous family life (Deut 5:16). As we read through the history of Israel the recurring theme is clear: obey (submit to) the commands of God and live! (1 Kings 8:58). We see the same thing echoed in the New Testament. Obey the essential principles of the law and prophets (Matt 5:19-20); follow (submit to) Jesus (Mark 1:17); listen to the voice of the Holy Spirit (John 14:26; Heb 10:16). As Jesus says, "Anyone who loves Me will obey my teaching. My Father will love them, and we will come to them and make our home with them" (John 14:23).

Then the Bible continues to make sure this principle of submission (voluntary subordination) permeates society by giving pertinent instructions to children, fathers and mothers. The first thing for a child to learn is this submission to the authority of his/her parents. Fathers therefore have the responsibility to practice moral authority in the manner that represents God the Father. Mothers have a massive role to play in this as well. They have to set an example for the children by validating the authority of the father. That this is not happening as it should implies that the world struggles both with misused authority by fathers and a lack of exemplary submission by mothers.

What We Do
How do we practice this in discipleship?

Richard Foster lists a few examples of acts of submission:
1   Submission to the Triune God, where we say as Thomas a Kempis did: "As thou wilt; what thou wilt; when thou wilt." In this we yield our body, mind and spirit for his purposes.
2   Submission to the Scriptures, where we yield ourselves to hear, receive and obey the Scriptures.
3   Submission to our family. In a healthy family, we consider and protect each other's interests. We listen, we share, we serve, and we create an environment of selfless sacrificial love.
4   Submission to our neighbours. We serve the common good of society through kindness, good deeds, support, hospitality, etc.
5   Submission to the body of Christ. As each person executes their specific calling, we serve the body of Christ and the world. Since life is not about us, but the mission of God, we focus on that and commit to that.
6   Submission to the broken and despised. We discover ways to identify with the downtrodden when we spend time with, help and empower them.
7   Submission to the world. We have a responsibility to the environment, so we should always try to make the world a better place. [27]

Most pertinently, we have uncovered the precious treasure of submission through discipleship. Those who commit themselves to the practice of submission experience a security, a freedom and a richness beyond what they ever had. What Richard Foster says about the freedom of submission is true. Nothing is so enslaving as the need to have things "my way".

Submitting to their mentors introduced new language and a source of moral authority for our group. You often hear statements like, "I won't do it unless my mentor agrees." These people are setting an example for their own disciples, who find it easier to submit to their authority in turn. The principle is clear: true authority flows from those who stand under authority.

You will also hear us making claims like, "My mentor knows everything about me." True submission implies complete transparency, so we hide nothing from each other, especially in the areas of money, sex and power. We also hear, "If I do step out of line, please speak to my mentor." This highlights a willingness to be scrutinised and to be held accountable.

A key commitment to the submission principle is submitting to the decisions of the co-disciples in the team. For example, if someone comes to the team to audit their use of money or time, the team speaks into the situation and the person corrects their behaviour. Key decisions are also brought to the broader council of the team. (Refer to chapter 2.4 (Transparency) for an elaboration on this point.) Some make great sacrifices to further the mission of the team, and not only their own mission. They submit to making their mission a sub-mission to the mission of others. (Refer to chapter 3.5 (God's Specific Assignment for Us) for an elaboration on this point.)

In this journey of submission, we focus on each other's attitudes towards our spouses, parents, church leadership, authorities… and above all, to God! Submission to accountability is essential to our discipleship movement.

Discussion questions

1 Have you had bad experiences with submission? What were they?

2 Have you experienced healthy biblical submission? Can you describe it?

3 In what areas do you need to practice more submission?

4 What do you stand to lose if you avoid submission?

Scripture to study • Ephesians 5:21-33 • Romans 13:1-7
• Hebrews 13:17

Books to read • Authority and Submission, *by Watchman Nee*

2.8 PUSHING AND PULLING

George Kellerman

Before deciding whether you want to commit to making disciples, ask yourself: "Do I want to grow as a person?" "Do I want to grow in my walk with God?" We have seen again and again that if you are not getting pulled and pushed in your walk with God, you are not growing like you could. The pulling comes from your discipler (the person who disciples you) and the pushing comes from your disciples. Your disciples push you when they ask you tough questions. If you want to grow in your walk with God, make disciples who push you closer to God. No pushing, no growing. Your discipler pulls you closer to God as they ask tough questions, holds you accountable, helps you make disciples, and so on. No pulling, no growing!

Many people who don't believe mentoring or discipleship is important change their minds after I tell them the following story.

A father saw his 17-year-old daughter (let's call her Tracy) walking hand-in-hand with a 19-year-old boy he didn't know. This was a huge shock to him. He realised this guy was nearing the peak of his testosterone levels, and he had no idea how physically intimate Tracy and her new boyfriend were. What was he to do? He decided to ask his friend's 13-year-old daughter to ask Tracy some pointed questions such as, "Are you and the guy kissing?" "Do you French-kiss?" "What are you going to do next physically?" "What will you do if he puts his hand under your shirt?" When she heard these questions, Tracy got nervous and looked for someone to counsel her on this subject. She wasn't comfortable speaking to her mom (or anyone else that much older than her), so she looked for someone more in touch with her generation. Thankfully, she found a wise 25-year-old lady who was a youth leader at the church. She confided in her and found answers to the questions the 13-year-old had asked her.

However, it wasn't just Tracy who found answers. The youth leader also realised that she herself needed advice on these sensitive issues. So she found a mentor for herself, who happened to be Tracy's 45-year-old mother.

The discipleship chain was thus established: the first generation 45-year-old mother discipled the 2nd generation 25-year-old youth leader at church, who discipled the 3rd generation 17-year-old daughter, who in turn discipled the 4th generation 13-year-old keen protégé.

This is the ideal discipling scenario: four or more generations of disciples. With four generations you get pulling and pushing in the 2nd and 3rd generations. These two generations learn more than anyone else.

This is what Jesus intended with discipleship and what Paul taught Timothy in 2 Timothy 2:2:

"The things you (2nd generation) heard me (1st generation) say, entrust this to reliable people (3rd generation), who will be qualified to teach others (4th generation)."

Discipleship is powerful when done in four or more generations!

Mentoring – The Good, The Bad And The Ugly

When I think back on the major life decisions I have made or biggest life-lessons I have learned, my disciplers and discipleship team have always played a fundamental role. I can share every major issue, question and decision in my life with a group of people who understand me best, who listen to the Lord and who speak into my life. To not have a mentor is unthinkable to me.

THIS IS THE IDEAL DISCIPLING SCENARIO: FOUR OR MORE GENERATIONS OF DISCIPLES

But there are many people who consciously choose not to have a mentor. The three reasons we see most often are an unwillingness to change, a know-it-all attitude and prior negative experiences with a mentor. The first two reasons are, to put it bluntly, just prideful.

The last one is more understandable, yet still not a valid excuse. When someone describes their negative experience, I usually ask them, "What did your mentor's mentor say?" If you have access to your mentor's mentor, it safeguards against many (though not all) negative experiences. It is dangerous being discipled by someone who themselves are not discipled. The same counts for you — you cannot disciple people if you yourself are not discipled. There is no integrity and moral authority in place if this is the case.

Defining Mentoring

We use the terms "mentoring" and "discipling" interchangeably since we believe they are essentially the same thing. When done right, both are whole-life coaching processes. Traditionally, at least in evangelical circles, discipleship is understood as spiritual coaching. But this is not what we find when we examine how Jesus invited people to follow him. He demonstrated the totality of Kingdom life and taught them on relevant life issues. His discipleship was holistic life-coaching, including all the dimensions of life, not only the spiritual. (See more on this in chapter 1.5 on holistic discipling.)

We also believe that the discipler, since he/she is a whole-life coach, should be in a more advanced life-season than the disciple. You tend to understand life better in retrospect.

Mentorship is a well-known concept in the marketplace, but here the "mentor" is more of an advisor, consultant or executive coach. This is a beneficial relationship to have, but it should not replace the role of a whole-life discipler/mentor. An advisor/consultant is usually a one-way relationship and rarely covers all the dimensions of life. The mentee considers the advice of the mentor but can discard it when it doesn't suit them. Communication mostly takes place at the request of the advisee — it is a one-way street. This kind of advisor is little more than a genie in a lamp, only useful when the advisee sees fit. The power is still in the hands of the person who rubs the lamp — the advisee. True accountability cannot exist in a relationship like this. This is far from the ideal two-way accountability where both the discipler and the disciple have the freedom to approach each other at any time. The discipler should always have the right to approach the disciple and speak into her life. We all need someone who can jump into our life and speak (sometimes hard) truths when they feel it necessary. The best person for this is your discipler/mentor.

Then there is the role of the coach, someone who helps you grow and develop mastery in a specific skill. A spiritual coach is someone who teaches you in biblical and other spiritually related matters. But this idea isn't limited to the spiritual dimension. Your coach could teach you a sport or musical instrument, or guide you in business matters. They can be anyone, of any age.

These roles are valuable, but none can replace the inclusiveness and the accountability of a whole-life discipleship relationship.

The Pulling

It is strange (and rather arrogant) when people talk about "being someone's mentor" as though it is a major accomplishment. The assumption that you can only be a mentor once you are someone impressive is both wrong and misses the point completely. I have had people ask me to mentor them, but with a subtle attitude that I should feel honoured to be able to mentor them. I quickly declined these "offers." Discipling or mentoring someone does not mean you have a superior position over your protégé. You are fulfilling the role of a shepherd and life coach, serving the needs of the person. It is a step of obedience towards the Lord. It is not a status to be achieved.

A discipler should see themselves as the servant of the disciple. Their job is to set an example, encouraging the mentee and keeping them accountable to the goal they set together. Whole-life discipleship is an exercise in empowerment.

What We Do

When I disciple a team of people, two questions consume most of my thoughts, prayers and time with God.

The first question I ask is, where is God taking each person, and how can I help them get there? As I lean into this question, I ask the Lord a few other related questions. To begin with, I ask God what he wants the disciple to focus on, what he is teaching him and calling him to, the traps on his path and how he can make more disciples. The Lord often gives me something to tell one of the guys, so I pick up the phone and contact him. My prayers in the morning focus on fulfilling God's dreams for these disciples. Taking action, I try to open gaps for these guys by helping them make disciples, providing chances in ministry or even trying to find them jobs. I invest as much as I can into them. I steer them away from relying on me for spiritual growth but facilitate them towards growing in maturity into Christ and fulfilling God's calling for their lives.

The second question I ask is, where is God taking the discipleship team, and how can I help the team to get there? As we are aiming to disciple teams and not individuals, God often directs and guides where the team should go. I try to discern where the Lord is leading us on a few levels. What theme does God have for us? What is the team's calling, and what steps must we take to fulfil it? Where are the holes within the team and how can we cover them?

It is hopefully clear by now that discipling and being discipled is not an occasional event. It is an ongoing life-on-life commitment.

The Pushing

A large percentage of my personal growth comes from interactions with my disciples. They constantly push me closer to God through the tough questions they ask. This can sometimes keep me busy for an entire week as I sit with the Lord and with my discipler to get the answers or an appropriate response. The Gospels record that Jesus was asked 183 questions, of which he only directly answered three.

He responded to the other 180 questions with questions of his own, stories or silence. [28] When my disciples ask me a question, I first consider a response question. Usually, my return question is, "What does the Lord say to you on this?" Doing this helps ensure that God is still the primary discipler of our disciples. Other times, silence is the best answer.

In my daily life (whether work or weekend) it feels like my disciples are watching me all the time. They often ask me what I do with my time, how I work and how I handle specific situations. Their innocent questions dig into my life, assess my behaviour and interrogate my motives. They challenge me to live a truly exemplary life. Now any life situation gains meaning as my disciples will learn (positively or negatively) from every move I make.

In the same way a first-time father has both feelings of deep endearment and the more concerned, "How on earth am I going to do this?" — such are my feelings when I think about my disciples. I care deeply about them. And the thought of the large responsibility I have to shepherd them and facilitate them towards Jesus often overwhelms me. That being said, I cannot imagine my life without them. They push me closer to God.

We need pulling and pushing in our lives so we can grow!

Discussion questions

1. What discipleship pushing-and-pulling have you experienced?
2. How can you increase the discipleship pull-factor in your life?
3. How can you increase the discipleship push-factor in your life?
4. Where is God taking your discipleship team, and how can you help the team to get there?

Scripture to study • 1 Peter 3:8-18

Books to read • As Iron Sharpens Iron, *by William Hendricks and Howard Hendricks*

2.9 THE TABLE OF SUPPORT

George Kellerman

"We are the average of the five people we spend the most time with."

The actual figure in Jim Rohn's claim above isn't as important as the principle it conveys: the people who are closest to you will shape you the most profoundly. So who are these five people in your life? More relevantly, were you intentional about choosing some of them to fulfil specific roles in your life? We don't mean to imply that all the people close to you are only there as tools or props in your life story. However, you should be intentional about who you allow into your close circle, and why. They might not be people you spend a significant amount of time with, but the time you spend with them should be significant. Are they shaping you positively? Will they hold you accountable, and rebuke you if necessary? Are they the people who have the most significant positive impact on your life? And which of these people can support you to reach your full potential in God's kingdom? Asking questions like these provide clarity on the state of something we call your "table of support."

"A Table of Support indicates the kind of people you should have close to you to make a real impact on your life and through whom you may make a real impact on other people." [29]

We have seen, from many counselling and mentoring meetings, that people who have a table of support in place seem to grow the most in Christ. They have the best support structures during times of difficulty, and we have found that they tend to make the best big decisions in life. We cannot walk this road alone; we need people to help us grow. We believe your discipler and disciples are the most important seats around your table, but those are just the start.

The table of support concept comes from Cassie's book:

"These people take responsibility to help you develop holistically in all spheres of your life: spiritual, emotional, social, intellectual, physical and even the environment of your life. So who do you have close to you? The table of support on the next page indicates the seven to nine people you should have close to you. They are:

- The discipler/mentor — he or she is the person who is our whole-life coach (if you want to differentiate between a discipler and a mentor, then see the discipler as a spiritual coach and the mentor as a whole-life coach). For me, both the discipler and the mentor have the same function: whole-life coaches.
- The disciples/mentees — these are the people we do whole-life coaching with.
- The coach — he or she is someone who trains us in a specific skill.
- The trainee — he or she is someone you train in a specific skill.
- The inner circle — he or she are friends who are real soulmates (same gender). Your spouse may not be one of these people. (Our spouses hold a place all of their own.)
- The family member — he or she is the person in the family who has very close emotional intimacy with us, almost like a soulmate within the family. This will be someone in the family with whom we will be totally transparent.
- The successor — he or she is the person who will take the baton of our mission in life and run with it when we are no longer around.
- The cross-culture friend — he or she is a person from a different culture to yours who can enrich your understanding of life by helping you see things from a different perspective.
- The hero — he or she is someone who we have the highest admiration for, though we may not be able to become like this person." [30]

Table of support

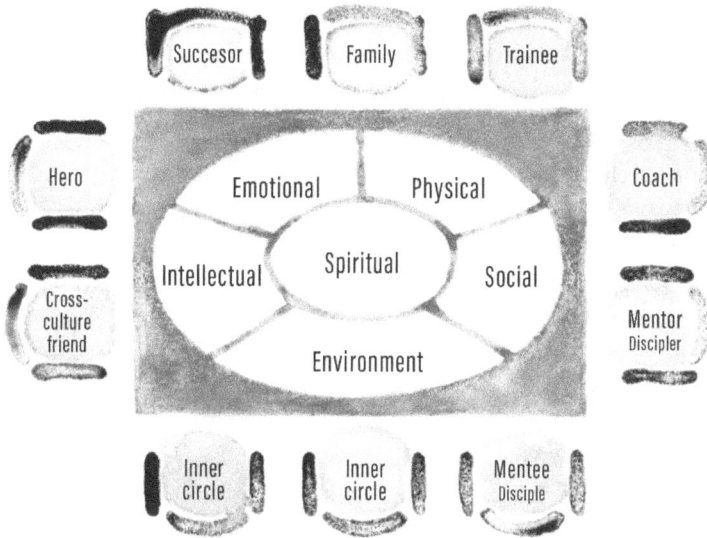

The following stories contrast two people with very different table of support experiences.

Cathy

Cathy's husband was active in disciple-making and gathered a table of support around him. Cathy saw the benefits of her husband's discipleship lifestyle, but it was never high on her priority list for her own life. After shelving her flourishing career for four years to be a stay-at-home mom for her two children, she resumed her job with enthusiasm. Before long she was excelling at work, but started to struggle at home. The energy and motivation she used to have to spend time with her children was a distant memory. Discipline became an issue, so she resorted to spoiling them instead. With her own paycheque she rediscovered a love for shopping, updating her wardrobe every other week. Her husband felt like he was living out his true purpose but worried that she seemed more concerned about trying to keep up with the Jones'. He knew he was not always the best person to speak into her life, but struggled to think of anyone else she could turn to. He realised that while he was benefitting from his table of support, Cathy needed her own one badly.

Cathy didn't have a discipler or mentor to challenge her with tough questions on parenting, purpose and stewardship. She had a group of close friends, but they were more likely to encourage her selfish behaviour than confront it. They weren't willing or able to hold her accountable to the real issues in her life. Cathy didn't have disciples whom she could selflessly pour herself into either. She was stuck in a rut and, without a clear table of support in place, there was little hope for her to climb out of it.

Hein

Hein was a prominent leader in his community. He led a non-profit ministry, organising and speaking at events, outreaches and programs. He was successful in what he did and was renowned for his speaking abilities. However, he came across as exceptionally task-orientated, so people struggled to get close to him. He impressed people from a distance but struggled to impact people up close.

During a conversation with his mentor, Hein realised he didn't have many people to challenge and empower him. Despite a good relationship with his wife and kids, he felt alone in many of his struggles. So he built a table of support for himself.

First, he asked a mentor figure he trusted to become his discipler and started meeting with him regularly. They discussed things like marriage, work, disciple-making and personal development. Hein was challenged on multiple levels and matured tremendously. He started discipleship relationships with a group of younger men, sometimes driving an hour to have lunch meetings with them. He was intentional about discipling them, praying for them, and made a point of attending important events in their lives.

Hein also invited friends and acquaintances he felt he could trust to form his inner circle. He shared his intimate struggles with them and asked them to hold him accountable on things like money, selfish ambition and sexual purity. Hein also coached others and received coaching to keep developing himself. He knew he struggled to connect with other cultures, which is especially important in South Africa. As uncomfortable as it was, he asked some cross-cultural acquaintances to become friends. They appreciated his honesty and openness and accepted his awkward request. After a year, Hein filled the seats around his table.

Tragically, Hein died of a heart-attack at the young age of 40. His funeral was a poignant, but significant and special day. Over 2,000 people attended, and those who spoke shared stories of a life well lived. Hein's discipler led the service and spoke of the son he lost. Hein's disciples talked about the dad they lost. Hein's inner circle talked about the brother they lost. Months later, people still shared how they struggled to come to grips with Hein's absence. He left a gap in these people's lives. Not only did Hein surround himself with a table of support, but he was also part of the table of support for many people. Hein's understanding of the importance of a table of support led him to become a deeply loved and most influential friend/discipler/disciple/brother to hundreds of people.

In our experience, we have seen echoes of these two stories in lives all around the world. Those who have a full table of support in place are living lives of significance, growing tremendously and finding real support in times of need. The people without a table of support tend to make more wrong decisions, and struggle to sort out the issues they face.

How the table of support looks for each person will be slightly different. The important thing is that each seat is filled. Some of the relationships will be formal, while others far more casual. Either way, we encourage formalising the relationship, even if it is relaxed in practice. The goal is intentionality and setting time aside to build the relationship. Formalising the relationship helps ensure this happens.

One person can fill more than one seat, but you should try to have as many different people fill the seats as possible. The principles and practical application of the table of support are more important than just ticking the boxes. People like Hein, who pursued the principle of the table of support, experienced noticeably enriched lives. We pray the same is true for you as you fill your table of support.

Look at the figure on the next page and see how many chairs around your table of support are full and how many are empty. Write down the name of each person at a chair in your life, then be intentional about filling the empty chairs. Ask possible candidates if they would be willing to play the relevant roles in your life. Don't be discouraged if some people say no — as you pray through this process, God will help you find the right people to fill the chairs around your table.[31]

Discussion questions

1   What seats around your table of support do you still need to fill?
2   How do you plan to fill those seats?
3   What do you lose out on with each empty seat?
4   What seat(s) on other peoples' table of support are you occupying?

Scripture to study • Matthew 18:15-18

Books to read • The World Needs A Father: A Trainer's Guide, *by Cassie Carstens*

2.10 CROSS-CULTURAL FRIENDSHIP IN DISCIPLESHIP

——•——

Carel Wandrag

We rarely question our own perspective on life until it is challenged by, for example:

- An honest conversation
- Reading an article or post in just the right frame of mind
- Spending time with people from a different socio-economic class
- Being part of a multi-ethnic discussion group.

However it happens, broadening your perspective is a critical part of discipleship. Some relationships and experiences have broadened mine tremendously.

A few years ago someone confronted my discipler with the following words: "The white church in South Africa should be disbanded". I consider myself part of the white church in South Africa, so hearing him recount his experience felt like a punch to the gut. After the shock settled, I was faced with serious questions about the relevance and value of the white church in the country I love so much.

One evening I was giving computer classes to two black ladies in a shack in Khayelitsha, the largest township in Cape Town, South Africa. As it got darker, one of the ladies stood up to turn on a light. Instead of flicking a switch, she had to unscrew the lightbulb from another room and screw it into the dodgy fitting above us. The fitting was hanging from threadbare wires in the roof and looked very unsafe, even to untrained eyes. I could not believe they had been struggling with this for months, but they had learned to live with it. I discussed the situation with them, and it was clear that they would appreciate some help. During my next visit, a little DIY was all it took to light up their home and our friendship.

In 2016 I was part of a hard-hitting conversation on reconciliation with a group of leaders. A coloured[B] pastor from a nearby town shared his longing to be treated the same way as the white pastors of the town. He lamented that when any of his white colleagues wanted funding for an initiative, the white businessmen of the town were quick to help and generous in their support. However, it was a huge struggle for him to get the same degree of support for similar projects. The suspicion and mistrust between the two groups was painfully clear.

That same year, students at universities around South Africa started the #feesmustfall movement. In the face of the stark inequality facing the country, a fee increase above the inflation rate pushed the students to mass action. An urgent cry for free tertiary education swept campuses around the country, with some of the protests even turning violent. A popular slogan during the protests was "Decolonise our education!" This baffled most white South Africans, myself included. It was only after a revealing conversation with one of my young black friends that it made sense to me. While I can't do his full argument justice, the main issue was the lack of African content and context in university syllabi. It is worth noting that his perspective was all but absent from the media coverage of the events.

My wife and I are friends with a white couple who chose to stay in a predominantly coloured neighbourhood. They have also adopted two boys, one from a Xhosa background and one from Congolese parents. Their choices about where to live and how to raise their children often challenge our thinking in a serious, but wonderful way. Through their lives, they remind us to be intentional about the decisions we make and why we make them.

B   We are aware that in some countries this term is demeaning. However, in South Africa, "coloured" is a nationally recognised race on the national census.

These and other similar experiences helped me understand the value of diverse relationships in a new way.

We gain invaluable insight. We all have cultural blinkers, and if we aren't exposed to situations that challenge our thinking, we may never learn the crucial truths that only multicultural contexts can teach us. I realised that I need close friends from different backgrounds. People who will lend me their eyes, hearts and minds to see, feel and think about everyday realities from their perspective. Even though I may understand it intellectually, I will never truly "get" white privilege as I wasn't on the receiving end of Apartheid. This kind of compassion only develops in deep and meaningful intercultural relationships.

I often ask myself what I can learn from people different to me, and how they can help me grow. The wisdom of Proverbs 27:17 (AMP) comes to mind: "Iron sharpens iron, so a man sharpens the countenance of his friend." My black friend helped me overhaul my understanding of the discontent of a large group of young people in South Africa.

My own context and often limited understanding can lead me to act on perceived needs, rather than the real needs of people. You cannot know the need if you do not feel the need. If I had not been in that shack as it was getting dark, I would never have realised their need for safe electrical wiring. It created an opportunity for me to help address a very real need in that household.

Our cross-culture friends help us to gauge the weight of the values we carry. In urban areas, career or financial troubles are perceived as serious crises. Alternatively, a shortage of relationships in rural life is a major concern. The values held dear by different cultures should help us evaluate the weight we assign to our core values.

My cross-culture friends take me outside my comfort zone. That, I have found, is the space where I learn the most. The further I am from my comfort zone, the more creative tension there is to help me to discover new things.

A message from a multicultural group is much stronger than a message from a homogenous group. The power of unity in diversity is often underestimated. This is specifically valuable in an environment of racial tension.

THE FULLNESS OF GOD CAN ONLY BE FOUND IN A MULTITUDE OF DIFFERENT PEOPLE

We should not forget that the media industry rarely shows us the whole picture. Their goal is to sell a story. They tend to focus on sensation and fear while ignoring or misrepresenting the realities at the root of the issue. By engaging with people who are closer to the events than ourselves, we can get a better understanding of how to be salt and light in the world.

Finally, I have come to realise that the fullness of God can only be found in a multitude of different people. To think that my way is the only way and that my reality is the only reality is both prideful and ignorant. We are all created in God's image, but his nature is too big to be fully replicated in any single group of people. We need each other to have a fuller experience of God. Without diversity we will never understand the different facets of the character of God. God wants to reach the ends of the earth. To do that with him we need to partner with others who can influence places which are difficult for us to reach.

So how do we put this into practice as disciples of Jesus?

The following is how the discipleship group I am part of is trying to apply the theory. We do not have it all figured out and are still working out the best ways to apply these principles every day. However, we consistently aim to demonstrate real love to each other and to the world, even more so in a very diverse context:

- We encourage each other to be more intentional about inviting people from different backgrounds to walk the path of discipleship with us.

- We remind each other how important cross-cultural and uncomfortable perspectives are to guard ourselves from living in a bubble of comfort.
- We listen to each other with true humility and an openness to learn and to grow.
- We search for expressions of God in people different to ourselves.
- We help each other see people through the eyes of Jesus. He loves us all the same and places the same value on each of us.
- We struggle with questions about things we are unwilling to accept in our lives but are tough realities in the lives of others. For example, why should other people's children go to schools I would never send my child to?
- We are intentional about taking ourselves outside our comfort zones. We need new and uncomfortable experiences to stay in touch with the calling that God has for us in a world in serious need of his love and salvation.
- We are embracing the dynamics of diverse groups while grappling with the best ways to do it. How do we become more inclusive in our meetings? How do we mentor a diverse group of disciples? Should there be more than one mentor in co-mentorship roles?
- We support people who are loving and impacting communities that would be difficult for us to reach. We build relationships with them and visit them in their own spaces so we can get a better understanding of the contexts they operate in.
- We partner in ministry with a variety of leaders in different cultures.

What does the Bible say about these things?

In the book of Revelation, John has the following vision:

> "After this I looked, and there before me was a great multitude that no one could count, from every nation, tribe, people and language, standing before the throne and before the Lamb. They were wearing white robes and were holding palm branches in their hands" (Rev 7:9).

John was able to distinguish a great variety of people in his vision. This leads me to believe that the diversity on earth will continue to exist in eternity in some form. And contrast that with the possibility that marriage might not even survive our earthly existence (Matt 22:30). The value of cross-cultural friends cannot be understated.

Will our willingness to love diverse people in the present impact our co-existence with them in heaven one day? Only God knows the answer, but I believe we should be serious about practising for heaven now. Loving well and embracing diversity are always worth pursuing.

We could also find biblical guidance for this from Peter's vision (Acts 10), or in the diversity of the early church leadership (Acts 13), but the most convincing biblical example is probably that of Jesus himself. As disciples of Jesus, we should always look at his example.

The 12 disciples were a diverse group. John — the beloved disciple — was one of the Sons of Thunder. Judas Iscariot became a traitor. Matthew was a tax collector, a group of people despised by the Jews at the time. Peter, meaning rock, also betrayed Jesus. Simon belonged to the Zealots — a group of fanatical Jewish nationalists that hated the Romans with violent passion. And we can go on. If business leaders had to create their best team to carry the fate of our faith, it is unlikely they would have chosen the type of people Jesus did. And still, the legacy of his disciples echoes around the world today.

Discussion questions

1 What are the dangers of not being enriched by other cultures?
2 Do you have cross-cultural friends? If so, explain your friendship with them; if not, what can you do to befriend people from a different culture?
3 Do we as a group have enough enrichment from various cultures? What can we do to increase our exposure to diverse cultures?

Scripture to study • Acts 10:9-23

Books to read • Muslims, Christians, and Jesus, *by Carl Medearis*
• Crucial Conversations, *by Kerry Patterson, Joseph Grenny, et al.*

2.11 PRIMARY FAITH COMMUNITY

—●—

George Kellerman & Cassie Carstens

Do we all need a primary faith community?

There is a stunning variety of Christian input available today. Between conferences, streaming services, ministry initiatives and podcasts, people wonder why they need to be part of a fellowship (church) on a consistent basis. Why not pick what we need from the available resources and privately live our Christian life? The Bible shows us that this is not a new question (Heb 10:25). So, why be part of a faith community?

The main arc of the Bible's narrative is told through the lens of faith communities. Heroes of the faith are found and formed in community, and there is a strong emphasis throughout the Gospels on the togetherness of the believers. This is perhaps best exemplified in the together-journey of the disciples. We read in Acts how followers of Jesus worked together to grow the movement, and the Epistles repeatedly refer to responsibilities and roles within the context of fellowship. Ephesians 4:11-12 mentions five distinct roles (apostles, prophets, evangelists, shepherds and teachers) members of the church can embody to equip believers to attain fullness in Christ. We experience the fullness of Christ when we practice our gifts in the community of believers.

Another convincing argument is the plethora of "one another" texts found in 90+ verses in the Bible. They make it clear that a Christian cannot be a lone ranger in the Kingdom. Here are a few examples:

- "… be at peace with each other" (Mark 9:50).
- "Love one another" (John 13:34).
- "Be devoted to one another in brotherly love…" (Rom 12:10).
- "… honour one another above yourselves" (Rom 12:10).

- "Live in harmony with one another" (Rom 12:16).
- "Accept one another, then, just as Christ accepted you..." (Rom 15:7).
- "... instruct one another" (Rom 15:14).
- "... have equal concern for each other" (1 Cor 12:25).
- "... serve one another humbly in love" (Gal 5:13).

We can also compare the benefits of following Christ corporately or individually. In his book, *Celebration of Discipline*, Richard Foster mentions four corporate benefits: confession, worship, guidance and celebration. We cannot do any of these effectively alone.

Here are a few more corporate benefits:

- Submission: Scripture repeatedly commands Christians to submit to their leaders and each other (Heb 13:17; 1 Thess 5:12-13; Eph 5:21).
- The purifying of the doctrine by identifying and destroying false teaching (2 Pet 2).
- The carrying of each other's burdens (Gal 6:2).
- The assistance towards perseverance (James 5:19-20).
- The value of being shepherded by spiritual leaders (1 Pet 5; Acts 20:28).
- The valuing of unity, equality and diversity (1 Cor 12:12-31; Col 3:11).
- The inspiration of testimonies (1 John 1:3).
- The test of love (1 John 4:18-20).
- The testimony of love: "By this all people will know that you are my disciples, if you have love for one another" (John 13:35).

The Message translation of Colossians 3:15 puts it so clearly: "Let the peace of Christ keep you in tune with each other, in step with each other. None of this going off and doing your own thing!"

God Speaks To Corporate Bodies

In chapter 2.3 (Journey Together as a Team) we mention that God reveals his intention to groups, communities and nations more often than he reveals them to individuals. If God primarily reveals his heart through community and people stop meeting together, how will we fulfil his designs? How will we hear everything he wants to say to us? Being part of a congregation does not guarantee you will hear clearly from God. However, not joining a community at all will limit your understanding of your role in God's bigger picture.

When considering your current or potential church affiliation, you should ask two questions:

- What is the God-given calling of this church community?
- What is (or might be) my role as a team member towards this calling?

Without clear answers to these questions, your commitment to any role within the church community will be unclear.

The Primary Faith Community

Beyond our table of support, which is essential for accountability, intimate spiritual development and care, we should all belong to a broader expression of the body of Christ. Unfortunately, many churches have become self-oriented and attractional. Leonard Sweet calls them ABC (Attendance, Buildings and Cash) churches. [32] Their main focus is no longer to empower for outreach. Instead of being part of the movement to establish the Kingdom, they are building their own kingdoms.

Sweet says the church should instead become an MRI (Missional, Relational and Incarnational) movement. How are we going to achieve this? How can we restore the church to its original intent, to further establish the Kingdom of God on earth?

The ABC dilemma has robbed the church of much of its empowering capacity, causing members to look for answers in other places. It has devalued the definition of the church to where it has little meaning in many places. The image and practice of church needs restoration to where it can once again offer capacity to impact the world and build the Kingdom of God.

We call this regenerated understanding of church the "Primary Faith Community" (PFC). A healthy PFC should do the following:

1 Help members worship in awe of God
2 Help members live and love the Bible
3 Help members practice Jesus together with others
4 Help members fill their spiritual cups
5 Offer members a strong sense of belonging
6 Help members kill self-centeredness, idols and prejudices in their lives
7 Provide nurture and care
8 Empower members for victorious living
9 Bring about transparency, vulnerability and accountability
10 Equip members for Kingdom building
11 Equip members for multiplication through discipleship
12 Stretch members for missions to the unreached.

When the above is true, a PFC should be the ideal spiritual environment for growth. It will provide most of the spiritual care, accountability and empowerment. Within this space, the table of support supplements the PFC by monitoring, mentoring, addressing immediate needs and deepening emotional intimacy.

We believe the way Jesus discipled accommodated all of this. He modelled discipleship in three different spaces:

- The Three: Jesus' inner circle — Peter, James and John (Matt 17:1-13).
- The Twelve: Jesus had 12 disciples as his core discipleship team (Matt 10:1-4).
- The Seventy: Jesus had other disciples beyond his core 12 (Luke 10:1-24).

Many ministries have seen growth in depth, community and multiplication when these spaces function together and overlap with each other. We are convinced that anyone should be able to launch into victorious Christian living from a PFC.

What We Did

We surveyed a group of Christians about their primary faith communities. This is what we discovered.

Local church and primary faith community disconnect

We first asked them to identify in which community or group they experienced most of the 12 elements of a PFC (as mentioned above). The options were:

- Their local church
- A sport club
- A ministry
- A gymnasium
- Short-term outreach
- A team at work
- A social club
- A discipleship network
- Their family at home
- Church they watch on TV or any other Christian gatherings.

Surprisingly (or not?), most of them did not select their local church as their PFC. As they were answering the survey, some realised how far their local church falls short of what God intended. Some people even needed a combination of Christian gatherings to provide what they need. We want to stress here that involvement in multiple spiritual communities is not a bad thing. The problem is when it impairs your level of commitment to a community with a God-given calling.

Certain church models didn't qualify

We next asked if they felt an attractional church could qualify as a PFC. (The attractional church is, according to Jared Wilson, a "ministry paradigm that has embraced consumerism, pragmatism, and moralism as its operational values.") [33]

The overwhelming response was no. Any church that primarily features the preacher and worship team only addresses a few elements. Intimate gatherings that foster participation typically meet more of the 12 elements of a PFC.

Passivity is deeply ingrained

We then asked two final questions: how their PFC helps them in each of the 12 elements, and how they help their PFC in each of the 12 elements.

Far fewer responded that they helped their PFC than the other way around. This implied a staggering reality — Christians seem less willing to contribute to being the "body of Christ" than they are to receiving from the "body of Christ". Has the theatrical orientation of the church created this apathy?

What can we take from all of this?

Firstly, it is important to commit to a community of faith. However, that community must embody most of the 12 elements we discussed to qualify as an authentic PFC. You should evaluate your community of faith to see if it qualifies (sadly, many churches don't even come close).

If your current community of faith doesn't reflect the values of a PFC, you have two options. Firstly — and ideally — you should make an effort to help reform your current community into a God-intended PFC. However, if they show absolutely no interest in becoming a PFC, you should consider looking for a new community, one that you can meaningfully contribute to and which will empower you to succeed in your Kingdom assignment on earth.

Discussion questions

1 After reading this chapter, how would you convince a friend to join a primary faith community if they say they would rather practice their faith in private?

2 We argue that we should not call a community a "church" or "primary faith community" if it does not meet (or intend to meet) most of the 12 key elements we discussed above. Does your church or primary faith community score well on these 12 elements? Why or why not do you say that?

3 What three things do you think your PFC needs to work on?

Scripture to study • Ephesians 4:1-16

Books to read • Pagan Christianity, *by George Barna and Frank Viola* • So Beautiful, *by Leonard Sweet* • Loving One Another, *by Gene Getz* • Serving One Another, *by Gene Getz* • Encouraging One Another, *by Gene Getz* • Praying for One Another, *by Gene Getz*

3

WORLD IMPACT (OUTWARD)

How the body of Christ can significantly impact culture

When Jesus said, "Freely you have received, freely give!"
he wanted to focus our lives outward.
As the Father sent him,
he wants to send us into this world as his ambassadors.
We have to make disciples of Jesus
and redeem all spheres of society
to operate under his Lordship.
In discipleship we encourage each other
to be the salt and light of this world!

3.1 OUTWARD PURPOSE / MISSIONAL COMMUNITIES

—•—

George Kellerman

Sport is a stellar example of how unity should present itself. In the teams I have played on, we shared a clear sense of camaraderie and belonging, and a clarity of roles and purpose. We suffered together and were transparent with each other. Just like it is in church, right?

As I compared my experiences playing sport to my experiences in the church, I had the troubling realisation it wasn't. Not at all. I experienced more unity while playing sport than I had at any point while at church. The question is, why?

Churches arrange many well-intentioned activities such as camps, shared meals, games and worship. They tend to fall under the banner of fellowship, and echo sentiments of "feeling welcomed", "being good friends" and "becoming family". The events weren't bad, but compared to what I experienced in my sporting days, something was missing. There was a shallowness to the interactions, as though they weren't quite real. I love the people in my church, and the activities were meaningful, but as far as building genuine unity went, they fell far short. There was a major disconnect between what we were doing and what the world needed. I rarely heard any urgency to impact the surrounding culture, to transform people and communities, and redeem our unique contexts. It felt like we were sitting in a massage circle rubbing each other's shoulders while the world was falling apart around us.

How can we spread the news of Jesus to the whole world if our teams are shallow and fake or if our involvement in church doesn't drive us to develop unity? How will we relate to a world craving authenticity if we struggle to be open with each other? No wonder the new generation, when challenged to join a church, responds with, "Why?"

Jesus' team of disciples could not afford to be fake. In John 17, Jesus prayed: "And may they be in us *so that* the world will believe you sent me… May they experience such perfect unity that the world will know that you sent me and that you love them as much as you love me" (John 17:21,23 NLT, emphasis mine).

Their unity was to be so bright a beacon that the whole world could see God's love for them and believe in Jesus. There was a clear "so that" (purpose) statement guiding them. Their common purpose was too challenging to allow them the luxury of shallowness.

Church activities often lack a clearly defined "so that" statement to give them purpose. We aim to be a family "so that" we can be a family; we have fellowship together "so that" we can enjoy fellowship together. There is no deeper intentionality in our times together as a group. There is no real purpose for us to become unified. There was a reason Jesus prayed for unity between his disciples, and why unity is such a strong theme throughout the New Testament: so that the whole world will believe the message of Jesus. The common purpose was to impact the whole world with the message of Jesus.

Our church teams rarely have challenging purposes. Take note of the challenge set to the disciple team of Jesus. It was not only to reach their neighbourhood or Jerusalem; it was also to reach the whole world. It was a crazy awesome purpose which must have sounded impossible, but it is coming true. Does your team have a clear and challenging "so that" statement?

WHEN TEAMS FOCUS ON INTERNAL GROWTH BUT HAVE NO SHARED PURPOSE, THEY WILL NEVER EXPERIENCE REAL FELLOWSHIP

When a body has a clear purpose and direction, all the limbs will move in beautiful synchronous unity. To keep the body moving and balanced when it runs, the eyes need to be focused on the destination. Staring at your feet or other limbs the whole time will probably land you on your face. Similarly, when teams focus on internal growth but have no shared purpose, they will never experience real fellowship. When a body, with all its limbs working together, is on the move towards a clear direction, it will experience unity, synchrony and fellowship. Is your team on the move? Does your team have a clear purpose?

Classroom Teachings vs. Halftime Talks

Unfortunately, many churches and small groups have become like classrooms and lecture halls. People arrive, receive knowledge and discuss things, then leave and go on with their lives. Gaining knowledge is a worthwhile exercise, but the focus of our gatherings should primarily be about taking action. I imagine when Jesus was with his disciples it was more like being in a halftime meeting than in a classroom. Halftime talks are generally filled with passion, purpose, intent and rejuvenation. Game plans are re-aligned or altered, and new passion is breathed into the team. The focus is on the game plan, and how to execute it as a team. I can still remember our halftime gatherings, and that feeling when the team gave it all together, suffered together. Blood, sweat and tears flowed as we strived to live out the game plan together.

Instead of looking inwards and craving input, church gatherings should be outward and action-focused. How can we best love others? How can we get them to know Jesus? Outward-focused followers of Jesus should be more concerned about other people's walk with God than their own. We aren't just meeting together for our own edification. We meet for the teams of people we represent, the teams of people we will play the game with until our next gathering. If we change our focus from in to out, the nature of our time together will also change. Instead of personal growth, it will become about how we can make disciples. Instead of holding theological debates, we will practice how to

WHEN A DISCIPLESHIP TEAM FOCUSES OUTWARDS ON THE GROWTH OF OTHERS, THE INWARD GROWTH OF THE TEAM HAPPENS NATURALLY

become a better team so we can make a deeper impact. We want more than just a Bible study. We want to figure out how we as a team can change the world! Are your meetings more like classroom teachings or halftime gatherings?

After a rugby game, people don't ask me "How was the halftime talk?" They want to know how the game went, and the same applies to discipleship. Discipleship is not the gathering itself. It is playing the game together. Discipleship happens between the gatherings. Limiting church or discipleship to the two-hour gatherings that happen once or twice a week is ludicrous. The gatherings should be spaces to realign ourselves to the game plan, and opportunities to encourage each other to live lifestyles that can change the world. Churches and cell groups that put 90% of their effort into gatherings and only 10% into the "game time" between gatherings are missing the point. Our focus and energy should always be on what is happening between the gatherings. I see many teams sitting for hours and hours talking when they should be out there playing the game. It is even sadder to see teams losing the game, holding half-time discussions, and persisting with the same faltering game plan. What a waste!

The focus in your discipleship team should be helping your disciples to help others become more like Jesus. If they do that, your disciples will start becoming more like Jesus. When a discipleship team focuses outwards on the growth of others, the inward growth of the team happens naturally. In our university student discipleship group, we saw this principle play out beautifully. While planning our bi-annual retreat camp, we were pondering how we could apply this outward-focused principle. "Instead of having our own camp, why don't we organise a camp for others?" one student asked. Great idea! Before long we were busy organising a camp for teenagers, and while it was a first for many of the students, it was a fantastic experience for them. They saw the impact in the lives of the youth and built new discipleship relationships. But the most valuable thing that came from the experience was observing the inward change in the hearts of the university students. Looking back, we realised a critical principle:

We learn best when we teach others.

I see it happening again and again: people grow the fastest when they train and disciple others. As the adage goes: if you really want to understand something, explain it to someone else. The best inward growth happens when we are outward-focused!

What We Do

Most successful companies share one thing in common: a mission statement clarifying their purpose. We need a team purpose statement that keeps us focused on the calling God has given us. Review it occasionally and refer to it to remind each other about the purpose of the team. If God is changing your goals, update your purpose statement, but ensure it remains front and centre of your actions as a team.

My discipleship team spends a large percentage of our time together strategising how and where we should make disciples. We pray together, make plans together, and help each other connect with people. We ask God to show us who we should invest in, and where to find people willing to talk about Jesus, or who might be open to being discipled. We discuss how we tried to invest in people since the last time we met. We re-invigorate each other to renew our efforts.

We play the game together. Sometimes we go to hospitals, the streets, or to pubs to live out the love God has been revealing to us through the Scriptures. When we realise we are too fat from knowledge, we take action together. We organise camps, climb mountains, and reach out to people we would not normally come into contact with.

We train others together. For a few months, we replaced our small group gatherings with a leadership training event, where instead of receiving training, each member of the team had to train another group. We grew more during that event than any other time!

We form missional communities. As the name implies, a missional community is a community (or team) formed around the same mission. They live out their mission (or secondary calling — see chapter 3.5) together. A good example of a missional community is 4Hope. 4Hope is a group of business friends who share the mission of building bridges between fortunate and less fortunate communities. They get together every month to discuss key needs in each community, pray together and make big decisions. Between the meetings they seek solutions and build partnerships to address the identified needs. They even founded a non-profit organisation to help address this mission God called them to.

Another example of a missional community is Legacy, an adventure program for high school boys. It is an amazing space for young men to discover what it means to follow Jesus through adventuring together. They also learn perseverance, leadership, and what healthy, Godly manhood looks like. Legacy was the way adventure-loving university students formed a community around the mission of mentoring and investing into the next generation.

Another example of missional community is when people move into a specific neighbourhood (or even into the same house) to address key issues within that neighbourhood. We use the term "missional community" to remind the team members they need to constantly realign themselves to the mission God has called the team to. The mission determines the agenda, the regularity of gatherings and the people in the community. There is a clear sense of purpose when these missional communities gather. And why is that? Because the mission is not shaped around the community. Rather, the community is formed and shaped around the mission.

We form catalytic teams. A catalytic team shares the primary calling of practising Jesus together and making disciples, but collectively helps develop each other's secondary callings. (See chapter 3.5 for an elaboration of what we mean when we talk about secondary calling.) When these teams meet, their focus is learning from and shaping each other's callings. Strategising, equipping and listening together are typical verbs describing the actions when these teams meet. Most of our discipleship groups are either catalytic teams or missional communities. These are the teams which really grasp the principle of living with an outward purpose.

Discussion questions

1. Are your gatherings like halftime talks, or more like classroom teachings?
2. How should the dynamics within your gatherings change to turn your group into a missional community?
3. What is your discipleship team's purpose statement? What is the reason you get together?

Scripture to study • John 17:14-23

Books to read • Missional Communities, *by Reggie McNeal*

3.2 **MULTIPLICATION**

•

George Kellerman

We were talking about what Christmas means one December evening, when my dad said, "We are going to do things differently this year." He was aware of the culture of greed so common around Christmas and wanted to inoculate us against it. "Since Christmas is about the gift of Jesus, we are going to buy gifts for other children." A few days later, we found ourselves shopping with three children who had never received Christmas presents. I didn't understand why the boy I was with spent more time in the girl's toy aisle but ignored it at first. After considering his options carefully, he decided on his present… a doll. Very weird, I thought.

"Why do you want a doll?" I asked him.

"I want to give it to my sister."

I was shocked to my core. The first opportunity this boy had to receive a Christmas present, he used it to get a gift for his sister. We thought we were doing something special for these three kids in giving them each a gift, but the boy taught us what giving really meant. He had a selfless giving mindset, and I realised that I wanted that mindset too.

When you have a selfless, giving mindset, discipleship becomes a natural outflow. There is no need to push discipleship if selfless giving is part of your DNA. To share, to be outward-focused, to invest in others and to make disciples all flow from the heart of giving. If no expectation is placed on your disciples to make their own disciples, they will develop a "getting" mindset. Eventually, they will learn it is okay to relax in a comfort zone, getting fat on input from their mentors. We want our disciples to see the Gospel lived out on the move, impacting others. Too many cell groups meet with the sole intention of feeling like a family and learning from one another, which can be healthy if it leads to multiplication, but if growth is stagnant, something is wrong. When we gather, we must keep the people we will impact — our potential discipleship family — in mind. Sharing, giving, and being outward-focused should be our DNA. Making disciples should be our DNA!

To keep these things in our focus, our discipleship team often asks each other challenging, practical questions, such as:

- "Who can you share this with?"
- "How are you making disciples?"
- "How are your disciples doing?"
- "How are your disciples making disciples?"
- "How can we help with disciple-making amongst your disciples?"

Questions like these might be awkward at first, but when we really grasp what it means to give, they will become the norm. A team with disciples has very different conversations to a team that has none. They are usually outward-focused, investigating how they can better impact their disciples. And as your disciples start making their own disciples, your conversations with them should shift from what they can learn to what they can teach. We should never stop trying to learn and grow, but we forget that having our own disciples pushes us to grow even faster.

Multi-Generational Impact

Multiplication within discipleship can be a challenging topic, but it really shouldn't be. Christ commanded us to "make disciples of all nations" and even showed us how to do it. Without intentional disciple-making, there would be no growth in his Kingdom. People sometimes use discipleship as an excuse to build their own kingdoms, but that is not what we are discussing here. We are talking about exponential growth of the selfless message of the Kingdom.

Exponential growth is very different to doubling (or addition). Doubling happens when a cell group splits in two, usually because the logistics of the group became inconvenient. This type of growth is slow and tends to have a single-generation impact. Instead, the multiplication we want is exponential, intentional, multi-genera-tional, and creates disciples instead of attendees. It has a broader reach, and a deeper impact on those involved.

While his recorded miracles were largely public affairs, Jesus spent most of his time with a small group of people, the 12 disciples. By focusing on many you will reach a few, but by focusing on a few, you will reach many. If you disciple three people each year, each of whom disciple three people the next year, you will have reached two generations and nine disciples in two years. If the nine of them each disciple three people the following year, and so forth, the whole world will be discipled in 21 years. Consider that for a moment. We can reach the whole world in 21 years! All it takes is for one person to start discipling with a generational mindset and instil that DNA in his disciples.

Developing A Grandfather Mentality

Generational impact in discipleship has nothing to do with physical family. The goal is for our disciples to make disciples of their own. When your disciples have disciples, you are the grandfather of a discipleship tree. We need to start thinking like grandfathers — at least three generations down the line. To impact many generations we must be eager to multiply, and willing to take care of our spiritual descendants.

It is exciting to see when generational discipling starts from a young age. In our movement, we have 20-year-olds who have already become great-grandfathers, having spiritual sons, grandsons and great-grandsons.

You may be equally comfortable discipling peers or older people, but in our experience, the best age group to disciple is usually about one generation younger than you. Their experience of what you are going through is recent, but looking in the rear-view mirror should give them a broader perspective. A happy marriage of 10 years is an ideal position from which to help newlyweds navigate the first phase of their married lives. Young working adults should not forget about the university students who might be struggling to find purpose in life. University students can ensure teenagers don't have to discover their identity by themselves. Even teenagers can help younger children as they try to come to grips with this cruel world.

Are you aware of your responsibility to the next generation? Are you thinking like a grandfather?

Discussion questions
1   Do you and your disciples have the "giving mindset"?
2   How well are your disciples practicing multiplication?
3   What assistance do you need with multiplication issues amongst your disciples?

Scripture to study • 2 Corinthians 9:6-15 • Acts 1:8 • 2 Timothy 2:2

Books to read • Multiply, *by Francis Chan* • Cultivating a Life for God, *by Neil Cole*

3.3 THE PROCESS

—•—

George Kellerman

The purpose of this book is not to limit discipleship to one specific method, or to turn it into a simplistic plug-and-play formula. Discipleship is the process of facilitating a team towards becoming like Christ. It plays out differently on each team, but there are some consistent principles we have taken from the way Jesus taught and lived. The diagram below illustrates how these principles work. They are loosely defined, but we have found that they help people identify where they are in the discipleship process and what they need to focus on.

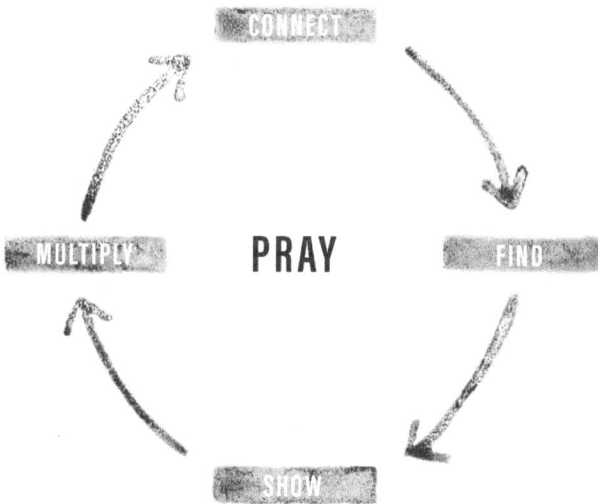

Pray

One of the questions I most enjoy receiving is, "How do I start with disciple-making?" It is always exciting to discuss this with people because it suggests that they are starting to take disciple-making seriously. "Where do I start?" is one of the easier questions to answer, because the Bible paints a clear picture of how Jesus started.

He started with prayer.

Reading through the Gospels, it is amazing how much time Jesus spent praying. Luke 6:12 notes that Jesus spent the whole night praying before he chose his disciples. One would think that a quick question would be all he needed to get a quick response from the Father. But no, Jesus spent the whole night praying for his disciples before he chose the 12 apostles. How much more should we not start our discipling process with prayer? Prayer is the place to start, and the place to return to throughout the disciple-making process. Prayer should be at the centre of your discipleship process, from start to finish. Refer to chapter 6.1 for more on prayer.

Connect

As you pray, God will show you who to disciple. If no person or group of people come to mind, make a list of anyone you know who has similar interests, passions or causes. Include people you interact with at work, at home, and other places you spend time with people. While making the list, ask God if you should intentionally build a relationship with any of the people on it. Alternatively, ask God if you should approach people whom you don't yet know. He might even call you to join an affinity group so you can connect with more individuals and groups. He may not answer your prayers immediately, but when he does, trust him and take action.

Occasionally it is just a matter of starting a conversation, but sometimes you will need a different approach. For example, a group of my friends felt God calling them to disciple teenagers. To create a point of connection, they organised camps and hikes and invited the teenagers to join them. What you do depends on your context — it might be easier for you to use sports, game nights, or communal meals. It doesn't matter what the activity is, provided you can spend quality time with the people you are called to disciple. We call these access activities because they give us access to connect with the people God has called us to pour our lives into. As you intentionally spend time with those people, you will be amazed where God leads you and how God connects the people who are seeking him to those who witness about him.

These access activities can be informal and organic (starting conversations with people you meet in the street or inviting colleagues home for dinner) or they can be more formal and structured (holiday programs, entrepreneurship training, Alpha courses, camps). These activities all provide opportunities to access more people. These are activities where God can use you to answer the prayers of lost people.

As you interact with people, some of your conversations will move to a deeper level, while others will never go beyond casual chatter. Taking a conversation deeper than sport, politics or the latest buzz is rarely easy with people you don't know well. As strange as it sounds, conversation is a skill. Some people are naturals, while others need to practise. If you are not comfortable taking a conversation deeper, ask a mentor or friend to teach you. It is important that we learn how to take conversations from casual to serious, from serious to spiritual, and from spiritual to scriptural. It will be fantastic to have conversations where the Word of God becomes "alive and active", even "dividing soul and spirit" (Heb 4:12).

Find

Jesus did a fascinating "discipleship training practice" with his group of disciples. This is captured in Luke 9:1-6, Luke 10:1-24, Matthew 9:35-10:42 and Mark 6:6-13, and reveals principles for disciple-making.

In Luke 10, the practice starts with prayer. "He told them, 'The harvest is plentiful, but the workers are few. Ask the Lord of the harvest, therefore, to send out workers into his harvest field'" (Luke 10:2). Next, Jesus gives a simple, yet direct command, "Go!" (Luke 10:3), echoing Matthew 28:19's "'Go and make disciples.'" The "connect" principle becomes clear in the next few verses, as it guides the disciples to use "hospitality" as a test for spiritually open households. Notice the non-threatening nature of seeking invitation (instead of forcing their way in or preaching from street corners).

Jesus reminds them that it will not always be an easy or safe road. "'I am sending you out like lambs among wolves'" (Luke 10:3). He also gives practical guidance and a purposeful, loaded command: "'Do not take a purse or bag or sandals; and do not greet anyone on the road'" (Luke 10:4), to teach them to rely on God and not try to be self-sufficient.

JESUS REMINDS THEM THAT IT WILL NOT ALWAYS BE AN EASY OR SAFE ROAD

Jesus then gives guidance to find the person (or household) who promotes peace. "'When you enter a house, first say, 'Peace to this house.' If someone who promotes peace is there, your peace will rest on them; if not, it will return to you. Stay there, eating and drinking whatever they give you…'" (Luke 10:5-7).

As David Watson puts it, "Persons of Peace [are the ones] God has prepared to receive the Gospel into a community for the first time." [34] They promote peace and are welcoming and open to you and your message. Sometimes you meet them immediately while other times you have to be patient. If there is a Person of Peace in the community, God will lead you to them eventually if you listen and obey his voice. It is always easier to make disciples if you are working with God. Look for the people he has been preparing rather than trying to force the Gospel on people who aren't ready. Even though a Person of Peace will not be behind every door you knock on, purposeful and intentional "knocking" is still a prerequisite to finding them. If you are not well received, move on and seek elsewhere because if you are persistent, you will find a person of peace. Prayer is critical to this process.

A friend of mine, Nic (not his real name), shared his story of finding a Person of Peace while disciple-making in a Middle-Eastern country. Nic met a Muslim man, Amir (not his real name) two years after arriving in the country and shared a story of Jesus with him. Amir seemed interested initially and asked for a copy of the Gospels (known as the Injil in Arabic). Nic thought Amir might be a Person of Peace and tried to meet him again. But after a few months of no response from Amir, Nic stopped approaching him. Then out of the blue, Amir contacted Nic again.

Amir had had an encounter with God. He shared this experience with Nic and asked Nic to help him hear and obey the voice of God by studying the Injil together. This was the start of a great friendship and discipleship relationship. With guidance from the Holy Spirit, Amir started sharing Jesus with others in his mostly Muslim community. Over the next two years, he started six groups who also discuss Jesus stories from the Injil. Multiple generations of disciples came from these six groups, and they have expanded into 38 groups at the time of writing. Thus far, 80 people from these groups have been baptised into a life of following Jesus. Nic does not know many of these 80 people. All he knows is that he needs to encourage and disciple the Person of Peace he found in Amir.

What was illustrated in this story is that the Persons or Households of Peace open their social network for the Gospel. I should not put my mind on discipling the entire network. I need to focus and pray to find the Persons of Peace God has prepared.

Show

Jesus was the ultimate example-setting discipler, but who discipled him? His Father God. God the Father is thus the ultimate discipler. Jesus often said he was only doing what he saw his Father doing and saying what the Father wanted him to say. When people asked him to reveal the Father to them, Jesus replied, "Don't you believe that I am in the Father, and that the Father is in me? The words I say to you I do not speak on my own authority. Rather, it is the Father, living in me, who is doing his work" (John 14:10).

While Jesus was discipling the 12, he was teaching them how to be discipled by the Father. He walked, ate, debated, joked and reached out to people with them. He shared life in all its fullness with them, modelled Kingdom principles for them, and sent them off to disciple others. As we disciple people, they need to see what this life with Jesus looks like.

My most memorable discipleship experiences have been when my disciples and I were doing things together. I have fond memories of outreaches, organising camps, and travelling overseas for training with them. We have shared meals, fun activities and holidays, and even spent a whole weekend on the streets trying to find a Person of Peace. Never underestimate the value of sharing your everyday life with your disciples. They will learn from how you work, play sport, and how you interact with your family. When one of the guys I am discipling wants to spend time with me, he arrives at my home with his pillow and toothbrush and lives with me for a few days. It is an incredible opportunity for significant conversations and doing life together. Life-on-life time with your disciples is the best way to demonstrate following Jesus and the disciple-making process. Some of their most life-changing lessons will happen when they see how you live.

In this phase, you need to invite your disciples to gather regularly. Your gatherings might be over a meal, reading the Bible together, or discussing questions, but whatever form they take, they should be learning opportunities. Your disciples need to learn how important taking initiative is in disciple-making, and they need to learn how to lead in a discipleship context. If they don't already know how, you need to teach them how to lead a Discovery Bible Study, small group gathering, and eventually, their own discipleship team. If they aren't yet comfortable introducing people to Jesus, that should be the focus of your initial gatherings.

Remember, we want to create disciple-making communities around Scripture and not around the teacher. Furthermore, our gatherings should be focused more on active obedience and less on content; more self-discovery and less persuasion and teaching. When we find the person or household to disciple, our role is to facilitate spiritual discovery through the Word. The main focal point for the "show" phase should be Bible engagement and discovery of scriptural truth for obedience. Everything else extra-biblical (such as books and other training materials) should be secondary. Stick to the Bible as far as possible. To help us facilitate Bible self-discovery and to help keep things very simple, we often follow a Discovery Bible Study (DBS) format. See an example of a thorough DBS in the appendix.

Multiply

Most of the time, people follow the dreams and calling of their bosses, parents, companies or churches. However, the focus of discipleship is all about developing the dreams and callings of the disciples. The dreams of the leader are not a focal point. Discipleship requires putting your dreams aside and developing the dreams of the team. To equip your disciples is to help develop their callings and develop how they make disciples. As good leaders are known by the actions of their followers, so good disciplers are known by the disciple-making of their disciples.

Please refer to chapter 3.2 on multiplication for more on what we mean by "multiply". Without repeating too much what was said in that chapter, I would like to emphasise the importance of this "multiply" phase. Too many disciples get stuck in the "show" phase. For non-believers, the "show" phase could take longer, but believers should move to the "multiply" phase as quickly as possible.

The first step is to make sure your disciples are multiplying by discipling others who also disciple others. There will be plenty of equipping needed during this phase. But once they are well established, what about starting a new discipleship stream? If you have the capacity, prayerfully consider discipling a new group — what about people from a different life context to your current discipleship group?

Hopefully, this will stir the dream of how discipleship movements can become a reality, and how you can get involved in a discipleship movement yourself.

Discussion questions

1. Where in the discipleship process are you? Are you in the pray, connect, find, show or multiply phase?
2. Where in the discipleship process are the people you disciple?
3. What is the next obedience step in the discipleship process you need to take, and what should your strategy be?

Scripture to study • Luke 9:1-6 • Luke 10:1-24 • Matthew 9:35-10:42 • Mark 6:6-13

Books to read • Contagious Disciple Making, *by David Watson and Paul Watson*

3.4 WITNESSING

—•—

George Kellerman

Scent Trail: Witnessing Your Fragrance

We can learn a great deal from tent caterpillars. They are constantly hungry and can strip a tree in a day or two. To sustain their voracious appetites, they have developed a brilliant method to ensure they survive and get the best food at the same time. While they are busy on one tree, they send out scouts to find a new source of food. Each scout leaves a scent trail as it leaves, to help it navigate back to the nest. If it finds a source of food, it eats itself full and returns to the nest, leaving a second scent trail. This second trail gives information about the quality of the food it just ate. The other caterpillars then compare the scent trails and decide if any of the scent trails are worth leaving the nest for. Once they figure out which scent trail is good enough, the rest of the colony leaves to follow the chosen scent trail.

It is not about following the caterpillar. It is about following the fragrance the caterpillar carried. This is what 2 Corinthians 2:15 is talking about when it refers to us carrying the fragrance of Christ. The fragrance the caterpillar lays down is strong enough to cause the rest of its colony to move into a new life. What fragrance do you leave behind? Is it one that people will risk following?

All aspects of our lives bear witness to who or what we follow. Mahatma Gandhi famously said the following when asked how to evangelise in India:

"Oh, I don't reject Christ. I love Christ. It's just that so many of you Christians are so unlike Christ. If Christians would really live according to the teachings of Christ, as found in the Bible, all of India would be Christian today." [35]

We are witnessing all the time. Those who eat a lot witness that food is important to them; those who are constantly on their phones witness to the importance of digital interaction in their lives.

Discrimination witnesses to a subconscious belief that not everyone is equal, and those who ignore the suffering around them witness to a focus on self above all else. Our lives and conversations bear witness to what we value and reveal the fragrance we carry.

Witnessing to people about Jesus is not a programmed event. It is how you live every minute of every day.

Witnessing Through Conversations

We witness about our idols.

"The place where your treasure is, is the place you will most want to be, and end up being" (Matt 6:21 MSG). If the treasure of your heart is partying, you witness that a good party is the most meaningful thing you can do. If sport consumes your life, you witness that sport is an idol worth worshiping. When your life reflects a total orientation toward Jesus, he will be the idol you witness about.

We witness about who we love.

A person in love does not struggle to talk about whom they are in love with. Similarly, many parents talk about their children at every chance they get. If we are infatuated with Jesus, we will struggle to stop talking about him.

We witness about what we experience.

You will be amazed at how much conversation with your friends revolves around experiences. Good or bad, work or play, if it meant something to you, you probably told someone about it. Social media is the prime witness of that. If we aren't spending time with Jesus and journeying with him on his mission, we won't have many encounters with him to talk about.

We witness about what amazes us.

Listen to someone coming from a scenic trip and you will hear how they marvel at creation. A movie that left a deep impact becomes the topic of discussion long after the final credits roll. Are we in wonder of our salvation? There are many amazing, unique attributes of the Gospel of Jesus. There is unending love without expecting anything in return, and fellowship with God without having to perform for it. We have access to overflowing life in spite of suffering and hardship, and the promise that instead of being the end, death is the beginning of joy. We will witness about these things and much more when we are constantly amazed at these masterful mysteries of Jesus Christ.

We witness about what would benefit others.

When a friend has health problems, we are quick to offer advice or a reference to a medical practitioner. Our selfless conversations are full of what is beneficial for the other person to hear. If we believe deep down that Jesus is the answer to the many voids and questions people have, we will most definitely witness about him more. "Do not let any unwholesome talk come out of your mouths, but only what is helpful for building others up according to their needs, that it may benefit those who listen" (Eph 4:29).

Healthy Tension Between Intentional And Organic Conversations

Have you ever been approached by someone trying to evangelise you? How did it make you feel?

It happened to me the other day. As he was preaching to me, he triggered a conversation in my head. One voice applauded his boldness, that he would share the things most important to him with a stranger. The other one pointed out how similar it was to being called by a telemarketer — like I was being manipulated into buying something I didn't want or need. It was an uncomfortable tension to be in — encouraged by his boldness for the Gospel but put off by his pushiness. I wanted to ask him to stop, because "I'm already on the inside, one of you guys", but decided against it.

While there is a time and place for it, "cold-call" evangelising often ends up being repulsive instead of attractive. It is often received as presumptuous, manipulative and pushy. On the other hand, I want to talk about what I love… and since I love Jesus, I love talking about him. This is where the conversations feel real, because they flow from my natural passion for Jesus. This is the state I want to be in — bubbling over from the fullness of God. As Jesus puts it, "the mouth speaks what the heart is full of" (Luke 6:45). However, most days I get to talk about Jesus much less than I would like. So I need to be intentional to create opportunities where I can talk about what and who I love. You will experience this healthy tension between intentional and organic conversations as you open your heart to the Spirit's prompting.

God Speaks... So Let Us Listen!

As we go about our daily lives, we interact with many people who need to hear good news. Our antennae need to be ready to receive promptings from the Holy Spirit about the who, when, what and how. Most significant opportunities I have had to share Jesus (his life, his love and his ways) were when I bumped into someone I did not plan to meet that day. If our antennae are up constantly, we are more likely to hear God when he speaks, and what he has to say. We can trust that God speaks to us regularly. As our sensitivity to promptings from the Holy Spirit grows, our opportunities to witness will grow.

AS OUR SENSITIVITY TO PROMPTINGS FROM THE HOLY SPIRIT GROWS, OUR OPPORTUNITIES TO WITNESS WILL GROW

God Draws People, Not Us

"No one can come to Me unless the Father who sent Me draws him [giving him the desire to come to Me]; and I will raise him up [from the dead] on the last day" (John 6:44 AMP). Drawing people to Jesus is dependent on God above all else. God draws people, not us. We should be aware of who is being drawn to God, and what our role in the process is. Paul understood that God opened the doors, not him: "And pray for us, too, that God may open a door for our message, so that we may proclaim the mystery of Christ, for which I am in chains" (Col 4:3). Luke 10 also teaches us to find the Person of Peace — someone who is welcoming, open to the message of Jesus and opens their social network to the messenger. (We will talk more about the Person of Peace in chapter 3.4.) As God's efforts are to draw people to Jesus, we must look for these people who are open and help them (and their relational network) be reconciled to God. We still have a responsibility to knock on the door, but the Holy Spirit tugs at the hearts of the people to help them open their door.

We Are Pointing People To Jesus, Not Converting Them

Since God is the one who draws people to him, he is also the one who does the converting. We cannot change people's hearts; only Jesus can change hearts. Our only job is to point people to Jesus. My thoughts during my interaction with the evangelist were not right, for a few reasons.

- Thinking "I am on the inside" assumes a clear line separating those "on the inside" from those "on the outside".
- It reveals that I subconsciously segregate people into those who make the cut and those who don't, which is not my job!
- With this kind of mentality, I am more likely to point people to the rules instead of to the God they are to follow.

It is as if I want to pull them across the "line of salvation", and when they are across they are safe and "on the inside". This is a dangerous way of thinking and has many flaws:

- It suggests that people need to perform to a particular standard to earn the right to be a follower of Jesus.
- It encourages judgement on who is "saved" and who is not.
- It encourages an intellectual approach to faith.
- The thicker the "line of salvation", the more difficult it is for people to meet Jesus.
- The thicker the line, the more (falsely) secure I feel being on the inside.
- It encourages Christians and denominations to fight about where the boundary-line is.

We are pointing people to Jesus, not a set of rules.
We are pointing people to Jesus, not ourselves.
We are pointing people to Jesus, not our culture.

It would be better to avoid pointing people to rules, steps, a specific ritual, a church, or even a religion. Rather, focus your energy on pointing to the Person who transforms lives. Our concern should be less about whether they are close to or far from Jesus, and more about whether they are moving towards him. Don't worry so much about the laws and legalities. Help them set Jesus as their true north and move towards him with unerring focus.

As a good networker introduces you to the right people, so a good disciple-maker should introduce you to Jesus. We can't force people to follow or get to know Jesus, but it shouldn't be too difficult or offensive to introduce people to him. When we model Jesus in our words and actions, we encourage people to gravitate towards him. Jesus will do the changing of hearts. We just need to lift him up and point people to him.

Salty Statements

To see if people are open to meet and get to know Jesus, we use what we call "salty statements" and "salty questions". As the term suggests, they are intended to evaluate if people are thirsty for Jesus. If we don't think the person is ready yet, we don't continue knocking during the conversation.

A salty statement is usually a response to a question indicating that God loves us, we love him, he speaks to us and that we obey him. It is important that the answer is in context so as not to seem contrived. For example, a friend was asked what he does for a living. Instead of describing his job, he replied, "I help people discover the plans God has for their lives." When asked about his weekend, another friend of mine responds with answers like, "I worked in the garden while trying to understand this thing about Jesus."

Hopefully, these statements will lead to other questions, which you can use to guide the conversation deeper. The world is hungry for meaning and longing for people willing to have the deep conversations that lead to it.

Salty questions have a similar impact to salty statements. I have often used questions like "What is your calling in life?", "What life questions have been occupying your thoughts lately?" or "How can I pray for you?" to test if the person is thirsty for a deeper or spiritual conversation. Many times, these questions are turned around, which gives you an opportunity to answer with salty statements. There is no trickery in these salty statements. The purpose is simply to see whether the person is willing to have a spiritual conversation or thirsty to meet Jesus.

Reflection Questions

To close this chapter, I would like to reflect on the Holy Spirit-inspired words of Paul in his letter to the Colossians. Please read the Scripture below, then reflect on the following questions (preferably with your discipleship team).

"Devote yourselves to prayer, being watchful and thankful. And pray for us, too, that God may open a door for our message, so that we may proclaim the mystery of Christ, for which I am in chains. Pray that I may proclaim it clearly, as I should. Be wise in the way you act toward outsiders; make the most of every opportunity. Let your conversation be always full of grace, seasoned with salt, so that you may know how to answer everyone" (Col 4:2-6).

- Are we praying for people who don't know Christ?
- Are we devoting ourselves to prayer?
- Are we watchful and seeing what the Lord wants us to see?
- Are we praying for open doors?
- Are we seeking the seekers?
- Do we know the mystery of Christ?
- Are we proclaiming?

- Are we proclaiming it clearly, in a way that is simple and understandable?
- Are we proclaiming the uniqueness of the Gospel?
- Are we acting wisely with the people we encounter?
- Is our motive when approaching people to get something from them, or is it about giving something to them?
- Are we prepared for opportunities when they arise?
- How do we take the conversation deeper?
- How can our conversation be full of grace and salt?
- Do we know how to answer everyone?

Discussion questions

1 What needs to happen for us to witness about Jesus more?
2 Is God speaking to you about a specific person/household who is open to the Gospel? If so, how are you going to approach this person/household?
3 What "salty questions" can you start adding to your conversations?
4 What are some good "salty statements" you can use?

Scripture to study • Colossians 4:2-6 • John 6:43-47
• 2 Corinthians 2:12-17

Books to read • Just Walk Across the Room, *by Bill Hybels* • The Master Plan of Evangelism, *by Robert E. Coleman*

3.5 GOD'S SPECIFIC ASSIGNMENT FOR US

George Kellerman

A friend of mine, Juan, told me one day that he was experiencing God speaking to him about a specific life calling. This was a normal topic for most of my friends, but what made it peculiar is that Juan had never talked about, or to, God before. He had never read the Bible, didn't go to church and had never really prayed before. When we spoke again a few days later, he asked me to teach him how to read the Bible. We read Ephesians 2:1-10 together, which is a passage explaining the Gospel in a concise way. I meant to focus our discussion on verses 1-9, but it was verse 10 that gripped him: "For we are God's masterpiece. He has created us anew in Christ Jesus, so we can do the good things he planned for us long ago" (Eph 2:10 NLT). After reading this verse, Juan got very excited. It confirmed what he heard from God about his calling. Not only did he discover that God could speak to him, but he also realised God has specific plans for his life. He decided on that day to follow the God who revealed these plans to him and started to walk the road God was leading him down.

We are not on earth simply to become good people preparing for heaven. We are on earth with a specific assignment.

> "This is the true joy in life, the being used for a purpose recognised by yourself as a mighty one; the being thoroughly worn out before you are thrown on the scrap heap; the being a force of Nature instead of a feverish selfish little clod of ailments and grievances complaining that the world will not devote itself to making you happy." [36]

Our Purpose Is Determined By God

Discovering your purpose and calling isn't hard, but a self-centred and individualistic process can trip people up.

> "Since God is the one who calls, His way, mind and heart should be examined. We have to understand God as our ultimate Father who created us for His mission... No one just automatically aligns with this mission of God. Everything in us naturally gravitates towards our personal desires, which are in opposition to God's design. We prefer to do our own thing. We prefer to be our own gods. Our natural tendency is to oppose God, not side with Him. [Because of this], a drastic turnabout is needed. [We need to turn away] from an egotistical orientation where we are frantically pushing [to get] our own way, securing our own rights and realising our own dream, towards a life that is reprogrammed by God and lived for others. This calls for an act of self-abandonment. Man has to discard his own dreams, plans and agenda in order to adopt God's dream, plans and agenda." [37]

Once, and only once, we are in submission to God's mission, can we discover the journey of our specific assignment — our secondary calling. Once we submit to our primary calling we can live out our secondary calling. To practice submission is to force my mission to become a sub-mission of God's mission. Most of us want to discover our mission, then try to squeeze God into the picture, instead of asking what God's mission is and finding our place in it. We start by looking at our gifts, abilities and passions, instead of first investigating God's heart and passions, and seeing how we fit into his picture.

The primary calling for followers of Jesus today is the same as it was 2000 years ago. The "together mission" — the Great Commission — and the Great Commandment hasn't changed; we are on earth to love God, love others and make disciples of Jesus. Only if we fulfil the primary calling of God, can we fulfil the secondary calling of our lives. Many people won't find their secondary calling in life because they don't live out their primary calling of making disciples. Your specific assignment on earth will render useless (or even damaging) results if no discipleship takes place in your life. If you don't live out your primary calling, you won't properly live out your secondary calling.

Our Purpose Is Determined By Context

Once you figure out what God wants to do, you need to ask what God is busy with in your context. Your calling is determined by context.

Have you ever wondered why you were born in this period of history? Or why you grew up in the country you grew up in? How different would your calling have been if you grew up in a different time or country? Maybe there is a specific reason you grew up where and when you did. Maybe there is a specific reason you find yourself in the context where you are now. We believe you are in your specific context for a reason. For example, I cannot ignore the fact that I live in one of the most economically unequal countries in the world (South Africa). Nor can I ignore the call to address the racism in the post-Apartheid period of my country.

Our area, community, workplace, family, place of education, people-group, season of life, social groups, and friends all make up our context. If it is difficult to analyse your context, rather think about your affinity groups. Affinity groups are groups you interact with on a weekly basis. In typical urban settings, an affinity group has a shared need, interest or cause. In a typical rural context, they have shared family ties, ethnicity or culture. Think about your context and the affinity groups you are part of and ask yourself: what would Jesus do in our context at this time in history?

Our Purpose Is Determined By Our Teams

We have now established the importance of figuring out what God is doing, and the context in which he is doing it. That means we can finally get to our specific role and assignment, right? Yes, but with one caveat: this must not become an individualistic exercise. We cannot see our calling in isolation. God typically works through teams rather than individuals.

Before we go on, don't let the word "team" limit you here. Your team can be any group you share a common goal with, be it family, a discipleship group, church or a leadership team. It might even be a sub-team within a bigger group. The important thing is that it is a group of people who self-identify with a shared Kingdom mission. If you feel alone in your specific calling, look for people with a similar calling, assemble a team, then go! Confirmation of your calling is most often found when other people share a similar call.

For every team we find ourselves in (or new one we want to form), we should ask two questions. What are God's intended purposes for the team, and what role do I need to play in it? It is particularly important that you ask these questions with your discipleship team. I encourage you to make a frequent habit of praying this simple prayer with your disciples/discipler:

"Lord, what is the purpose of our team for a time like this?"

As God is a team (Father, Son and Holy Spirit), it makes sense that he thinks and directs his Kingdom rule through teams. I believe God uses a guerrilla warfare approach for his Kingdom: small teams of warriors, constantly on the move with a specific purpose. That purpose becomes the focus of our team, which in turn guides our individual secondary calling.

We must constantly remind ourselves to avoid a mindset preoccupied with my calling, my mission and my dream. Rather, become occupied with our calling, our mission and our dream. Your calling in life is nested in your team's mission, which is rooted in God's mission.

This approach does not reduce the importance of our individual and unique callings. In an ideal team context our individual callings merge, not clash. Our team's calling should reinforce our individual callings. I have seen great scenarios where every team member is aware of each other's individual callings, and then work together on the individual callings and team calling.

Jesus teaches us we are co-creators with him. As we discover our calling and live out our purpose, we better understand the meaning of "being Christ's ambassadors". While he did the cardinal work on the cross, Christ makes his appeal to reconcile the world through us. "All this is from God, who reconciled us to himself through Christ, and gave us the ministry of reconciliation: that God was reconciling the world to himself in Christ, not counting men's sins against them. And he has committed to us the message of reconciliation" (2 Cor 5:18-19).

As God made Adam and Eve in his image as a creator, so we are assigned to build God's kingdom with him as co-creators and ambassadors on his behalf. We don't do this in our own capacity, but through obedience to and the releasing of the Spirit in us. What an amazing privilege to co-create and represent Jesus in his mission!

Within the context of a discipleship team, we have the best chance to fully live out our primary calling. Also, we most definitely have the best chance within our teams to discover, be supported in and fully live out our secondary callings.

I would like to pray with Paul, Silas and Timothy, "for you, that our God may count you worthy of his calling, and that by his power he may fulfil every good purpose of yours and every act prompted by your faith. We pray this so that the name of our Lord Jesus may be glorified in you, and you in him, according to the grace of our God and the Lord Jesus Christ" (2 Thess 1:11 NIV 1984).

What We Do

Since we believe that God has a specific assignment for our lives, we conduct weekend workshops to help people discover their life mission statement. Through this process of self-discovery, reflection, prayer and asking the right questions, we regularly see lives realigned to God's intended purposes. We have seen career changes, service projects started, NGOs birthed, and many disciples made.

Discussion questions

1. What is God's primary mission, and where is he now on that mission?
2. What would Jesus do in your unique context at this specific time in history?
3. What are God's intended purposes for your team(s) within this context?
4. What is your role within each team's calling? What is your specific role within God's mission?

Scripture to study • Romans 15:14-22 • Esther 4

Books to read • The Purpose Driven Life, *by Rick Warren*
• Experiencing God, *by Henry T. Blackaby, Richard Blackaby, et al.*

3.6 **REDEEMING CULTURE**
(Counterfeit Idols & Counterflow Teams)

—●—

George Kellerman

Disengage From Counterfeit Idols And Re-engage With Counter-flow Teams

The rhythm of our time, the idols of our time and the culture of our time all numb us from the needs of our time. The following song expresses this so poignantly:

Nero's watching video while Rome begins to burn
Nero's wearing roller skates so he can quickly turn
Get away from all he does and what to see or what to hear
Nero's wearing headphones and they stretch from ear to ear
Nero's got a private world for which the heart may yearn
Nero's watching video while Rome begins to burn

Tension on the TV, a world out of control
Wounded people weeping, they never touch his soul
Nero's changing channels, Nero's moving on
Nero's feet are moving to a very different song
Oh Nero, can't you hear them?
Don't you ever feel the pain?
The words go through his ears
But they never touch his brain

He's moving out, he's moving up, he's always moving on
Nero moves his body to a thousand different songs
Nero is the product of an advertiser's dream
He took in all the slogans, he's part of the machine
Nero, do you realize
There's another world outside

Where the poor
Keep getting poorer
And the hungry
Have just died [38]

Jesus calls his followers to see and feel the real needs of society. We cannot bring about change if we are unaware of the problem. However, instead of being change-agents, most Christians have become the conformed ones — conforming to the norms of culture and forgetting the needy.

"Religion that God our Father accepts as pure and faultless is this: to look after orphans and widows in their distress and to keep oneself from being polluted by the world" (James 1:27).

These two practical commands complement each other. Looking after the needy opens your eyes to the enticements of the world, and keeping yourself from being polluted by the world opens your eyes to the real needs of society. These two "religious" commands are the recipe for a people group to redeem a culture.

Keep Ourselves From Being Polluted By Counterfeit Idols

Christians struggle to remain unpolluted by worldly culture because the same idols that rule the secular world rule the Christian world. The Old Testament is littered with stories of the Israelites becoming polluted by the false gods of other nations. (Deut 32:15-20; Jer 8:19; 13:25; Amos 2:4) The same thing happens with Christians today. Most people claiming to worship God also worship other false gods. Maybe not Asherah, Baal or Chemosh, but certainly one (or all) of the gods Money, Sex and Power (terms made popular by Richard Foster in his book, *The Challenge of the Disciplined Life: Christian Reflections on Money, Sex and Power*).

Timothy Keller shares similar sentiments in his book *Counterfeit Gods:*

"Our contemporary society is not fundamentally different from these ancient ones. Each culture is dominated by its own set of idols. Each has its 'priesthoods', its totems and rituals. Each one has its shrines — whether office towers, spas and gyms, studios or stadiums — where sacrifices must be made in order to procure the blessings of the good life and ward off disaster. What are the gods of beauty, power, money, and achievement but these same things that have assumed mythic proportions in our individual lives and in our society?" [39]

As we start following God wholeheartedly, we realise that we are still enchanted by Money, Sex and Power. We might surrender our lives to God our Provider but still struggle to surrender our monetary excess. We might have repented of our sexual sins many times but still regularly struggle with lust. We aim to be servants like Jesus, but still ambitiously seek success. It might be more difficult to escape the enslavement of these foreign idols than we first thought.

These false gods are dangerous not only because we invite God's wrath when we worship them, but also because of the ease with which they enslave us. And we rarely escape their fangs.

Enslavement To Beauty And Sex

Everywhere you look it seems as if culture is pointing to sex as the ultimate fulfilment. The bombardment of sexual remarks, jokes, visuals in the media and general conversation urges everyone to seek this "fulfilment". Not that the natural sexual desire the Lord has created in you is wrong, sinful or dirty in any way. Rather, sexuality becomes your god when sexual desire becomes your primary motivator. This is evident in an endless yearning for sexual fulfilment and fantasies. Beauty and sex consume our headspace and become the primary thing we seek. It becomes a drug, an addiction. We see these symptoms in our culture in the countless accounts of:

- Pornographic practices and addictions
- Eating disorders
- Affairs
- Cosmetic surgery
- Emotional attachment or total dependency on a partner
- Profitable dating and casual sex websites.

Considering the list above, it is clear that the sex god has enslaved our culture.

Enslavement To Power And Achievement

Similar strongholds are clear with the god, Power, who also goes by the name Achievement. Our culture glorifies any type of rising to the top. Never mind who you step on or cheat to get there; if it is survival of the fittest the ends justifies the means, regardless of who it hurts. Our culture adores striving to ascend into success, while Jesus repeatedly calls us to become the least and descend into greatness (see chapter 4.4). Many Christians are still slaves to success; it is just hidden by the context of church or ministry. The symptoms of the enslavement to Power and Achievement appear in various forms within our culture:

- Your whole life built around performing and impressing a few individuals
- Employers becoming higher priority than your spouse or children
- Pursuing leadership positions for the sake of controlling decisions or feeling more important because of it
- Bullying at schools and in the marketplace
- Christian leaders misusing their positions to control and manipulate people
- Selfish ambition towards significance, often at the expense of close relationships.

From the above, it is clear that the ladder of success still enslaves many.

Enslavement To Money

And now for the famous one, the one that even has a specific name in the Bible: Mammon, the god of Money. Oh, how sneakily this one enslaves us! Mammon has two middle names: Comfort and Security. A yearning for money is rarely a simple desire for more fancy printed paper — it is rooted much deeper. We crave the comfort, security and ability to gratify our desires that money brings. The Comfort and Security gods have a numbing and demobilising effect. Money enslaves, and the symptoms of that enslavement to Money and Comfort are prolific in our culture.

WE SET OURSELVES UP AS THE HOLDERS OF OUR FUTURE SECURITY, AND THAT IS A STRESSFUL POSITION TO HOLD INDEED

The recognition or security offered by a safe, stable job lures many people away from their calling. The pull of being more "secure" outweighs the uncertain pursuit of their calling.

People constantly seeking to make things more secure for themselves. But the sad reality is that more worldly security often leads to less trust in God. This hampers our freedom in serving Jesus. The world believes that security brings more freedom, but the irony is that worldly security brings more anxiety. We set ourselves up as the holders of our future security, and that is a stressful position to hold indeed.

People live for weekends and holidays. The shallow fulfilment during these "happy" times drives people to spend all their energy recovering from and preparing for the next "happy" time.

Most people spend their "free" time on themselves, using weeknights and weekends for relaxation and comfort. And all of this while the world is busy bleeding. Watching series, gaming and social media are not wrong in and of themselves, but it is the time-wasting and numbing effect that make these activities so catastrophic.

Comfort enslaves those who struggle to break free from the grip of complacency. It trades the immediate gratification of selfish desires for an inability to see and act on the real needs of others.

Freedom And Life Overflowing

To avoid creating a grim picture of life, we want to point out the good news. Freedom from these enslavements is possible. Ultimate freedom and joy are possible! Jesus said he came to set us free. He came to save us. It is for freedom that he set us free (Gal 5:1). Jesus did not promise life would be easy, nice or pleasant, but that we could have it in abundance (John 10:10)!

Jesus provides us with everything for our enjoyment (1 Tim 6:17). And we can live this amazingly joyful and free life if Jesus becomes our sole provider of joy and freedom. Jesus knows our calling and what is best for us, but we will miss it if we follow our own ways (Prov 16:1-4). Thus, we can only walk in this overflowing life if we follow Jesus and his ways for us.

Freedom is not doing whatever I want whenever I want. True freedom is being free from my selfish desires — available to do whatever Jesus desires. But if we are serving (amongst others) the gods of Money, Comfort and Security, we are not free to do what Jesus asks. Many decisions in our lives are influenced by the need (or addiction) to serve our comfort. This limits our flexibility to go where God calls us because the fears of uncertainty and discomfort reign in our hearts. Additionally, the numbing effect of Comfort cripples our ability to see the real needs and sufferings of others.

So how do we break free from the counterfeit idols of Money, Sex and Power?

We first need to disengage from our old habits. Hebrews 12:1 says to "throw off everything that hinders and the sin that so easily entangles. And let us run with perseverance the race marked out for us." God's seriousness about disengaging from a poisonous culture can be clearly seen in his request to completely destroy all the idols upon entering the Promised Land. He even went as far as commanding them to wipe out entire cities or cultures to prevent them from infecting the Israelites (Num 33:52). There was a rich young man who asked Jesus what he still had to do to get eternal life. Jesus told him to sell everything he had. The young man refused (Mark 10:17-31). The Israelites and the rich young man needed a clean break from the old culture before they could establish a new one.

So does this mean you need to lock yourself in a monastery to prevent anyone from influencing you? No! A secluded life is of little use. Disengagement from our culture needs to take the form of a cultural detox. After the detox, we can re-engage society with transformational intentionality. As disciples of Jesus, we are not only called to be on the defensive. We are meant to be on the offensive — to be the trendsetters of new cultures (Matt 5:13; John 17:15-18).

Re-Engage With Counter-Flow Teams

The principles of Jesus are radical and usually contradict secular principles. As disciples of Jesus, we should live in contrast to the prevailing culture, and need to get comfortable being uncomfortable in society. We must confront culture, go against the flow where needed, and start new counter-flows.

The teachings and life of Jesus are full of confrontational encounters with culture. Jesus spoke out against the prevailing Roman culture, and even more passionately against the religious culture at the time. The radical nature of his teachings led many people to try and kill him, and the same happened with his disciples. They were persecuted and killed for the radicalness of their beliefs and principles. Jesus even said that, "small is the gate and narrow the road that leads to life, and only a few find it" (Matt 7:14). He was indicating that the majority will go with the flow (broad road) and miss the real life altogether. Only a few will choose the difficult path, the narrow road, and find real life.

Throughout history we see how God calls and uses small groups of people who go against the flow of society, countering it with a radical set of new principles to bring about massive transformation.

GOD USES SMALL TEAMS TO START MOVEMENTS We see these examples on many occasions in the Bible, most notably in the stories of Daniel and his three friends, David and his mighty men and Jesus with the 12 disciples. Note the size of these groups. These are small groups. God uses small teams to start movements.

We need to start counter-flows within our contexts, be it business, church, friends or school. We need to form counter-flow teams! Imagine believers forming teams around specific counter-flow areas (youth, business, medicine, motherhood, media, sport, etc.) to pray, discuss and strategise how to create a counter-flow culture within their context. This could be the start of radical societal transformation — the kind Jesus long planned for those following him.

What We Do

A group of us have started conducting time audits on each other. We recognised the danger of surrendering to the cultural belief that time belongs to us and we can spend weekends on whatever we choose. We started a counter-flow team by sharing our average weekly time schedule with each other. We did this to help each other maximise our time given to God and others by spending each minute with purpose and intent. This simple exercise brought much freedom to our lives and helped us challenge the accepted cultural norms.

We have seen counter-flow student groups demonstrating how student life can be about impacting and investing in others over investing in yourself and seeing life as a party.

We have seen counter-flow businessmen empowering the lives of people in the community rather than maximising the profits for individuals.

We have seen counter-flow families living out a family calling in the community rather than being comfortable, secluded and succumbing to the "American Dream".

We have seen counter-flow couples who redefine the way they spend weddings, birthdays and Christmas rather than falling prey to the sentimental materialistic culture of our day.

These teams have shifted culture to a different flow through the love they embody within their context. We need more of these counter-flow teams!

Discussion questions

1 In what ways are you still enslaved to Money, Sex and Power?
2 How can freedom be gained from this?
3 What counter-flow team are you a part of? What counter-flow teams should you start or join?

Scripture to study • Galatians 5:13-26 • 1 Corinthians 5:1-8 • Mark 10:17-31

Books to read • Counterfeit Gods, *by Timothy Keller* • The Challenge of the Disciplined Life, *by Richard Foster* • Counter Culture, *by David Platt*

3.7 REDEEMING ALL SPHERES OF SOCIETY

—•—

Cassie Carstens

A study investigating how the U.K. public views the church found that four out of five non-Christians don't believe churches are making a positive difference in the world. A similar 2007 study by the Barna Group in the U.S.A. discovered only 16% of non-Christians aged 16 to 29 years had a "good impression" of Christianity. [40]

Frustration that the world is not changing for the better has reached boiling point in the hearts of so many. Does it mean that God does not want to change the world? Does it mean that the church will never have the capacity to change the world? What is the problem? Is it our fate to live in an ever-deteriorating world, or is there any hope that followers of Jesus could make the world a better place? Can we succeed in bringing heaven to earth?

Before we discard the possibility of changing this world into a better place, we ought to remember what the early church did.

Historical Eras Of Hope

In *The Rise of Christianity*, Rodney Stark describes the remarkable growth of the early church. From around 7,000 believers at the time of Acts 2, the church grew 40% per decade over 300 years, until they accounted for 33 million of the 56 million citizens in the Roman Empire. According to Stark, the main reasons for this phenomenal growth were:

- Christians lived significantly different to the rest of the world
- Christians had deep compassion for each other and for people in need
- Family lives were arranged according to biblical principles
- Christians strongly condemned racism and classism
- Christians were reliable and hardworking. [41]

And all the above happened without the people having the New Testament in their pockets! Can this growth in Christianity happen again? Can Christianity be known for the five reasons mentioned above? It might be a stretch, but we should study what can once again bring a phenomenal impact in the world.

If the early church awakening seems impossible and too far back in history to try to replicate, we can also look at more recent awakenings. Several revivals have been recorded recently, like the one in Fiji in 2001:

In July 2001, Christians [in Fiji] joined together for three weeks of prayer and Bible teaching… Since then, there has been a reduction in poverty, a reduction of beggars in the street... and a reduction in crime... tourism has vastly increased, and the economy has progressed well beyond what other countries and banks expected... As a postscript to the coup in 2000, most of the hostage takers have since become Christians, and inside the prison there is now a Christian Fellowship that meets regularly, and some of the members of parliament who were held hostage go into the prison and lead worship services for the hostage takers and others. The repentance has been so genuine that those who go into the prison say that the sense of the presence of the Lord is far greater inside the prison than outside it. There is now a willingness, shown by all people, from children and young people through village chiefs right through to the Prime Minister and the President, to humble themselves before God and their people, in stark contrast to what had been the norm in Fiji. At the beginning of 2004, the Fijian government inaugurated a year of prayer for the nation. Everyone was asked to set aside at least one week to repent, to seek the Lord, to make a new covenant with God and be reconciled to others." [42]

From this story, we should gather hope for the redemption of our societies.

Understanding The Gospel

When it feels like the world is falling apart, it is tempting to ignore the redemption of the world and focus solely on the redemption of souls. To impact the world significantly, we should remember our holistic understanding of the Gospel.

- Landa Cope says we have taken the holistic message preached in the Old and New Testament and reduced it to an entry point into the Kingdom. [43]
- Martin Luther reiterates by saying: "If you preach the gospel in all aspects with the exception of the issues which deal specifically with your time, you are not preaching the gospel at all." [44]

When God reconciled the world to himself through Christ (2 Cor 5:19; Col 1:20) he reset the world to its original intent. He did not only want to restore individuals to the image of his Son (Rom 8:29). He wanted Christ's transformational power to permeate everything. He put the church at the centre of it all (Eph 1:22 MSG), of which he is the head (Col 1:18) and in which he lives by the Holy Spirit, which is the deposit of heaven (Eph 1:14). "When everything and everyone is finally under God's rule, the Son will step down, taking his place with everyone else, showing that God's rule is absolutely comprehensive — a perfect ending!" (1 Cor 15:28 MSG).

Jesus' calling was comprehensive. Beyond spiritual salvation, he came to offer psychological, sociological, economical and physical freedom from oppression. His assignment was to announce the Jubilee year; to proclaim good news to the poor, freedom for the prisoners and recovery of sight for the blind. He came to set the oppressed free (Luke 4:18-19).

Christ came to redeem the lost, both people and cultures. "As the father has sent me, I am sending you" (John 17:18; 20:21). His disciples' assignment is the holistic transformation of the world into the Kingdom of God.

Disciples As Change Agents

"... the whole church [needs] to take the whole gospel to the whole world." [45]

Our call as followers of Jesus is to incarnate this world with the character of God and the principles of the Promised Land. God wants his Kingdom to invade all society with his presence. Mark Foreman says that Christ's Kingdom invasion should travel on the pathways of society, which includes government, education, technology, business, the entertainment industry and more.

"To effectively transform culture, a separatist approach will never work. The believers in that culture must become incarnate. They must travel in the veins of society, risking temptation and compromise, for the sake of loving the people with God's love." [46]

Rather than offering to get people into heaven, we should devote ourselves primarily to get heaven into people. Augustine of Hippo puts it beautifully.

"You are the body of Christ: that is to say, in you and through you the work of the incarnation must go forward. You are meant to incarnate in your lives the theme of your adoration — you are to be taken, consecrated, broken and distributed, that you may be the means of grace and the vehicles of Eternal Charity." [47]

Why Do We Not Impact The World Significantly?

When my discipleship team tried to answer that question, they came up with the following reasons. This is not a complete list, but it is a good place to start. As you go through this list (either by yourself or with your discipleship team), identify which of these points resonate with you and add any others that come to mind.

No clear sense of who we are (identity)

If we are confident in our identity as representatives (ambassadors) of God, we should step into our role as a royal priesthood (1 Pet 2:9) and enculturate the world with heavenly principles.

Living without a biblical worldview

Worldviews determine our thinking and our behaviour to a large extent. Some live with a fatalistic worldview that leaves all responsibility to God while others hold a secular worldview that leaves God out of the equation. As Christians, we should live with the worldview that we are stewards and co-workers with God, establishing his Kingdom on earth. Landa Cope agrees with this in part 3 of her book, *The Old Testament Template*, where she summarises the worldview that Christians need to transform society: "A belief in a supreme Christ, God's view of the nations, a biblical view of vocation and biblical strategies." [48]

Dualism

Despite the letters in the New Testament clearly illustrating how we should put the theory of the Gospel into practice, one of the main reasons we do not change the world lies in dualistic thinking (some call this Evangelical Gnosticism). We think praying is holy but playing is carnal; we separate Sunday life from Monday to Saturday life; we do business with a set of non-biblical principles, but then pray for God's blessing on the work of our hands. Integrating biblical principles into everything we do is essential if the world is to change.

Development-(wealth)-centred instead of relationship-centred

The mission moved from relationship-centeredness to building-centeredness. We want to build homes instead of living in tents.

We accumulate our wealth in monetary terms and not in relational terms.

Not living under the control of the Spirit

To live under the control of the Holy Spirit is to have the mind of Christ and the heart of God beating in our hearts. Things that disturb God disturb us. We would live with a holy discontent until all is restored to God's original intent. We would also have a clear sense of Kairos — God's opportune moment for things.

Individualistic Christianity

God created us to be interdependent. This is clear from the first pages of the Bible. Sin has separated us, and this tendency to live without interdependence has matured in the Western world over the last three centuries. The problem is that we were created to be one member of a body (1 Cor 12), with diverse giftings that complete the whole. When Christians rediscover how to work in unity, we can address most of the world's needs. There will be no more orphans because all will be adopted; no one will be jobless because we will apply our entrepreneurial skills for the benefit of all as we practice our collective design.

WE ARE CONVINCED THAT THE ONLY STRATEGY THAT CAN CHANGE THE WORLD IS THE ONE THAT JESUS LEFT AS HIS GREAT COMMISSION

No urgency

We have no urgency because we do not live with a watchfulness for the second coming of Christ. Jesus taught us to be watchful and laborious in our preparation of his second coming (Matt 24 and 25). We have no urgency to make the most of every opportunity because the days are evil (Eph 5:16).

How To Start A Movement

We are convinced that the only strategy that can change the world is the one that Jesus left as his Great Commission.

It starts with a total heart transformation that invades all the spheres of your own life. It then spills over to your closest spiritual relationships to form an exemplary guiding community that demonstrates transformation in a small way. This example teaches key principles of faith practice, which then provide the guidelines for larger expansion. The expansion should always be a growth in depth and a growth in width.

Let's expand a little more on some key elements of transformational movements:

Transformation within

Nothing will change in the world if the transformation does not change our own lives first. That is why God speaks to our hearts first. It is the transformation of our hearts that transforms our first circle of influence, which ripples out in ever-widening circles of influence. This means we should emphasise personal intimacy with God first! God always calls us to himself first before sending us to do anything on his behalf.

Intimacy with God, worshipping him in everything and discipling others towards growing in Christ precedes our understanding of stewardship, and creates in us the eyes to see as he sees. It prepares our hearts to feel as he feels, birthing in us the obedience to become his co-workers. It all starts with an intimate relationship with God. Intimacy moves us to join God on his mission, articulated in the specific and unique assignments we receive from him.

The first healing that should take place is our personal inner healing (spiritually and emotionally). Then we should soak ourselves in the Word of God and walk with the Spirit so that the fruit of the Spirit will prepare to influence the lives of others.

As we walk with God and ask him for direction, we will see that God sends different people on different assignments. If all followers of Christ obeyed their assignments, the world would see the hand of God at work in all spheres of society.

A guiding community

My personal transformation will not be credible if it does not translate into change in my first sphere of influence, namely my family and my most intimate circle of disciples. This community should set the example for the rest to follow, which is what we see in the first church in the book of Acts (Acts 2, 4 and 13). They demonstrated how they cared for each other, and the world changed.

This guiding community (or counter-flow team, as discussed in chapter 3.6 on Redeeming Culture) is then modelling the transformed world. The example of the group is influential, and it increases the workforce for the transformation of all. People are more convinced by demonstration than by proclamation. When reality is seen and felt, it is convincing.

The guiding community is a force to be reckoned with when they reach a critical mass that influences all spheres of society. As Jack Dennison puts it:

> "Transformation… is about reaching a critical mass of believers who are so empowered by the gospel of Christ that they change everything they touch — family, workplace, schools and business. As this critical mass is achieved, the power of the living God brings significant changes to the problems that plague our cities today — poverty, crime, addictions, gangs, divorce, violence — and a dramatic increase in the things that characterize the Kingdom of God — mercy, justice, prosperity for the poor and compassion." [49]

A study by the University of Pennsylvania concluded that the point of critical mass to change a group's way of thinking is 25%.[50]

If we want to change a sphere of society, we must pray strategically for this critical mass to form.

Identify key principles

The "guiding community" (whether it is a discipling team, a counter-flow team or a local church) should move beyond the experience of Kingdom in their own midst. From that Kingdom encouragement, they should see their mission not only to evangelise souls, but cultures and spheres of society as well. How should we do this?

Identify the key principles that have gone wrong in a specific sphere. To prepare the way for a counter-flow culture, the largest stones need to be removed, as explained in Isaiah 62:10. We meet in teams to pray about these large stones in our cultures and contexts. These stones refer to the cultural traits blocking the way for heaven to come in that area. When you walk closely with people who also seek a counter-flow culture in your context, you will see how quickly the Holy Spirit identifies those stones to your team. For example, education ought to prepare us for life, but it has regressed to equipping us almost exclusively for work and the accumulation of money.

Landa Cope summarised key biblical principles for the redemption of different spheres of society. [51] You could, for instance, take the biblical principles for economy and discuss how to apply them where capitalism is the dominant economic system.

Then set out to rectify the wrong. Be intentional, focus by specialisation and be creative in taking initiative to redeem specific spheres of society.

Partner and strategise to impact society

To have a large impact in the various spheres of society, it is necessary to partner with other teams/communities/groups. Initiate these conversations. Invite other groups or join groups which already have momentum. Be alert to see where God is moving already. There might be a critical mass you need to join. Strategise on the best ways to impact society. Share resources, share ideas, share vision, broaden the tribe, and become the critical mass that transforms societies.

Seven spheres of society

The Seven Mountains movement addresses seven spheres they identified as moulders of society: the arts/entertainment, business, education, family, government, media and religion. Although we should be conscious of the danger of a dominion theology — that we should have power over all these spheres, which undermines the cross theology — we should not refrain from trying to redeem all aspects of life. God wants his principles to reign everywhere, whether or not we hold powerful positions in the world.

Create models of hope in society

We have a long way to go before all spheres feel the impact of followers of Jesus, but many movements and ministries focus on doing things God's way. Here are some pioneering initiatives in the different spheres:

Education: the Calling Academy is an affordable private high school that prepares boys to become good fathers and leaders in the future. [52]

Governance: there are many Christian parties in the world, but most fail in good governance because they struggle to integrate biblical principles with practical application.

Family: there are a number of active family, father- and motherhood initiatives all around the world, such as Focus on the Family, The World Needs A Father, Family Foundations, Family For Life. [53]

Sport: the ReadySetGo Movement has brought sport bodies together from around the world to redeem sport and to reach the world of sport. [54]

Agriculture: Foundations for Farming (previously known as Farming God's way) is an initiative to focus farmers away from pure commercialisation and towards the triple bottom-line of People, Planet and Profit. [55]

Arts: YWAM has several arts initiatives in Switzerland, South Africa, Slovakia, Australia and elsewhere doing great work. [56]

Business: Crown Financial Ministries functions with the mission of "equipping servant leaders to live by God's design for their finances, work and life... to advance transformation." [57]

Media: Lars Dahle wrote a brilliant paper for the Lausanne Movement Congress in Cape Town (2010) titled "Media Messages Matter: On Global Technologies, Global Trends, and Gospel Truth". All Christians involved in media should discuss this paper. [58]

As the salt and light of this world, we simply have to make the presence of the followers of Jesus felt, like in the early church. It is time for a new era in history where the church builds schools, hospitals and roads again. We want the world to know the body of Christ cares not only for people, but also about the conditions they live in. We have the message that Jesus came to bring heaven to earth. Now we must prove this message is believable!

Discussion questions

1 Do you have hope that the world can change?
2 Do you believe discipleship is the answer? Why or why not?
3 We mentioned seven barriers to impacting the world significantly. Which barrier is the most urgent in your team/ context?
4 Where do you see yourself in the movement to change the world? Are you part of a modelling community?
5 How much do you know about the key principles to transform the spheres of society you are involved in?
6 Different models of hope are mentioned. Can you share one model of hope that you have come across? If not, describe your dream model of hope.

Scripture to study • Isaiah 58:6-12 • Isaiah 61:1-2 • Luke 4:18-19

Books to read • An Introduction to the Old Testament Template, *by Landa Cope* • Discipling Nations, *by Darrow L. Miller* • So Beautiful, *by Leonard Sweet* • Transform Your Work Life, *by Graham Power and Dion Foster* • Convergence, *by Brett Johnson* • Transforming Society, *by Brett Johnson*

4

SURRENDER TO GOD (INWARD)

Knowing the value and strength of humility and love

*Inward cleansing is necessary to produce
an unpolluted outward discipleship impact.
It is about emptying ourselves and surrendering to
God so that God can be more in and through us;
about understanding who we are in Christ
and how our lives should be re-shaped for Christ;
and about being filled with the love of God
and living that love selflessly.*

4.1 PRIMARY IDENTITY

—•—

George Kellerman & Cassie Carstens

The Special Forces have a specific technique called HALO ("High Altitude Low Opening") for jumping deep into enemy territory. To minimise the risk of aircraft or paratroopers getting shot down, the paratroopers jump from beyond radar range, anywhere between 4,500 and 12,000 metres. They then free-fall to as low as 600 metres(!) and land behind enemy lines, ready to continue their mission.

This is a very accurate picture of what it means when we become citizens of God's kingdom. When we decide to follow Jesus, we become citizens of heaven. We are dropped from heaven into dangerous territory behind enemy lines. Earth becomes our temporary mission, our assignment.

Paul tells us in Ephesians 2:6 that "God raised us up with Christ and seated us with him in the heavenly realms in Christ Jesus". As Erwin McManus puts it, "it's as if at the moment of our conversion, we were lifted beyond time into eternity. Seated with Christ in the heavenly realms, we can't get much higher in altitude than that". [59] We become heavenly citizens because we are born from above.

This is what Jesus explained to Nicodemus in John 3:3 — that he can only experience the Kingdom of God if he is reborn from above. Interestingly, the Hebrew word translated as "born again" can also mean "born from above". Jesus wasn't just telling Nicodemus he would become a new man. He was helping him realise that the source of his identity would be heaven. We're not just "born again Christians". We are "born-from-above Christians". When we become reborn from above, we take on a new identity. We become heaven people. This is who we are.

Our new identity invites us to shift our mindsets from earth-bound creatures to citizens of heaven on a temporary mission to earth. "In the same world where we were once at home, we are now strangers and aliens. Where once we were enemies of God, we are now behind enemy lines." [60] While we are strangers in this world, we are ambassadors of a different Kingdom. With the knowledge of where we are from, we can build a deeper understanding of who we are.

Identity: False Or True Self

From this perspective, our identity as Christians should be clear:
1   We are born of the Spirit (John 3:6);
2   We follow Jesus (1 John 2:6), we identify with him, align ourselves with him and associate with him; and
3   God's calling is written on our hearts by the Holy Spirit (John 16:13).

The sad thing is that many Christians forget their heavenly lineage, aligning themselves with worldly values and setting themselves worldly goals. This was the case for Israel as well, which is why God wanted them to practice all kinds of disciplines to remind them of their identity. One of these disciplines was hanging a "mezuzah" on the doorpost of their front door (Deut 6:9), a reminder of their identity every time they leave or enter the house. (A mezuzah is a piece of parchment framed in a decorative case, inscribed with specific Hebrew verses from the Torah.) We need reminders of who we are on a regular basis to anchor ourselves and operate from a heavenly perspective.

When we lose our alignment with Jesus, we align ourselves with half-truths, pseudo solutions, coping mechanisms and life orientations that lead us astray and cause countless problems. Richard Rohr reminds us that so many people still live from the "false self". The false self is an internal construct we create in response to our contexts and social groups as we grow up. It often stems from hurts and the expectations of others, leading us to build our identity on what we have, what we do and what others think of us. However,

Rohr reminds us that the false self is not bad or inherently deceitful. It is quite natural. It just does not go far enough, and it often poses as, and thus substitutes for the real thing. [61]

Many Christians operate from this internal contract. We base our value and security on the value of what we own, the prestige of what we accomplish, or how many people like us (or our posts on Facebook).

So many of us try "live up to the Jones'" or "fake it till we make it". We buy cars and homes beyond our means, study one degree after the other or spend every ounce of energy to climb the corporate ladder. It can also be more subtle; we focus on having self-esteem and confidence and acquiring this in earthly ways, instead of knowing Jesus and becoming more conscious of him in us.

WHEN YOUR IDENTITY IS BASED ON SOMETHING SO TEMPORAL, YOU WILL ALWAYS BE INSECURE ON SOME LEVEL

This type of thinking and lifestyle has a major flaw. When you base your identity on status, achievement or acceptance, you will always live with the fear that it could be taken from you at any moment. You can lose the competition, go bankrupt, or even lose friends and family. No wonder so many people feel worthless when faced with loss — their sense of identity and value is stripped away with the loss of the thing(s) sustaining their false self. When your identity is based on something so temporal, you will always be insecure on some level.

So how do we find our identity? In being dead to ourselves and resurrected in Christ, we find our true selves (Mark 8:35; Gal 2:20). Jesus lives in us. Jesus is our unchangeable identity!

If we don't intentionally work against the dictates of this world, we become what the people around us want us to become. We act and behave how the world wants us to behave. To fit in, we hide parts of who we really are behind masks — sometimes without even realising it. We find it easier to hide than to delve into the depths of what makes us who we really are. Or maybe, we just haven't made time to meet the real person behind the masks we wear.

Since there is no higher status than being a child of God, it is misguided for an heir of God (Gal 4:7) to try to build their identity on what they have, what they do or what others think of them. But this is what so many of us do. We operate from a worldly perspective because the starting point is all wrong. Until we realise that we are living from the false self, we struggle to realise God's kingdom. We are "ever hearing, but never understanding; [ever] seeing, but never perceiving" (Isa 6:9, Matt 13:14).

Our restoration comes when we start to function from our true self. The true self is the created or recreated and intended expression of God in us. It is the understanding that I am the beloved, uniquely and sufficiently gifted to reign on earth as the representative of heaven.

God intends for us to live from our true self. In Colossians 3:9-10, Paul says we "have taken off our old self" and "have put on the new self, which is being renewed in knowledge in the image of its Creator". He also points out distinctions between the false self and the true self in Ephesians 4:22-24:

"Put off your old nature which belongs to your former manner of life and is corrupt through deceitful lusts, and be renewed in the spirit of your minds, and put on the new nature, created after the likeness of God in true righteousness and holiness."

Central to this process is filling our minds with the love of Christ and the fullness of God. As we do this, it renews the spirit of our mind and frees us from the deceit of the world. Out of that renewed mind comes new attitudes, emotions and practices which clothe us with righteousness and holiness. And this new person you become draws even closer to reflecting the likeness of God himself.

Romans 8:29 (MSG translation) tells us that, "God knew what he was doing from the very beginning. He decided from the outset to shape the lives of those who love him along the same lines as the life of his Son. The Son stands first in the line of humanity he restored. We see the original and intended shape of our lives there in him."

In Ephesians 4:13 (AMPC translation), Paul says the goal is:

"... that [we might arrive] at really mature manhood (the completeness of personality which is nothing less than the standard height of Christ's own perfection), the measure of the stature of the fullness of the Christ and the completeness found in Him."

Jesus is the shape of the true me God intended for this world. If we follow Jesus and live according to his example (1 John 2:6), we will find we become more like him. As we become like him, we become more like our true me, and closer to the identity God has intended for us!

Most epistles in the Bible start by reminding us of who we are before it tells us what we should do. We are called God's holy people, but sometimes, like in Romans and Ephesians, the description of who we are is much more elaborate. In some cases, it is formal (Phil 1:1; Col 1:2), while in other cases it is extremely intimate (1 John 1:3; 3:1). You are children of God!

One of the most outrageous claims in the Bible is that the One who created the galaxies of stars calls us by his name. In 2 Chronicles 7:14 it says: "If my people, who are called by my name..."

It is phenomenal to consider that this is our primary identity. In the Old Testament, we are called the people/nation of God, and in the New Testament we are even called "children of God"! The apostles are filled with joy at this truth:

- Galatians 4:7: "You are no longer a slave, but a son, and since you are a son, God has made you also an heir."
- Colossians 2:9-10: "For in Christ all the fullness of the Deity lives in bodily form and you have been given fullness in Christ, who is the head over every power and authority."
- Colossians 3:3-4: "For you died and your life is now hidden with Christ in God. When Christ, who is your life, appears, then you will also appear with Him in glory."

- 1 John 3:1: "How great is the love the Father has lavished on us, that we should be called children of God."

God has no half-sons, half-daughters or grandchildren. There is no partly belonging to God. When we belong to God, we have full belonging in him. No trace of emptiness exists. We don't need to work towards a higher level of belonging. When you were born, there was no effort from your side other than accepting breath. You were in full dependency. Similarly, when born from above, you are dependent on God for your belonging as his son/daughter. No work from your side, only acceptance and surrender to that truth.

To help us understand the fullness of our identity, it is worth distinguishing between our "primary" and "secondary" identity. Our secondary identity (see next chapter) should flow from and affirm our primary identity.

Our primary identity is our Godly lineage. It simply blows my mind to hear how God associates with us, incorporates us in his plans and risks his reputation with us! This thought should fill us with amazement every day!

Our primary identity is that we are children of God, followers of Jesus and temples of the Holy Spirit.

Discussion questions

1 Without saying where you are from, what you like or what you do, answer the following question: "Who are you?"
2 Are there temporal (or variable) things on which your identity is based? If so, what comes to mind?
3 How real is being a child of God for you? How does this impact your daily life?
4 What should you do practically to live more consciously of your primary identity?

Scripture to study • John 3:1-21 • 1 John 3:1-10

Books to read • The Barbarian Way, *by E.R. McManus* • Emotionally Healthy Spirituality, *by Peter Scazzero*

4.2 SECONDARY IDENTITY

—•—

George Kellerman & Cassie Carstens

A friend of mine, Carel, felt called to facilitate reconciliation conversations between people on opposing sides of racial divides. But to turn this calling into a reality, he would need an extra day in his week. How would that be possible working at a big insurance company which expected 40-hour work weeks (minimum!)? He asked his employer for permission to work four days a week instead of five. After several attempts and difficult conversations, his boss eventually granted his request. He took a pay cut and risked being demoted, but by challenging the leadership at his work he defied the cultural norm of a 40-hour work week. He followed his calling and rejected the dictates of culture. Even though his context did not appear to give him any options, he made a choice anyway which altered the course of his life.

When we don't know exactly what we are on earth for, we drift along in life. Life just happens to us. We become spectators of our own lives. Like a rudderless boat adrift at sea, we let the current take us wherever it will.

I often get frustrated when I watch movies because I don't want to just observe the action, I want to live it. By following Jesus, we have every reason to lead a fascinating life. Jesus has the most adventurous plans for our lives, more than we can dream up ourselves. With Jesus, this exciting life is possible. Not necessarily an easy life, or even a fun life. But a brilliant, intentional, meaningful life.

When we forget we are in a war and on assignment (or when we forget to remind ourselves we are on mission), we become tame. As Erwin McManus puts it, "We have not been prepared to take on any great quest, to battle any great enemy, or even to pursue the great dream for which we have been born... Christianity has become docile, domesticated, civilised." [62]

Christians blend in with culture when they are meant to stand out. In so many cases, what we believe and how we live rarely correspond. Outside of Sunday services, I hardly ever hear Christians offering a different way of thinking and talking about the world. We speak with a worldly language — a domesticated language. We get indoctrinated by the world and live by its values, instead of being trendsetters ourselves. The sad reality is, many of our homes are not Christian homes. They are secular homes occupied by Christians.

We see this when Christian parents feed their children the same message as the rest of the world: be successful, get to the top, make money! We see this when everyday conversations at home follow the same pattern as trendy Facebook posts.

THE SAD REALITY IS, MANY OF OUR HOMES ARE NOT CHRISTIAN HOMES. THEY ARE SECULAR HOMES OCCUPIED BY CHRISTIANS

Dr. Edwin Louis Cole said that people without an organised system of thought will always be at the mercy of people who have one. Christians without an organised system of thought are at the mercy of the surrounding culture. If they do not choose their principles, culture will choose for them. Have you ever taken the time to work through your thoughts and principles and decide how you should live your life? Have you ever considered which truths to hold on to when all else fails around you? Have you ever come up with a personal philosophy of life? What foundational principles do you live from? Have you sat with Jesus on these questions? If not, be very careful; culture might well choose those principles for you.

I can think of no better story about a group of people who stood by their heavenly values and challenged the norms of culture than Daniel and his friends. When the Babylonians captured and subdued Israel, the king recruited Daniel and his three friends to form a special group of administrators in his palace. They were trained in the philosophies, pagan ideas and the norms of this new regime. They even received new Babylonian names. The aim was to indoctrinate them. But Daniel and his friends stood firm and set a trend themselves. They knew who they were and where they came from — they were born from above. The Babylonian kingdom was a temporary assignment. They chose not to be governed by the king's orders when it went against their values and beliefs. And they were willing to die because of it. Even with the pressures of the court of the king, the furnace death-sentence and the lion's den, they chose to live differently.

To live a different identity demonstrating different values, we must be intentional about it. We learned from the previous chapter that our primary identity comes from God. It is not something we can earn or work towards. It is an adoption offer made by God to accept us as his son or daughter and join him in his Kingdom. This is our primary identity. Our secondary identity requires choices and actions from our side. Our secondary identity is our unique being and assignment, flowing from and affirming our primary identity.

Our secondary identity is determined by:
1   **The Past:** What you inherit after filtering your past.
2   **The Present:**
    • The values you associate with,
    • The friends you hold close to you, and
    • The choices you make in all spheres of your life.
3   **The Future:** Your life mission, determined by your calling.

The combination of these three themes make you uniquely different. They make you who you are and point towards a unique difference only you can make in this world. As you work through these things — your heritage, your values, your friends, your choices and your calling — your identity will become clearer and truer.

Let's start the journey towards a solid, secure and unique identity by looking at each contributing factor in more detail.

The Past

At some point in their journey, most people long to go back to their roots and discover where they come from. Discovering who your forefathers were and what they did, or learning the meaning of your family name and given name opens new insights into yourself. It fosters a sense of identity. However, as we work through our history, we should filter the good from the bad and reject some things while accepting others.

Take me for example. My dad is of white Afrikaner heritage and my mom is a white woman of British descent. I had to sift through history and reject the bad things bundled with those histories, such as Apartheid, oppression, racism and colonialism. On the other hand, I choose to accept the entrepreneurship and the hard-working values of my ancestors. I especially embrace the courageous efforts of some in my lineage to rid the Dutch Reformed Church denomination of its racism and lack of leadership. All of us have good and bad in our heritage. What we choose to accept and what we reject plays a huge part in forming our identity.

The Present

Values

In the present, we should first make sure that the values we live by are Kingdom values. Values are the filtering system that dictate your mind and should dictate your emotions, which in turn influence your decisions and the resulting behaviour.

NOT JUST WHAT WE BELIEVE, BUT WHAT WE DEMONSTRATE WITH OUR BELIEF, IDENTIFIES WHO WE ARE

So many people call themselves Christians, but do not live Christian values. Paul laboured to help the early church understand the difference between a worldly value system and the Christian value system. In Colossians 3, after explaining that "Christ is your life" (Col 3:4), he encourages them to stop doing things that identified with their old lives like lust, self-absorbed living and grabbing whatever caught their fancy (Col 3:5 MSG). He then contrasts the values of a new life defined by Christ: compassion, kindness, humility, quiet strength, discipline, even-temperedness, being content with second place, being quick to forgive (Col 3:12-13 MSG). The point he wants to make is that Christian values and worldly values are dramatically different!

When we ask: "What were the key values Jesus lived by?" then: "What are the values that my community lives by?" we often see a vast difference. This should not be! If we are followers of Christ, we should live by the values of Christ, and not only say amen to the words of Christ. Not just what we believe, but what we demonstrate with our belief, identifies who we are.

People with whom we associate

Secondly, our identity in the present is determined by the people with whom we associate. The Xhosa belief that "People are people through other people" (in Xhosa: "Umntu ngumntu ngabanye abantu") is just as valid in the body of Christ. The values of the people we surround ourselves with shape our values, and vice versa. Our *perceived* identity is also determined by the people with whom we associate. This is clear from the life of Jesus (Mark 2:13-17; Luke 15:2). Being intentional in deciding with whom we associate is also being intentional about determining our identity. We discuss this further in chapter 2.9 when we work through the table of support.

Choices

Thirdly, our identity in the present is determined by the choices we make in every sphere of our lives. Deuteronomy 30:19 encourages us to choose life so that "you and your children may live"! Our choices and the commitment we make towards them largely determine the footprint of our life. It is essential that we become more intentional in life. The philosopher William James said: "When you have to make a choice and don't make it, that is in itself a choice." This is one reason why so few people rise above their circumstances. They passively float along with the current of their culture. If we want to find our own identity, we need to swim upstream. Every choice we make and execute redefines the direction of our lives.

More on choices

We have to make good choices in all the dimensions of our life: spiritual, physical, emotional, social, intellectual and environmental. And since the dimensions are interlinked, a bad choice in one dimension could weaken your whole life just as a good choice in another dimension may strengthen it. This is why we call discipleship whole-life coaching. When we disciple someone, we must coach them in all the dimensions of life. (See chapter 1.5 on holistic discipling for an elaboration on this point.)

It is important to remember that choices have consequences. To choose one thing is also to choose against other things. When you choose a healthy lifestyle, you also choose against unhealthy lifestyles and practices. If you want people to consider you with respect, you should avoid getting drunk, especially in public. Choosing to live hospitably removes stinginess from your life.

You should discuss this thoroughly with your disciples. Choosing Jesus has radical implications! (Luke 9:57-62; Luke 14:26; 1 Cor 7:29-35).

Also, fundamentally, making a choice isn't complete until you put it into practice. It is no good choosing a healthy life but never exercising and still eating junk food more often than not. Making a choice cognitively is only the first step; you still have to carry out that choice practically. Intentionality is therefore the watchword!

The Future

Our main purpose or calling in life will also shape our future identity. This means that once we discover our calling in life, we should lean hard in that direction until it receives most of our energy. We put such a high value on discovering our calling that we dedicated two chapters of this book to it: chapter 1.3 (The Cost of Disciple Making) and chapter 3.5 (God's Specific Assignment For Us).

In Summary

Let the identity of the prophet Daniel inspire us.

Even though he was a captive, he displayed character and virtues from a different kingdom — a heavenly Kingdom. Even though he was a prisoner of war, he knew he was born from above. He aligned with God's truths and principles, confident God had called him to be an ambassador on a special assignment. His primary identity was secure.

Daniel also had a unique and secure secondary identity.

The past: He inherited an Israeli nation in captivity, but still chose to see his people not as a captive nation, but as the chosen nation of God.

The present: Daniel's values were aligned to Kingdom values. He did not waver even when his values went directly against the king's orders. His fierce dedication to the Lord saw him praying three times a day, even when he knew it could get him killed. His friends (Shadrach, Meshach and Abednego) stood shoulder to shoulder with him and refused to bow down to the golden statue in the face of a fiery death. Not only were they a group of friends following their own unique set of values, they were also the ones setting a new trend for others to follow. Daniel did not allow the world to dictate his identity. He made difficult and obedient choices throughout his life, through the reign of multiple kings, challenging each of them on multiple occasions.

The future: Daniel obediently followed God's unique calling on his life and changed kingdoms because of it.

It is clear that Daniel was secure in his primary and secondary identity. Hopefully, his life story is an inspiration for you today. May you know who you are and become the unique person God intended you to be.

Discussion questions

1   What are the four most important values by which you live?
2   If you could choose four friends that represent who you are, who would they be and why?
3   Describe the person you want to be in 200 words. Where have you not yet become that person? What keeps you from becoming that person? What are the first steps you should take to becoming that person?

Scripture to study • Deuteronomy 30:11-20 • Colossians 3:1-17 • Daniel 1

Books to read • The Call, *by Os Guinness* • The Purpose Driven Life, *by Rick Warren*

4.3 HUMILITY

—•—

Cassie Carstens

This is one of the biggest unseen battles since time began: the battle between pride and humility. In the words of Andrew Murray:

> "All the evils of fallen angels and men have their birth in the pride of self. On the other hand, all the virtues of the heavenly life are the virtues of humility… What is then, or in what lies, the great struggle for eternal life? It all lies in the strife between pride and humility: pride and humility are the two master powers, the two kingdoms in strife for the eternal possession of man." [63]

It is pride that Satan instigated in paradise. It is pride that separates man from God. It is pride that separates man from man. It is pride that causes war and separation in relationships. The calamitous world with its unbearable pain is a result of one thing: pride!

This battle wages every day in government offices, companies, churches, sport fields, schools and homes as people are trying to find their position in the pecking order.

The only hope against this goliath of demolition called pride, the only cure for this sickness of pandemic proportions, is in humility. It is this virtue in Jesus who "made himself nothing" that won the battle for us. It is this virtue that can nullify the power of pride! This virtue alone can restore broken relationships with God and our fellow men. It is the essential heavenly medicine that turns hell on earth into heaven amongst us.

This is therefore the ultimate struggle in which we must be victorious, the one thing for which we should strain our spiritual muscles, stretch for and desire to embrace. This is the virtue in which we should soak ourselves and the main characteristic for which we should strive. This is the key area in which we should surrender our flesh to be destroyed by the Spirit. This should be the main thing we should ask of God, and the one thing we should sacrifice all else for. Humility should be our prized endeavour — knowing that our endeavour is a surrender, not an effort in our own strength! The real challenges in combating pride and chasing humility are deviousness, cultural prejudice and the hidden nature of both.

Deviousness

Pride frequently clothes itself in humility and humility, when reflected upon, can feel like an achievement. Seeking humility is a tight-rope walk and allowing yourself to relax can lead right back into pride. The focus should always be on striving and not arriving. We should continually refocus and realign on striving to make sure that our humble efforts remain humble. Standing on humility is like standing on an exercise ball. When you focus on your own humility you will fall off. But if you focus on others and Christ, away from the ball, you will remain balanced. The Holy Spirit is the calibrating mechanism, the "core muscle strength" to whom we should listen.

Cultural prejudice

The prevalent focus these days on "what I want" and "what is beneficial for me" demonstrates a clear bias to the self. This, by implication, makes it difficult to develop a humble, selfless orientation. Self-condemnation is the last thought of today's culture, neglecting Romans 3:10-12 which claims that "there is no one righteous... no one who seeks God... they have together become worthless... there is no one who does good." We simply do not attend to the fact that we are all evidently sinful. We seldom see the self-denying humility of the Bible in modern-day Christians. Exaltation of the self has become the centrepiece of our lives, instead of the self-crucifixion taught by Christ. We ought to question ourselves but trust God's truth about our sinfulness.

Hiddenness

Is it possible to see humility or pride? Both pride and humility are root issues, and you cannot see the roots of a tree. You can only see its fruit. So what are the fruits borne from the trees of pride and humility?

Andrew Murray says: "All manifestations of temper and touchiness and irritation; all feelings of bitterness and estrangement — have their root in nothing but pride." [64]

I would like to add a few more fruits to the tree of pride:
- A demanding spirit
- A selfish attitude
- Constant scepticism
- Not being teachable
- Always comparing
- Unconsciousness of sin
- Never doubting oneself
- Envy
- Gossip
- Lack of brokenness
- Impatience
- Ungratefulness
- Unforgiveness
- Self-consciousness

In contrast, the tree of humility bears the following good fruit:
- Contentment
- Service
- Trusting others
- Honouring others
- Brokenness
- A listening disposition
- A teachable disposition

- Commitment to a mission beyond self
- Patience
- Appreciation
- A forgiving heart
- Selflessness

By comparing these fruits, we can discover how often our hearts demonstrate pride.

Each of us struggle with different fruits of pride. In my life, pride often manifests through irritability, impatience, ungratefulness and self-consciousness. This tells me that there are depths of pride in my innermost being that contaminate me to the core. When I see these bad fruits in my life, they remind me to get the soul-destroying pride eradicated. It helps me to acknowledge that these bad fruits originate from pride, which leads me to carry my pride to the cross for salvation and substitution.

Defining Humility

I like Andrew Murray's definition of humility:

> "It is simply the sense of entire nothingness, which comes
> when we see how truly God is all, and in which we make
> way for God to be all. When the creature realises that this is
> the true nobility, and consents to be with his will, his mind,
> and his affections, the form — the vessel — in which the
> life and glory of God are to work and manifest themselves...
> as God is the ever-living, ever-present, ever-acting One...
> in whom all things exist, the relation of the creature to
> God could only be one of unceasing, absolute, universal
> dependence." [65]

Humility is therefore the disposition of entire dependence on God. It is a deep realisation and attitude of emptiness, which needs to be filled by God. Believing we can fix our own pride, or anything else, for that matter, is pride in itself. Deep humility can only be attained if Jesus sorts out our pride.

We See It In Jesus!

Where do we see pure humility? We see it in Jesus! We see this in his life.

Firstly, coming from a position of equality with God, he made himself nothing (Phil 2:6-7). Then in his life on earth he was "meek and lowly in heart" (Matt 11:29 KJV). He never for a moment thought of seeking his honour or asserting his power to vindicate himself. His whole spirit was that of a life yielded for God to work in and through. He counted himself the servant of God to complete the Father's intent for his mission. He also counted himself the servant of men, that through him, God might do his work of love.

We hear this in what he says about himself:
- "The Son can do nothing by himself" (John 5:19).
- "By myself I can do nothing… I seek not to please myself, but him who sent me" (John 5:30).
- "I do not accept glory from human beings" (John 5:41).
- "I have come down from heaven not to do my will, but to do the will of him who sent me" (John 6:38).
- "My teaching is not my own" (John 7:16).
- "I am not here on my own authority" (John 7:28).
- "I do nothing on my own" (John 8:28).
- "I have not come on my own; God sent me" (John 8:42).
- "I am not seeking glory for myself" (John 8:50).
- "The words I say to you, I do not speak on my own authority" (John 14:10).
- "These words you hear are not my own; they belong to the Father" (John 14:24).

We hear this in his teachings:

- In his first public speech on the mountain (the beatitudes) he says that the blessed ones are the meek and the poor in spirit (Matt 5:3,5).
- Pointing out a child in the crowd, he says that the greatest in the Kingdom is like that child (Luke 9:46-48; Matt 18:3-4).
- He warns the people not to take the seat at the head of the table (Luke 14).
- He washed the feet of his disciples and then told them to continue to treat each other the same (John 13:14).
- And when he teaches at the "Last Supper" about leadership, he says that the first should be the servant of all (Luke 22:24-27).

If we want to be humble, we must yield to him in perfect resignation and dependence, in full consent to be and to do nothing of ourselves. This is the life Christ came to reveal and impart in us.

If we feel that this life is too high for us and beyond our reach, we are right. However, it should then urge us to seek it in him; it is the indwelling Christ who will live in and through us. It is God who works in us all!

Embracing Humility

Defining moments determine our lives. Two defining moments set me up for my journey of combatting pride.

The first moment was when I was alone on a prayer mountain in South Korea early one morning in 1995 and God intervened. There was a long flight of stairs on the mountain with a small plaque at the bottom saying: "Steps of Penitence: Confess a new sin on every step." The first thing I did was to check if anyone was watching me (all hypocritical pastors fear people will learn that they too are sinners). Then I started the process.

The first thing I wondered was, "Do I even have any sin to

confess?" But I remembered 1 John 1:8 which reminds us that if we say we do not sin, we deceive ourselves, so I had to start by confessing that thought. I continued by confessing my shortage of love, and on steps three and four my reserved obedience. I confessed my lack of thoroughness on spiritual disciplines and then, running out of sins to confess, I started to re-confess the sins of my youth. Then all memory of my sins dried up.

I was on about step 14 and at least 25 more steps beckoned! For a moment, I felt great! It seemed like I did not have enough sin to make it all the way up the stairs. It **THE MORE PRIDE YOU HAVE, THE LESS YOU CAN SEE YOUR SIN!** was a comforting thought that I had less sin than other people! As I was enjoying the warm embrace of this delusional moment, God barged in harshly: "Firstly, your biggest sin is pride! Secondly, the more pride you have, the less you can see your sin! Thirdly, you are quick to see the sins of others because of your pride!"

I was shocked! Because of the depths of my pride, I simply could not see my sins. For the first time in my life I confessed my pride, and as I confessed it, the scales fell off my eyes… and I could see! I could see the multitude of my abysmal sins. They were staring me in the face, and they were ugly!

Step by step I confessed the sins I had never been able to see before. Remorse overcame me. I was convinced that I was the worst sinner ever! At the end of the flight of stairs I fell to my knees and begged God for more steps, more grace, more forgiveness. I was broken! Stumbling to my feet, I made a lifelong commitment to fight pride and seek humility every day of my life. I wanted to stay close to and conscious of my sins. I then knew my enemy and was determined to fight it with everything I had! The journey had just begun.

The next occasion was about 12 years later. One night while in Atlanta, I had a dream. I was standing on the edge of a big cliff when I heard Jesus calling me. I wanted to respond, so I looked up to see where Jesus was calling me from. He was nowhere to be seen, so I called back: "Jesus, where are you?"

"Here I am!"

Confused to where the voice came from, I shouted again: "Where are you, Jesus!"

"Look down! I am here, far below you!"

I looked down and at the bottom of the cliff, an enormous distance away, I saw a tiny figure calling me. I called down, "Jesus, what are you doing down there? Come up here!"

"What are you doing up there?" Jesus replied. "Come down here. You are too high! Come down to where I am!" And then the devastating words: "The student is not above the teacher, nor a servant above his master!" (Matt 10:24).

I realised I did and thought many things that were above the master. I had to come down! My estimation of myself was far too high.

Maybe we all need defining moments to remind us we are too high and need to come down. These two incidents helped me towards the first step in embracing humility. Desire and seek humility earnestly!

Growing In Humility

There are many activities that can help you grow in humility. The following is far from a complete list, but will help you think about how you can intentionally seek humility:

1 **Marvel at the awe of God the Father, Christ and the Spirit.** The bigger God grows in your perspective, the smaller you become in your own eyes. It was Spurgeon who said: "No subject of contemplation will tend more to humble the mind, than thoughts of God." [66]

2 **Fight your pride and your ego!** After receiving the Nobel Peace Prize, Mother Teresa took the most humble, filthy responsibility in Kalighat (scraping human faeces from the

bedsheets of the dying) for three days. When asked why she did this, she said: "You must be careful of your ego. It is simply the most dangerous thing in the world!"

3   Spend time with the poor and the humble. You cannot spend effective time with the poor and humble with a chip on your shoulder — it makes you very aware of the excess in your life. It inspired me to want to strip the excess "stuff", activities, expectations and thoughts I carried around with me.

4   Allow your wife/children/enemy to tell you what is wrong with you. I once invited my wife to do this with me, and she easily came up with a list. This list destroyed my ego. And when I complained to God, he sided with her! Your enemy is someone who can also open your eyes to things you will never be able to see otherwise. Refraining from self-defence in the light of these accusations will humble you significantly.

5   Submit yourself to the decisions of others. It looks like this discipline is one of the most difficult of all. See more on this in chapter 2.7 on submission.

6   Acknowledge your fears. This can be challenging, especially in a culture that paints fear as something to be ashamed of. Acknowledging your fears keeps you grounded in your humanity and encourages you to lean on people close to you for strength and courage.

7   Allow humiliations. Saint Francis once said the following to Brother Leo: "Above all the graces and gifts of the Holy Spirit which Christ gives to his friends is that of conquering oneself and willingly enduring sufferings, insults, humiliations and hardships for the love of Christ." [67]

8   The disciplines of self-denial, submission and service are some of the most powerful disciplines for forming humility. This is covered in other parts of this book.

Desire it Most Earnestly!

"What is the spiritual fruit you desire most eagerly?" God asked me one day in my devotional time. It was as if he was holding a wrapped gift in front of me but wanted to find out if I would appreciate it if he gave it to me. As I mentioned a few (like love, joy, patience, compassion), it felt as though God was not happy with my choices. He wanted me to desire — and wanted to give me — his very best gift. As he unwrapped and revealed the gift he had in his hand, I saw that it was humility. I pulled back from it immediately, but he kept moving towards me with this gift in hand.

"If you want me, take this gift first. Without this gift, you will not have me."

I then started risking the prayer: "Above all, Lord, give me humility. Teach me to desire this and seek this with my whole heart!" Every human part of me fights against praying this prayer, so I know that I need to keep stretching towards it!

Discussion questions

1   Thinking back over the last week, what fruits of pride do you need to confess?
2   This chapter suggests eight ways to grow in humility. Choose two of these and describe how you are going to practice them.
3   Humility is described as "the disposition of entire dependence on God." What can we do in a very independent age to create this disposition?

Scripture to study • John 13:1-17

Books to read • Humility and Absolute Surrender, *by Andrew Murray* • Calvary Road, *by Roy Hession*

4.4 DESCENDING INTO GREATNESS

—•—

George Kellerman

One of my dearest friends described in the following way why he believes in Jesus:

"Jesus and the Bible teach all the time, with no exceptions, to deny ourselves, to humble ourselves, to become less, to go down. To die to self is the only way to live. If the Bible spoke about anything that fed my ego, I would doubt it was the truth. I would also doubt it if there was a ladder of deeds I could climb to reach God, because I can never reach him. He is holy, and I will never be. The only way to reach him is to allow him to reach me at my darkest — a sinful, helpless and broken person. The stronger has the power to reach the weaker; the helpless and weak person cannot step up and reach the stronger" (Bassem Emad).

Bassem believes truth is found in ultimate humility, which he finds in Jesus. His words reminded me again of what Jesus said, "Self-sacrifice is the way, my way, to finding yourself, your true self" (Matt 16:24-26 MSG).

To simplify this paradoxical Kingdom principle and to examine your heart, ask yourself the following questions:

"What am I STRIVING towards?"

"What is my GOAL in life?"

Many people strive upwards. They want a higher position, more status, more importance and more respect at work. They chase money, comfort and power, constantly feeding their egos. The world believes you should ascend into greatness.

With all our mega churches, pastor-centred churches, televangelists and Christian celebrities, Christians seem to strive in much the same way. The goal is to ascend into greatness, and as long as we are waving the banner of Christianity, it all seems justified. But this is a dangerous way of thinking.

The temptation of selfish ambition is incredibly dangerous. Many cultures consider it a virtue, but consider the list of hideous behaviours it is compared to in the Bible (emphasis mine):

"The acts of the flesh are obvious: sexual immorality, impurity and debauchery; idolatry and witchcraft; hatred, discord, jealousy, fits of rage, *selfish ambition*, dissensions, factions and envy; drunkenness, orgies, and the like. I warn you, as I did before, that those who live like this will not inherit the kingdom of God." (Gal 5:19-21)

And, "For where you have envy and *selfish ambition*, there you find disorder and every evil practice" (James 3:16).

Selfish ambition is even more dangerous in Christian- or church-related things. The activities might seem (and even be) positive for the Kingdom, but the Bible urges us to "do nothing out of selfish ambition or vain conceit" (Phil 2:3).

JESUS WAS IMPLYING THAT IF YOU WANT TO BECOME THE GREATEST, YOU MUST BECOME THE LEAST IMPORTANT!

What about God's kingdom, then? Can we strive for greatness, or to become someone important in God's kingdom? This is exactly what the disciples asked Jesus (Matt 18:1-4, and similarly in Matt 20:21-28). They wanted to know which of them was the greatest disciple in the Kingdom of heaven. The question was not about the greatest person in the world, but the greatest disciple in the world. Jesus' reply was so staggering that even today, many people still do not grasp it. He said that if you want to become the greatest, you should strive to "be the least". In their society, children and servants were the least important people — the lowest of society. Jesus was implying that if you want to become the greatest, you must become the least important! You should strive to put others above yourself all the time, to think more of others and less of yourself. Don't aim upward (even in Christian circles); you should strive to go lower, to go down, to become the least.

Jesus spoke of John the Baptist as the greatest man to walk this earth, yet in the same breath, said that whoever is least in the Kingdom of heaven is greater than John (Matt 11:11). Greatness in God's kingdom is reserved for the least. We should strive to descend into greatness!

Considering what we have read, it is clear that Jesus was intentional about becoming the least. He focused his life on becoming the least. In chapter 53, Isaiah accurately prophesied how the Messiah would be received on earth: "a man despised and rejected by men, a man of sorrows, and familiar with suffering… he was crushed… he was like a lamb… he was a servant… he poured out his life unto death."

Jesus knew ultimate greatness lay in loving others selflessly and sacrificially. Jesus came from heaven, stooping from his God-position to meet us on earth. He lowered himself further to become human, equal to us, then lowered himself further to become a servant. He lowered himself even further to die for us; the most shameful death possible in those times. All the time he was descending into greatness.

This descending journey is exactly what Philippians 2:5-8 refers to:

"… have the same mindset as Christ Jesus:
Who, being in very nature God,
    did not consider equality with God
something to be used to his own advantage;
 rather, he made himself nothing
    by taking the very nature of a servant,
    being made in human likeness.
 And being found in appearance as a man,
    he humbled himself
    by becoming obedient to death
    even death on a cross!"

As Christ-followers, we are to have the same mindset (Phil 2:5). However, even striving for humility or selflessness can become self-serving and self-focused. We must develop a habit of self-denial, releasing us to love others and God more purely. The first step is to surrender our selfish desires, ambitions, dreams and anything that feeds the ego. Surrendering the self (the ego) is necessary to love God and others with a pure love which implies a daily surrender to the leading of the Spirit (Gal 5:16-17).

The famous words of C.S. Lewis are rightfully often repeated in discussions on humility. To paraphrase his principle: "Humility is not thinking less of yourself, it is thinking of yourself less." [68] Becoming the least is a process of reducing the amount you think about yourself so you have more capacity to think first of others.

Andrew Murray echoes this in his book, *Like Christ* (chapter 25):

> "Loving life, refusing to die, means remaining alone in selfishness: losing life to bring forth much fruit in others is the only way to keep it for ourselves.
>
> There is no way to find our life but as Jesus did, in giving it up for the salvation of others. Herein is the Father, herein shall we be glorified. The deepest underlining thought of conformity to Christ's death is giving our life to God for saving others... It is a death in which all thought of saving self is lost in that of saving others." [69]

We are not "becoming nothing", for a better spirituality. We are descending into greatness for the sake of others.

To come back to the earlier question: "What should your goal in life be?" Striving to love others selflessly should be the goal. This is becoming least; this is the way, and the life found in the cross!

The words of Paul to Timothy should make more sense now:

"The goal of this command is love, which comes from a pure heart and a good conscience and a sincere faith" (1 Tim 1:5).

Discussion questions

1 Are you striving to ascend into success or descend into greatness?
2 What does Jesus mean by becoming "the least"?
3 How did Jesus become the least?
4 How can you become the least?

Scripture to study • Philippians 2:1-11 • Matthew 18:1-4 • Matthew 20:20-28 • Isaiah 53

Books to read • Lead like Jesus, *by Ken Blanchard & Phil Hodges* • Descending into Greatness, *by Bill Hybels* • The Freedom of Self-Forgetfulness, *by Timothy Keller*

4.5 LOVE PRINCIPLES: OUR CODE OF CONDUCT

—•—

George Kellerman

Introduction

In one of the last recorded conversations with his disciples, Jesus left them with the following, "A new command I give you: Love one another. As I have loved you, so you must love one another. By this everyone will know that you are my disciples, if you love one another" (John 13:34-35). The way that followers of Jesus love one another should be a thing of beauty for others to emulate. But when last did you hear anyone compliment a discipleship group or church on the way they love each other? Where are the people who love the way Jesus loves? Where are the disciples whose extravagant love for others makes them stand out? Maybe then, people will see who the real disciples of Jesus are.

Where have we lost the plot?

Nothing is 100% evil. Satan is not the creator, so anything he twists to evil was once good. Besides, something that is 100% evil would be easy to detect and attack. Evil is usually good that has been twisted. We are most often misled by things that look and feel righteous (and might even be 99% righteous) but are evil at the core. If Satan could choose one thing to corrupt, it would be the most powerful weapon followers of Jesus have: the ability to love.

When challenged, Jesus summed up the entire law in one sentence: "Love God with all your heart, mind and strength, and love your neighbour as yourself." When Paul refers to the three great concepts of faith, hope and love, he labels love as the greatest. Paul also said, "The goal of this command is love, which comes from a pure heart and a good conscience and a sincere faith" (1 Tim 1:5).

The entire Gospel can be summed up in this one word — love.

Love is how we relate to one another. It is what drives us to action. It is a way of life. It is what sustains us. It is where we find our belonging and acceptance. It is the inner fuel for the outer action.

It should not be surprising then, that it is high on Satan's agenda to corrupt the world with a warped understanding and practice of love. Unfortunately, he has been largely successful. Love is one of the most misunderstood and warped concepts in the world, both within and outside the church.

Paul also felt that the church in Philippi needed reminding:

"And this is my prayer: that your love may abound more and more in knowledge and depth of insight, so that you may be able to discern what is best and may be pure and blameless for the day of Christ" (Phil 1:9).

We must fight the deception and redeem the way we love. It isn't enough to simply love more; we need to love differently. If the love is polluted, then simply loving more will increase the pollution. The question we must answer is, what is the difference between the world's type of love and Jesus' type of love?

God has given us many pointers as we seek to understand this important question. In his first epistle — also the Bible's most concentrated analysis of love — John points out a few clear differences which we have summarised into the four points below (1 John 4:7-21):

- Externally sourced love vs. eternally sourced love (1 John 4:7-8, 12-13, 15-16)
- Exchange love vs. one-directional love (1 John 4:10-11,19)
- Expectational driven love vs. intentionally driven love (1 John 4:18)
- Exit love vs. sacrificial love (1 John 4:9-10).

We will explain these differences in more depth over the next few chapters. Understanding these differences will also reveal and clarify the true gospel of Jesus Christ. It shows what makes the Gospel truly unique — all the more reason to be amazed at the love and life of Jesus.

One of the guys I am discipling brought this question to our team:

"Every team has a code of conduct, which guides how members should behave and the standards they should live by. What is our code of conduct?"

As a discipleship team, we ought to sharpen and shape one another in how we love. Discipleship means nothing if we don't help each other love the people around us in the right way. Our code of conduct is simple: love each other, and love people outside our circle. We want to love in a way that is eternally sourced, one-directional, intentionally driven and sacrificial.

Before we take a deeper look at the nature of this love, you need to bear the following in mind. Spending your life learning the theory of love is meaningless if it does not flow into action. Before John explains the uniqueness of God's love in 1 John 4, he specifically warns his readers about the following: "Dear children, let us not love with words or speech but with actions and in truth" (1 John 3:18).

4.5.1 EXTERNALLY SOURCED LOVE VS. ETERNALLY SOURCED LOVE

—●—

George Kellerman

Who defines, determines and fulfils your life?

The one who defines and determines our life is our god! One of the most repeated phrases in the Old Testament is, "I shall be their God and they will be my people". We find the same thing in the New Testament, where the Epistles frequently start by stating who we are in Christ before asking us to live according to that identity. Followers of Jesus know who they are and who determines their lives — they are children of God (1 John 3:1), and as their King, Jesus (and nothing else) determines their lives (1 John 2:4-6).

If any person or thing besides God defines our identity or determines our lives, the Bible calls it idolatry. God should be the only source of joy, significance and fulfilment in our lives. That right belongs to him alone — no one else! This is why the first law of Moses is crystal clear: "You shall have no other gods before me." And this is why 1 John finishes with the resounding words: "[Jesus Christ] is the true God and eternal life. [Therefore] dear children, keep yourselves from idols" (1 John 5:20-21).

Gary Thomas points out some practical applications of this in his book, *Sacred Influence*. [70] God — not your marital status — defines your life! Marriage becomes idolatry:

- If you are trying to find your primary refuge in your spouse
- If you have centred your hope on him/her
- If your security depends on your spouse's approval
- If you do almost anything to gain your spouse's acceptance
- If you care more about what your spouse thinks of you than what God does
- If you worry more about getting acceptance from your spouse than obeying God.

If you are doing these things, you have given to man what belongs to God alone. Effectively, you are turning marriage into idol worship, and you both lose! (This principle also applies to any relationship/friendship.)

If we allow God to occupy our hearts with this truth, we will not look to others to make us happy or unhappy. Other people will then not own the right to make us happy or unhappy. This right would be given to God alone. Our happiness and fulfilment will then be sourced eternally and fill us internally. Love becomes an inside-out process and is never determined by external forces.

No Greater Love

Is there any greater affirmation of acceptance and value than being called a child of God, the King? Is there any greater love than that of the God who is love? Not in this universe!

If we are unwilling to be children of God, we choose to live as orphans, and are settling for an insatiable desire for acceptance — acceptance in people, in things or in power, but everything falls short. However, when we accept God as our Father, we can love from the complete acceptance we receive from him. We can live a love-driven life, driven by the completeness we find in being loved by God our Father. We will also more clearly understand what Paul meant when he wrote, "The Spirit you received does not make you slaves, so that you live in fear again. Rather, the Spirit you received brought about your adoption to sonship. And by him we cry, 'Abba, Father'" (Rom 8:15).

If we do not choose to be a child of our heavenly Father and get to know him, love's fullest potential will always be out of our reach. That is why 1 John 4 clearly explains that everyone who loves has been born of God and knows God. But whoever does not love does not know God, because God is love. Paul also refers to this love in his letter to the Ephesians:

"And I pray that you, being rooted and established in love, may have power, together with all the Lord's holy people, to grasp how wide and long and high and deep is the love of Christ, and to know this love that surpasses knowledge — that you may be filled to the measure of all the fullness of God" (Eph 3:17-19).

External And Idolatrous Love

People love making idols from tangible things. This was a common theme in the Bible and is just as prevalent today. While most Western cultures no longer create and worship effigies (such as the golden calf), we are just as guilty as those who do. Anything that replaces God at the centre of our lives or acts as a gatekeeper to our happiness and worth becomes an idol.

Not that you should no longer enjoy anything else in life — far from it. Rather, it is dependence on people and things as the source of our happiness that is the problem. When we cannot find it with God, we look to external things to supply us happiness and worth. Anything can become an idol: people, sport, work, recreation, possessions, food — the list is endless. Simply put, idolatry happens when an object of healthy affection becomes an irreplaceable source of happiness and affection. When a thing becomes an idol, we usually find we are giving it an inordinate amount of attention, energy or resources. Worse than that, these things or people become the gods of our love and happiness. "I can't imagine life without you" or "you complete me" are good indicators a person or thing has become an idol in your life.

The issue here is replacement. If we aren't plugged into God's love, we turn to these things to satisfy our need for love. Loving like this gives other people or things the right that should only belong to God. God alone should be our ultimate source of happiness, fulfilment and significance. When we give our love to idols, we cut ourselves off from God, the sole supplier of real love.

Impossible Situations

We are all faced with situations where it seems impossible to love. A broken home. Unreasonable friends or family. A soul-crushing job. Extreme injustice and massive clashes of worldviews. Whatever it is, we have all experienced a private version of hell. However, as tough as these places are to face, they act as mirrors to the source of our love. Sometimes, we allow ourselves to believe our ability to love will diminish in the face of these realities. We give in to the assumption that the measure of our love is dependent on other people, not on God.

When we give anyone but God the power to determine our level of love, we are practising idolatrous love. This is why the world's type of love is easily angered, irritated and offended — because it is dependent on people for what only God can provide.

Undue Pressure

When others become the centre of our life orientation instead of God, it puts undue pressure on them. They are not free in our love.

What starts as something beautiful becomes an impossible burden to bear. Instead of a love that breathes, our love starts suffocating the object of our affection.

When we make someone the centre of our life orientation, it burdens them with supplying us happiness and fulfilment, a difficult and unfair duty to maintain. Sadly, this form of idolatry is also most common where it is most damaging; between spouses, and between parents and children. It is particularly unfair on the children. We see it when the child is "all the parent has left". In time, being the primary source of happiness becomes too much for the child to handle, resulting in fear, depression or rebellion. A parent who thinks they are giving real love by making their child the centre of their world is practising idolatrous love.

Eternal Love

The opposite of external idolatrous love is eternal love. As Cassie puts it in his book, *The World Needs A Father: A Trainer's Guide:*

> "It is clear, God and God alone should be the source of love. If you are therefore looking for pure love, do not look anywhere else. This releases your children and wife from the fear of trying to create love in you. You already have it abundantly in your relationship with God… Only God should be given the power to make us happy or unhappy. Only God can provide the love the world needs. His eternal source of love is unlimited. He wants to fill us with his love. We should love the world with this love only!" [71]

When God is our source of love, the situation we find ourselves in should not matter. With him as our source our love can keep on flowing, regardless of what stands against us. How often is our love not swayed and influenced by the mood and actions of others? If God is our source, it should not matter whether other people love or don't love us; our love can keep on flowing to them.

Wood Ants

Wood ants have an incredible method of warming their nests. A dedicated group of ants bask in the sun, soaking up the heat. They then go back to the nest and radiate the heat they stored to warm up the other ants. Like the sun, God is our constant source of love. Love flows from him, through us, to others. The flow is constant and overflowing. Because we are drawing from his love, not our own, there is no chance of burnout or running out of love. The effort and energy all come from him. Our only job is to soak it up and pass it on. In 1 John 4:16 it says, "And so we know and rely on the love God has for us. God is love." As we bask in God's love, it compels us to love others.

When we try to love from our own capacity, we realise that to love selflessly will always be a struggle. We even wonder if we will be able to love selflessly at all.

In short: if we rely on our own love, we won't.

We can only love selflessly if God loves through us. 1 John 4:7 says that "love comes from God." God is the source of love. To be filled by God — filled by his love — is the only way in which you can love people purely. This is what is meant by being filled with the Spirit. The Spirit fills us and loves through us, and we just need to do our best to not get in the way. The more we partake in God loving others through us, the more we partake in God himself.

"No one has ever seen God; but if we love one another, God lives in us and his love is made complete in us" (1 John 4:12). This is echoed a few verses later: "Whoever lives in love lives in God, and God in them" (1 John 4:16).

To learn to love like God, we need to let God love through us.

Discussion questions

1 What are the biggest idols in your life?
2 What makes the world's love different to God's love?
3 Can you think of some people or things that dictate (have become the gods) of your love and happiness?
4 Is there a person whom you have made the centre of your life orientation? If so, what are some practical ways you can free them from the pressure of providing you fulfillment and happiness?
5 In your own words, what is the difference between externally sourced love and eternally sourced love?

Scripture to study • 1 John 4:7-21 • Romans 8:14-17

Books to read • Equipped to Love, *by Norm Wakefield*

4.5.2 EXCHANGE LOVE VS ONE-DIRECTIONAL LOVE

—•—

George Kellerman

Currency Of Exchange

One of the biggest differences between the way we love and the way God loves is in the principle of exchange. In short, we want to love in such a way that the object of our love feels no obligation to pay us back for our love. Instead, we often love based on a cycle of exchange. One of the best explanations I have seen of this concept is in Cassie's book. Here is the whole passage:

> When a pre-marital counsellor asked a young girl what she normally did to get her loved one to do what she wants, she responded, "I just smile and look cute." It was clear that she worked with an exchange cycle: She smiles … he responds … she smiles again. But what if he does not respond to what her smile is trying "to buy?" It is important to see that love that is used as a currency of exchange creates the fear that "my currency will devalue to the extent that it cannot buy what I want anymore." Or it leaves us uncertain on who owes who, and how much is owed. The credit-debit way of dealing with love has never taken away fear. It never will.
>
> The fear is driven by the anxiety that I may not have the currency to buy love or appreciation. This is often experienced by wives and children who feel that they do their level best, but are not appreciated. The problem is often that they trade in a different currency. They give love in a specific way, but the receiver clearly trades in still a different currency.
>
> So many fathers or mothers with marriage problems feel that love only comes from their side. Well, it should! They feel that their love deserves more. My response is, "True love

deserves nothing, but false love always deserves everything." And more, because it is a trade-off with the trader always wanting the best deal. A child is free from fear if they know, "I never need to pay anything back to my Mom and Dad, because the grace they gave was a free gift, not a loan." Pure love that creates no fear is a love that is one-sided, unilateral in its giving, generating undeserved grace irrespective of its return. [72]

It isn't easy giving one-sided or one-directional love. But it is worth pursuing, because that kind of love creates an atmosphere in which someone can flourish.

One-Directional Love

Pure love flows in one direction. It does not act in response to anything, nor in hope of what it might receive in the future. It moves like a one-way street, a telegraph, a waterfall — in one direction.

John points out that this is the way God loves us: "He sent his one and only Son into the world that we might live through Him [one-directional love]. This is love: not that we loved God [we did not give God anything], but that he loved us and sent his Son as an atoning sacrifice for our sins" (1 John 4:9-10).

Usability

Compared to pure love, exchange love always expects some sort of "return on investment". When the object of love no longer offers the "value" it did previously, exchange love produces disappointment. Sometimes, the person is mature enough to realise the nature of the exchange love under the disappointment and repents of it. However, more often than not, the exchange love goes undetected, and we act from a place of disappointment (at not getting what we want) instead. Sometimes we discard the object of love in an outburst of anger or pain. Other times, we try to manipulate them into giving us the value again. A wink, a smile, smooth talk, flirtation or an act of kindness are all ways of manipulating someone to a desired behaviour. Those things aren't always bad in themselves, but when used in an exchange-love cycle they become a problem. When you are using good things to "earn a return" on your love, the object of love is actually yourself. You self-love. That kind of love is exchange love, not one-directional love. In his challenging book, *Equipped To Love*, Norm Wakefield puts it this way:

> "The world values things and people based upon their usability… When a world-ling says he loves his wife, he probably means that she does for him what he wants her to do most of the time and when he wants her to do it. As long as she makes him happy and comfortable, she has value to him which he expresses with the term 'love'". [73]

Norm's insight is both revealing and devastating. "Love" is all too often based on the value the object of our love offers. If you can't imagine how this applies to you, consider the following statements:
"You make me so happy."
"Thank you for doing (insert appreciated action here)."
"You are so beautiful."
"You are such a good parent to our children."
"Thank you for providing for our family."

Again, none of those things are inherently bad, but they illustrate the types of value we attach to people. If you want to evaluate how connected your love for a person is to their "usability", try the following mental exercise. Take a minute to identify the things you find most attractive about the person you love. Then imagine them no longer able to do/be like that. As you strip them of their "usability", what does that do to their value in your eyes? Will your love decrease?

Jesus' Love Is Defined By What It Gives

In stark contrast, one-directional love focuses on giving and serving. In the predominant Scriptures referring to love, the words "give" and "love" are often found in relationship to each other.

"For God so loved the world, that He gave His one and only Son" (John 3:16).

"There is no greater love than to lay down one's life for one's friends" (John 15:13 NLT).

"To love" and "to give" seem to be almost synonymous terms in the Bible.

But how often do we find this one-directional kind of love? Almost never. And this is why the world is in such a mess. Most of our love has a selfish "getting" inclination to it. When we do show great love, we want people to see it. When we serve someone wholeheartedly, we at least want a thank you. When we serve sacrificially, we want others to return the favour. When we serve until it hurts, we want blessings from God. All of these loving acts have some measure of expectation to them. This is selfish love, not real love. It is actually a loan; I will love you now, but I expect to receive love back later. Love that is loaned is not love at all. Love is defined by what it gives, and only that.

When last did you just give? When last did you just love?

> "Agape love, says Anders Nygren, is unmotivated in the sense that it is not contingent on any value or worth in the object of love. It is spontaneous and heedless, for it does not determine beforehand whether love will be effective or appropriate in any particular case." [74]

If love is defined by what is given, the more difficult it is to love, the more opportunity there is to practice one-directional love.

Cassie retells Norm Wakefield's deeply challenging story in his book.

"Norm Wakefield had a serious wake-up call to expectation-less love at the birth of his fourth child. As soon as his fourth child was born, he embraced the baby together with his wife with hugs and kisses and tears of joy. As the baby was taken away to be cleaned, Norm grabbed his wife's hand and gave God praise in a prayer of exultation:

"Thank you Jesus for this great gift. This is perfect. We cannot imagine a better gift from you. Thank you so much for your unmerited grace and the marvellous gift of this baby to us. The baby is so beautiful, so precious, so perfect. Thank you, thank you, thank you, we praise you, we honour you, and we praise you! Amen."

As they finished this prayer, the doctor arrived beside them with the cleaned baby and said, "I am so sorry." Norm responded, "Sorry about what?" Then the doctor broke the news. "Did you not see the baby has Down Syndrome?" Even as this astonishing news shocked Norm, he immediately heard the voice of God instructing him, "Pray the same prayer now! — exactly the same prayer that you prayed two minutes ago. 'The baby is so beautiful, so precious, so perfect. Thank you, thank you, thank you!'" Norm was stunned. He could not pray that prayer. Then he heard the shattering verdict from God, "You evil man. You do not love the baby. You love your image of the baby. You love your expectations for the baby, but you do not love the baby. Your love embraces your expectations, not the baby. Your love embraces yourself and your own desires, not the baby. You have self-love, not real love." Norm then discovered that he really loved no one. His love for his wife was self-love and so was his love for his children. He imprisoned them in his own contractual love. (Do we not all love like this?)" [75]

This story challenged my thinking. By the standards of exchange love, a mentally handicapped child has a lower capacity to meet expectations. And by those standards, if she can't meet his expectations, Norm's love for his daughter should be less than that for his other children. But in Jesus' type of love, those very limitations are what allow him to love her one-directionally. She is the one who can bring forth the most love from him. [c]

Norm explains it as follows:

"When Jesus says, 'I love you,' He means that I am of value because of what I draw out from Him — the love of His Father — Everyone's value comes from their ability to draw out what God puts in — His kind of love — thus bringing glory to God." [76]

Norm's fourth child will draw deeply on the love God deposited in him as a father. That his child had Down Syndrome created the opportunity for Norm to draw more love and bring more glory to God. And this adds value to Norm's life because of the opportunity it offers to discover and practice one-directional love.

If love is defined by what is given, love is not determined by the receiver, but by the giver.

I remember spending two days at Mother Teresa's Home for the Dying in India when I was 13. Mother Teresa and the others at the home invested all their time and energy taking care of people in the last few months of their lives. They helped them die better. There was nothing glamorous about it. I often caught myself thinking, "What

---

C   This is a challenging example because Norm's reaction might seem to imply that some people are worth less than others. To be clear, we believe everyone has the same intrinsic value no matter who they are or their situation in life.

is the point of all this effort? They are going to die anyway." Mother Teresa's patients offered her nothing. They didn't leave her care to go change the world, or even end up with noticeably longer, more meaningful lives. There was no measurable outcome of the love she gave — a vast majority of the people in the home died anyway.

While there, we helped with anything that needed doing. After washing the bed sheets, we had to place them carefully on the roof to dry. The nuns instructed us to avoid leaving creases because ironing was a luxury and therefore not allowed. Despite working with great care, one of the nuns took us aside later that day and pointed out that some of the sheets had creases in them. In a stern yet loving rebuke, she repeated Mother Teresa's words; "Always respect the poor!"

Her reprimand puzzled me. We did our best not to wrinkle the sheets but couldn't remove all of them. And besides, what was the point of being so meticulous? The sheets would be creased soon anyway. Whose life would change because of one crease?

Looking back on my time there, I realised at least one life did change. Mine.

That deep, unassuming love the nuns had for the dying, not expecting anything in return, impacted me deeply. The value of their love was not determined by any tangible outcome; who got better, who changed. Their love was not determined in any way by their patients (the receivers), but by themselves (the givers). Their primary concern was with how much one-directional love they could give. And the Home for the Dying was full of that.

I still find myself in situations today where I struggle to see the point of my love. When I love my friend but know he probably won't stop doing those things that are ruining his life. When I love my enemy, who won't appreciate it (at best), if he doesn't just use it against me. When I love someone who is too disabled to offer anything but their presence in return. When I love a stranger who won't even notice me. When my love feels pointless, I remind myself that one-directional love is not determined by the receiver's response, but by the giver. And the more one-directional it is, the more God's love shines through.

If love is defined by what is given, there is no point trying to earn God's love or acceptance.

So many people approach God from an exchange love perspective. They cannot fathom how God could possibly love them because they believe they don't deserve it. They are convinced they only earn God's love by doing good deeds. Not only is that untrue, but it is also a mockery of God, because it indirectly suggests that he also operates in an exchange love paradigm. It assumes that God only loves you for what he can get from you. This is a crooked understanding which leads to misguided beliefs, such as God blessing some more than others because of their deeds. God does not only give acceptance to those who earn it. He loves incessantly, and one-directionally. If you reject him, he still loves you. If you disobey him, he might discipline you, but he still loves you. When you worship him, serve the poor or give millions to missionaries, he still loves you the same way. There is nothing you can do or not do to change the nature of God's love for you. God is consistent, and gives one-directional love, no matter who you are or what you have done.

If love is defined by what is given, we shouldn't love God for what we can get from him.

It is scary realising we only love God for what we can get from him. Eternal life, blessings, favour, peace and significance were some of the reasons I followed Jesus. What are your reasons for following Jesus? Are you following him for what you can get from him or are you following him for what you want to give to him? When I noticed how much my relationship with Jesus looked like exchange love, I started asking myself tough questions. Is my love for Jesus for his benefit, or for mine? Is there any part of my love for Jesus that isn't based on some sort of exchange? Am I really loving Jesus at all?

I also started wondering about our motives when we approach God with our desires and requests for healing, miracles and blessings. Do we offer confessions and prayers for our enemies with the same urgency we give to our requests and desires? Do we practice obedience hoping God will see our efforts and give us the desires of our hearts? It is not wrong to ask things of God; in fact, it is encouraged. However, we must be aware of the nature of our prayers. Do you spend more time asking for things or giving back (confession, praising God, prayer for others)? This question will help us become more aware of the attitude of our hearts toward God.

We also need to understand that God does not need anything from us. We can never give back to him in the measure he has given to us. Our giving to him or our love for him, however, can be done in an increasing measure. And the way to increase the love given to God is to increase in our love given to people (as alluded to in 1 John 4:20-21). And that love is measured not just in quantity, but in its direction. As our ability to love people with a one-directional love grows, so our ability to love God increases.

Discussion questions

1   In your own words, what is the difference between exchange love and one-directional love?

2   Identify behaviour in the last week where you practiced exchange love.

3   Identify behaviour in the last week where you practiced one-directional love.

4   In practical ways, how can you love without trying to get anything in return?

Scripture to study • Ephesians 2:1-10 • 1 John 3:13-18

Books to read • Equipped to Love, *by Norm Wakefield*

4.5.3 EXPECTATIONAL LOVE VS. INTENTIONAL LOVE

—•—

George Kellerman

To improvise on stage in front of people is one of my greatest fears. Thankfully, I know I am not the only one. The improvisation theatre community encountered this issue so often they coined the term "failure bow". It started with trapeze artists, who would occasionally make a mistake they couldn't recover from and fall to the safety net below. After climbing out of the safety net, they would bow before the crowd, and the crowd would give a great cheer.

In improv theatre, the greatest threat to creativity and a quality show is the fear of failure.

Failure itself is manageable. But the fear of failure is crippling.

To overcome the fear of failure, the improv trainers create an atmosphere in which the actors are free to fail. Mistakes weren't ridiculed or chastised; they were met with a failure bow. The trainers even encouraged the actors to shout things like, "I failed! Woo hoo!" after a failure. As silly as it sounds, when the other actors cheered along it lightened the mood on stage and deflected shame. The gesture acknowledged the mistake, but it also acknowledged the bold attempt and the learning that took place.

We tested this at a youth camp a few years back. The teenagers were free to look goofy, free to make mistakes and free to fail. The one rule was that mistakes had to be acknowledged with a failure bow. It was a great atmosphere, and we saw that the kids — even the awkward, unpopular ones — felt free to be themselves. I experienced a glimpse of heaven that weekend. Thinking about it, I realised the power and importance of this atmosphere at home. Imagine living in an environment where you are encouraged to become the best person you can be, with no fear of failure. Pursuing it together must be heaven on earth.

What would life be like if we lived without fear?

"There is no fear in love [dread does not exist]. But full-grown (complete, perfect) love turns fear out of doors and expels every trace of terror! For fear brings with it the thought of punishment, and [so] he who is afraid has not reached the full maturity of love [is not yet grown into love's complete perfection]" (1 John 4:18 AMPC).

Why is John so convinced that love is on the other end of the spectrum to fear? I find this interesting because "trust" is more commonly understood to be the opposite of fear.

While the Bible speaks of fear in many places (Ps 23:4; Ps 56:3; Prov 29:25; Mark 5:36), the context is usually in relation to the future, or of the unknown. But in his letters, John frames fear in the context of people. Within relationships (such as in 1 John 4), the opposite of love will always be fear.

John goes on to say that fear brings with it the thought (or expectation) of punishment. What does he mean by this? What fear is he referring to here? Why would you fear punishment from another person? Only when expectations have been set and not met. Expectations create fear. As we relate to people we can, unfortunately, create fear.

When we set a standard for our acceptance and love, we create potential for failure. We create space for fear to flourish. When acceptance depends on performance, it will always result in fear.

If this sounds a lot like the previous section, it is because the same issue is at the root: expectations. The fear cycle starts with expectations:

- Expectations drive performance,
- Performance inevitably leads to disappointment,
- Disappointment causes shame,
- And shame drives fear.

When we reach shame and fear, we set new expectations and the fear-cycle starts again from the top.

The performance-driven life many of us lead is a direct product of fear. And unfortunately, it isn't something we leave behind at work. The insane obsession with performance is evident everywhere; at school, at home, in our friendship groups, and sadly, even in the church. We perform to get accepted by friends, approved at work, or even be loved at home. The irony is that the fear driving our performance is often the same fear we are trying to "perform away". We are terrified we will never reach the mark, but because that mark is often unclear or unrealistic, our frantic efforts only emphasise our failure.

In a fear-driven environment our actions are rarely good enough. And the more we fail (however unreasonable the goals), the more we see ourselves as failures. It is no wonder depression and burnout are so prevalent in First-World countries. Contrary to popular belief, burnout isn't just the result of an excessive workload. The relentless need to perform is a huge contributor to burnout. It is the chronic stress of too much to do and no scope to fail.

What expectations do your parents hold that you are afraid of disappointing? Or your friends? What are the expectations you hold for yourself? What expectations do you think God is holding you to? It is time for us to turn the fear-cycle into a love cycle, but we can only do that if we stop raising expectations as a qualification for acceptance.

Does God Have Performance Expectations?

Let's go back to John's claim that "there is no fear [fobos] in love" (1 John 4:18). If God is love, and "God's perfect love casts out fear", we can draw the logical conclusion that God should not be the cause of fear. However, some people argue that the Scriptures encourage us to "fear" God. They back up their argument with Scriptures like Matthew 10:28:

"Do not be afraid [phobeo] of those who kill the body but cannot kill the soul. Rather, be afraid [phobeo] of the One who can destroy both soul and body in hell."

There are, however, two distinct meanings for the use of the word "fear/afraid" in the Bible. The Greek word for "fear" in Matthew 10:28 is "phobeo", which more closely translates to "reverence". The word for "fear" in 1 John 4:18 is "fobos", which refers to "terror" or "alarm". It is an important distinction, because while John is saying there is no "terror" in love, Matthew is encouraging us to revere God.

So if there is no fear in love, what of performance expectations? As we stated earlier, hiding love behind expectations always creates fear in the beloved. Fear that their performance might not be good enough to earn the love; fear that the expected standard might change. Performance expectations always result in fear. Consequently, it would no longer be possible to say that "[God's] perfect love casts out fear." Claiming that God has performance expectations assumes God does not love perfectly.

God will never exert fear with his love. He will never require performance to get his approval. He loves you, just as you are, intimately, perfectly and unconditionally.

God not having expectations is not the same as him not having intentions, however. Nothing we do or don't do will make him love us more, or less. But he does nudge us towards becoming the best people we can be. God intends the best for us, and if we are obedient to his intentions, he will guide us towards our God-ordained purpose.

Hope

The best place to practice intentional love free of expectations is within our discipleship teams. One way we practice that is to no longer use the word "expectations". Instead, we prefer to use the word "hope". Just as God has intentions for us, so we have hope for our disciples. It provides a goal to strive for but avoids creating expectations. On the one hand, we encourage each other to live out our purposes as a team, and to live perfectly, just as our heavenly Father is perfect (Matt 5:48). On the other hand, our love between each other needs to stay the same, regardless of whether we succeed or fail. There is a healthy tension here; we strive for perfection but need to maintain our "expectation-less" love for each other.

How do you encourage your disciples to walk in their God-ordained purposes? With strict performance expectations, or with intention and hope?

Let's revisit the idolatry principle we discussed earlier. When we set expectations for people, we are carving an image of what we want them to be like in our minds. Consider one of your loved ones — a family member, a partner, a disciple. If you are honest with yourself, you will realise you have a subconscious set of expectations you want them to live up to. If they fit the image you created for them in your mind, it usually makes you happy. However, if they don't meet your expectations, the image shatters, and you feel upset or hurt. We go through relationships without ever realising the expectations we hold our partners to. Sometimes, we even marry the image of a person, rather than the person themselves. In essence, you are marrying an idol you created. As you can imagine, the shock and pain when your spouse breaks from the image you created of them can be intense.

If you interrogated your love for others honestly as you read this chapter, you should be aware of some of the expectations you have set for others. It is a tough reality to accept, that we rarely love without imposing expectations. The question is, if we shouldn't love by creating expectations, how are we supposed to love?

Love Driven By Intentionality

In his book, Cassie describes what a love driven by intentionality looks like:

> "When love has intent instead of expectation, the giver of love is not in it for what he can get, but for what the receiver of love can become. The one who loves does not live with an

open hand to receive, but instead with a finger pointed at the optimal potential the person can reach or a lifting thrust that pushes the person to reach the dream. The receiver of love is the beneficiary. This is what 1 John 4:12 implies when it says: Then God's love is made complete in us!

This is what Norm Wakefield had to discover: his Down Syndrome daughter would never meet the list of expectations for a normal child, but this daughter could meet the full, though limited, potential that she was born with. Love would then drive towards that potential so that the one who is loved can be benefitted, not the one who loves. A child is free from fear if he feels, "There are no selfish expectations from my parents' side, only selfless intention — an intention that I (the child) will optimise. I am the beneficiary. I am free to move towards that ... as far as I want to." There is no fear in love." [77]

Loving The Person Beyond The Person

When we love intentionally, we are able to love the person beyond the person. This type of love has the long term in mind. You aren't just loving for what is; you are loving for what could be. A simple example is when you discipline a child. In the short term it is unpleasant and may not seem like love to the child. But in the long run, healthy discipline teaches a child how to behave, building their character. This kind of love looks different in an adult context, but the principle is the same. We must love intentionally, even if it involves discomfort or discipline, to help others reach their optimal potential in the long run.

Be careful not to fall into the world's view of love, which is all about satisfying desires. A perfect example is parents who give their kids whatever they want whenever they want it. This is not real love.

Real love is serving people's real needs, not simply taking care of their happiness.

When a parent is unwilling to discipline their child, it shows a lack of understanding of real love. The same could be said of people who struggle to correct or rebuke their friends, and turn to people-pleasing instead. Jesus sets a very different example. From turning over the tables in the temple courts, to telling one of his disciples to "get behind me Satan", he clearly had a different vision at heart. While he rarely provoked it, Jesus wasn't afraid of confrontation as a means to liberate the person behind the person.

As we are encouraged to lay our lives down for others (1 John 3:16), we are also encouraging them to lay their lives down for others. Similarly, as we are encouraged to become broken and humble, we want to help others become broken and humble. The need for holiness is a greater need than the need for happiness. If we really love people, we will facilitate holiness and humility in them. Unhappiness is sometimes the cost in the short term, but in the long term, joy is the ultimate reward.

> *Influencing people to become what they want to become*
> *is people-pleasing.*
> *Influencing people to become what you want them to*
> *become is manipulation.*
> *Influencing people to become what God wants them to*
> *become is intentional love.*

To love a person beyond a person can also mean that the benefit of your actions flows to other people through the person you are loving. This could mean standing up to a bully to prevent him from bullying others. It could mean challenging a person to share their story in front of a large crowd because you know it will help many who listen. Or it could mean reporting an abusive individual to prevent harm to other people.

These acts are all loving the person beyond the person. To practice this love is to look beyond the immediate person, immediate results and immediate response. It calls for us to plan ahead and create opportunities for people to change for the better. Some people call this "tough love". We like to call it "intentional love".

Discussion questions

1 In your own words, what is the difference between expectation-driven (performance-driven) love and love driven by intentionality?
2 In what relationships are you still living with fear? What are the expectations in these relationships? How can you get rid of the fear and expectations that drive the fear?
3 Name some expectations you think God has for you which you fear you are not living up to. How might this change with your new understanding of intentional love?
4 How can you practice more intentional love this week?

Scripture to study • 1 John 4:18

Books to read • The World Needs A Father: A Trainer's Guide, *by Cassie Carstens* • Equipped to Love, *by Norm Wakefield*

4.5.4 EXIT LOVE VS. SACRIFICIAL LOVE

●

George Kellerman

A little girl, Annie, was in an accident and lost a lot of blood. She needed a blood transfusion from someone who matched her blood type, and she needed it quickly. The hospital did not have her blood type in stock, so the doctors tested her family. Her little brother, Billy, was the only one whose blood type matched. The doctor knelt down to Billy's level and looked him in the eye.

"Billy, we need your blood. It will save your sister's life. There is life in the blood."

Billy thought about it with wide eyes, then nodded. He was given a bed next to his sister, and the doctors connected a blood transfusion apparatus between them. After some time, Billy started to feel a bit drowsy. He looked over at his sister, who was starting to look less pale, and called his mom over.

"So Mommy, when is it going to happen?"

"When is what going to happen, Billy?"

His lip quivered a little.

"When am I going to die?"

"Nobody is going to die, Billy." His mom stroked his head gently. "Both of you will get up from these beds in no time."

"But Mommy, you said that you needed my blood to save Annie's life."

Billy's mom blinked away the tears as she realised what her son had done. When he said yes to the doctor, he wasn't just agreeing to a blood transfusion. In his mind, he was giving his life for his sister.

That is sacrificial love. A love that forsakes the self and gives to others, no matter the cost to self. Few things are more beautiful than experiencing love like this. In moments like this, you get a sense that it can change the world. Movies like *Braveheart, Blood Diamond* or *Hacksaw Ridge* stir us because of the people sacrificing themselves for others. And as I watch these movies, I dream of having the same heart: being able to disregard myself, and always put the interests of others first. Even, should it be necessary, to the point of death. This kind of love moves us and changes us.

Many people start out with good intentions, such as giving of themselves to others. However, as the cost of their love increases, the good motives fade. Instead of giving of themselves to everyone, they start setting limits to make it easier for themselves.

"I will only give of myself to loved ones."

"I will only give of myself if the other person is willing to give of themselves."

"I will only give of myself up to a certain point."

This is the world's kind of love. A love with limits, a love that gives up when the cost gets too high. That is why we call it "exit love". This is a love that opts out, that quits. In some cases, divorce is the result of one or both people just opting out. Their own happiness is more important than their partner's happiness. "We are just not happy anymore" describes an unhappiness with what they are receiving, and as a result the giving reached a limit. It is a love that gives as long as the other person also gives of themselves. It is a love where I must first meet my own desires before I take care of others. I can only love as much as I have been loved or will be loved in return.

Jesus's love is different. His love has no limits, and the people who carry this love will love without limits. These people love selflessly and sacrificially. "There is no greater love than to lay down one's life for one's friends" says John in his epistle (John 15:13). Jesus' love constantly looks to the best interests of others, while disregarding the self. The focus is on serving others, not serving yourself. It is a love that goes beyond accepting enemies, and into loving, blessing and serving them. 1 Corinthians 13 describes this as follows: "It does not envy, it is not proud. It does not dishonour others, it is not self-seeking... It always protects... always perseveres. Love never fails."

The love that Jesus came to show is a love that does not diminish when it faces difficulty and hardships. It loves when no one sees you. It loves even when it experiences suffering. It loves enemies. It loves even when opposition rages against it.

Love In Suffering

People who understand Jesus' love are those who are able to face darkness and pain and are still able to love in a powerful way. They endure and embrace the suffering that is a catalyst for Jesus' love to shine through. There is a character of perseverance, toughness and boldness about these people. They love in spite of adversity, and sometimes you even get the feeling they love because of it.

During the second century after Christ, a fatal epidemic broke out in the Roman Empire, wiping out around 30% of the population. During the plague, followers of Jesus risked their lives to take care of the sick in quarantined areas. The love they demonstrated by risking their own lives to take care of others brought many people to the love of Christ. Estimates point to over 50% of the world following Jesus during that time. [78]

"By this everyone will know that you are my disciples, if you love one another" (John 13:35).

Suffering is the best amplifier for what is going on in our hearts. When suffering, persecution or hardships come our way, most people try to escape. People who truly grasp Jesus' love, however, look suffering in the eye and ask, "How can God and his love be glorified through this?"

Suffering is the ideal stage for God's love to be displayed.

Norm Wakefield said: "The typical worldly concept of God's goodness is that God is watching out for our comfort and happiness." [79] People say, "God is good" and "I am blessed" when things are going well. But how often do we hear those phrases during suffering? The God-centred concept of God's goodness is to form us into his image. In this way, suffering takes on a whole new meaning.

As unpopular as this perspective of suffering is, our Christian growth will always be limited until we accept it. And if suffering is meaningful, suffering for the sake of others is even more so. Suffering builds character; suffering for others enables us to love sacrificially. Instead of running from suffering, we should learn to embrace it. This is why people go to dangerous and difficult places, risking their lives to share the sacrificial love of Jesus. They have not only embraced suffering themselves, but have also learned the value of sharing the suffering of others.

Strongest Power

I hope that as you start practising these things, you come to understand another mystery of Jesus' love — as opposition to love increases, so Jesus' love increases. The more difficult it becomes to give, the more valuable when the giving takes place. The more evil tries to oppose love, the stronger the love will grow when it remains steadfast.

Jesus' love is the strongest power in the world.

If it increases when difficulty increases and opposition rises, nothing can rise above it. Opposition thus creates opportunity for love to increase and opens new avenues for God's love to be displayed.

When we start leaning on the selfless love of Jesus, we become powerful in the most beautiful way.

We often look to miracles, dreams, healings or other supernatural interventions to change the world. But these things don't have the power to sustainably change the world. Without the love of Jesus, they will fail eventually. The strongest power to change the world is sacrificial love, the type that Jesus came to reveal. When we understand and practice the real love of Jesus, then will we be able to change the world.

How Is this Love Possible?

Sometimes, it sounds too good to be true. Is this type of love an unattainable and impossible love? If we try to do it in our own power, yes. It is entirely impossible. But when we surrender to God and allow him to love through us, the possibilities of this love are endless. The self will almost always be the greatest barrier to love. It is the self that enslaves us. Surrendering to God assumes us letting go of our own desires and "natural" behaviour. Sometimes we get to pick the pieces of ourselves up again; sometimes we must leave them behind us for good. But before we can allow God to love through us, we always have to be willing to lay EVERYTHING down. This, in its essence, is the Gospel of Jesus.

Once we learn how to lay ourselves down, we become free to love others sacrificially. When there is no self to get in the way, there is no need to protect or defend. We are free to give and serve others wholeheartedly.

As Mother Teresa said, "A sacrifice to be real must cost, must hurt, and must empty ourselves. Give yourself fully to God. He will use you to accomplish great things on the condition that you believe much more in his love than in your weakness." [80]

Discussion questions

1   In your own words, what is the difference between exit love and sacrificial love?
2   How will you practice more sacrificial love this week?
3   How should we move from "avoiding suffering at all cost" to "embracing suffering for real benefits"?

Scripture to study • 1 Corinthians 13

Books to read • Strength to Love, *by Martin Luther King Jr.* • A Path Through Suffering, *by Elisabeth Elliot* • Equipped to Love, *by Norm Wakefield*

5

INTIMACY WITH GOD (UPWARD)

Living an awe-inspired life

Discipleship needs to propel us upward, God-ward.
The biggest danger to us spiritually is that
we regress into idolatrous self-worship.
Our mind, soul, spirit and strength need to be
consumed with God-honouring thoughts and acts.
We need to avail ourselves fully to get to know him,
to worship him and build his Kingdom.
We need to learn how to live an awe-inspired life.

5.1 WHO IS GOD?

—•—

Cassie Carstens

As followers of Jesus, our eyes should remain focused upward. It is from studying, discovering, experiencing, and ultimately knowing God that we grow. We must get to know the One to whom our spirits should be attuned.

Even at the tender age of 20 years old, C.H. Spurgeon was convinced that a deep study of God bore great fruit: [81]

- An improved and expanded mind: no single contemplation is more pregnant with wisdom than a study of our God.
- A humbled mind: a study of God helps our "pride to drown in its infinity as our thoughts are lost in [his] immensity." The truest response is to turn away with the exclamation: "I know nothing!"
- Comfort: "I know nothing which can so comfort the soul; so calm the swelling billows of sorrow and grief; so speak peace to the winds of trial, as a devout musing upon the subject of the Godhead."

Concurring with Spurgeon, I would like to add that a study of God:

- Lifts us in divine adoration: as we study God, our astonishment should grow as we learn how the Creator of the universe stooped so low to reach us.
- Purifies us: as we seek God, we live in his presence (*coram Deo*) and are thus moved away from our own sinful desires (Ps 119:9).
- Re-orientates our lives around God: life tends to mould our thinking and living to the pattern of the world, instead of where we should be; living from, through and towards God.
- Calibrates our attentiveness: like a sheepdog, we should focus our attentiveness on God so that we can move with his

heart and develop the mind of Christ in us. As we focus, we should start picking up on what is on his heart for a specific time and place (also known as reading God's Kairos time).

Growing up in a society intently focused on immediate satisfaction, we lose out on discovering the width, breadth, height and depth of God. This leaves us with dangerous misperceptions of God; that he will disappoint us, or that he gets boring and is not worth the effort. The problem is not with God; it is with our understanding and expectations of God.

We hope that the rest of this chapter (indeed, the entire book) will move you away from disappointment or apathy and lift you into amazement of God. We pray that your heart and mind will be humbled, that you will be moved to adoration, and your prayer life and contemplation of God grow deeper and broader.

The Bible describes God in multiple ways. We will summarise them in three broad concepts: God is awe-inspiring, God is relational, and God is on a mission, and assigns a role for us in his dream.

1. God is awe-inspiring!

Some Psalms express how awe-inspiring God is in better words than we can find (e.g. Ps 92-94; 96-99; 104). What should inspire the awe of God in us is the sheer number and variety of viewpoints the Bible gives on God, both complementary and contrasting. At times it states that God is high and transcendent (Isa 57:15), yet the same verse tells how he is low and imminent. At times it says God never changes (James 1:17), yet also shows how God frequently changes (Jer 18:7-8). At times it says God is mighty, as well as expressing how he is meek. (Revelation 5:12-13 refers to angels using words like "The Lamb" in their worship-language to God.) At times it says God is a holy judge and simultaneously testifies about his forgiving grace (Hos 11:9 AMP).

The biblical perspective from which we approach God makes all the difference in how we understand and experience him. When we ponder on the holy justice of God, we are moved to fall down in absolute adoration and worship. But when we dwell on his grace and forgiveness, we want to jump with joy in celebration of our salvation! When we think of God as powerful (Ps 147:5), it could either give a sense of security or reverence at his power and strength. On the other hand, thinking of God as a humble servant of all (Mark 10:45) can help us feel understood (Heb 4:15), or overwhelmed that God was so gracious as to even associate with us at all.

CONTEMPLATING THE CONTRASTING QUALITIES OF GOD ALSO HELPS US REALISE HOW GOD'S LOVE FOR US WRESTLES WITH HIS HOLINESS AS A SINLESS GOD

Contemplating the contrasting qualities of God also helps us realise how God's love for us wrestles with his holiness as a sinless God. The Bible invites us to move in our contemplation of God from perspective to perspective, into a deeper understanding of the richness of God (Eph 3:18). Drawing us into his width and breadth and height and depth, it invites us into the tension of the salvation drama.

In an effort to grasp the diversity of God's character, we sometimes describe him as the compilation of tensions between paradoxical virtues which culminate in the cross. It is at the cross that the holiness and empathic grace of God collide; and it is at the cross that this tension broke apart the Son and with that the veil separating us from the holiest of holies. It is in the tension at the cross that we should often dwell.

God is so awesome! How can we find words to describe him? Paul is rendered almost speechless by the end of Romans 11:33-36:

Oh, the depth of the riches of the wisdom and
knowledge of God!
How unsearchable his judgments,

and his paths beyond tracing out!
"Who has known the mind of the Lord?
Or who has been his counselor?"
"Who has ever given to God,
that God should repay them?"
For from him and through him and for him are all things.
To him be the glory forever! Amen.

2. God is a relational God!

First God interacts with Adam and Eve, then he reveals himself as the God of Abraham, Isaac and Jacob. He calls out to Israel: "They will be my people, and I will be their God" (Jer 24:7). Then the climax of his relational heart is expressed to us through Jesus. "For God so loved the world, that he gave his only Son… [and the] Spirit himself bears witness with our spirit that we are children of God… by whom we cry, 'Abba, Father!'" (John 3:16; Rom 8:15; Rom 8:16 ESV). God desires an intimate relationship with us!

There may not be a better description of the astounding depth to which God stooped in his love than in the book of Hebrews:

"… he has spoken to us through his Son, to whom he has given ownership of everything and through whom he created the universe. This Son is the radiance of [God's reflected Sh'khinah glory], the very expression of God's essence, upholding all that exists by his powerful word; and after he had, through himself, made purification for sins, he sat down at the right hand of [the Majesty on high [revealing His Divine authority]]" (Heb 1:3 CJB, AMP).

It is astonishing to imagine how the One who holds galaxies in his hands, for the sake of having a relationship with us, shrank into humanity to save us and make us worthy of that relationship!

John describes this intimate relationship in 1 John 3:1-2:

"See what great love the Father has lavished on us, that we should be called children of God! And that is what we are!… Dear friends, now we are children of God, and what we will be has not yet been made known. But we know that when Christ appears, we shall be like him, for we shall see him as he is."

And he continues in chapter 4:7-8:

"Dear friends, let us love one another, for love comes from God. Everyone who loves has been born of God and knows God. Whoever does not love does not know God, because God is love."

This is why the author of Hebrews says: "Both the one who makes people holy and those who are made holy are of the same family. So Jesus is not ashamed to call them brothers and sisters" (Heb 2:11).

Oh yes, God is a relational God! He is defined by selfless sacrificial love! His love flows like water — always to the lowest point! He is the only source of pure love. He is love!

3. God is on a mission with his dream and assigns a role for us in it!

From a lighter perspective, the Bible is basically the logbook of God's mission. It describes how the mission starts (Genesis), and how the mission will end triumphantly (Revelation). It details all sorts of victories and disappointments, and the different plans (from the prophets to Jesus, from the law to grace) God used to ensure the mission succeeds. We are following Jesus as he leads this mission until he hands over the Kingdom to his Father (1 Cor 15:24).

Ephesians 1 describes God's dream beautifully:

> "For he chose us in him before the creation of the world to
> be holy and blameless in his sight. In love he predestined us
> for adoption to sonship through Jesus Christ, in accordance
> with his pleasure and will — to the praise of his glorious

grace, which he has freely given us in the One he loves. In him we have redemption through his blood, the forgiveness of sins, in accordance with the riches of God's grace that he lavished on us. With all wisdom and understanding, he made known to us the mystery of his will according to his good pleasure, which he purposed in Christ, to be put into effect when the times reach their fulfilment — to bring unity to all things in heaven and on earth under Christ" (Eph 1:4-10).

Jesus invites us to join him on this mission in John 20:21-22:
"'As the Father has sent me, I am sending you.' And with that he breathed on them and said, 'Receive the Holy Spirit.'"

Throughout the Gospels, Jesus describes our role in God's mission. Sometimes he was explicit in his guidance, like the conversations with his disciples or his sermons. He was also fond of parables, such as the workers and talents, and the story about the sheep and the goats (Mat 25:14-46). Jesus is very clear: God is doing something massive, and he wants us to be part of it.

Our assignment is to build God's kingdom as his co-workers (2 Cor 6:1), with him being the head and us the body (Eph 4:15-16). We try to bring heaven home in all spheres of society, so that everything will realise God's original intent. We are led by the Spirit and the Word (Eph 6:17) to accomplish the tasks set before us.

As we search the Word in humble obedience, with a deep desire to know God better and glorify him more, not only will our adoration of him grow, but his presence will shape us more and more into the image of his Son (Rom 8:29)!

Discussion questions

1 When you think about God, how do you see him? Do you mostly think of him as a king, a prophet, a friend, a servant, an advocate, a father…?

2 Which of the qualities or characteristics of God should you reflect on more?

3 In this chapter we wrote about three specific aspects of God: his majesty, his interaction with us and his mission. Which of these do you attend to the least?

4 Share with each other what each of these characteristics of God mean to you personally.

Scripture to study • Romans 11:33-36

Books to read • Knowing God, *by J.I. Packer*

5.2 BARRIERS TO INTIMACY WITH GOD

—•—

Cassie Carstens

In his writings, John encourages us to seek an intimate relationship with God. He says that we know God because we are born of God, that we are in God and God is in us. The language he uses is intimate, and urges us to get deep into God, to abide in him.

However, many Christians we speak to don't have this consistent intimacy with God. Some point to a specific incident that broke their intimacy, while others say they have "lost their first love". They can point to moments of intimacy with God, but those moments are blips on an otherwise silent radar.

So what are the barriers preventing us from enjoying a close relationship with God? We work with 10 broad types of barriers below, but there may well be others unique to your situation that don't fit one of our categories. Use this section as a starting point as you figure out what is keeping you from rich intimacy with God.

1 An Attachment To Self (Pride)

If you want deeper intimacy with God, you have to fight against self-absorption.

While narcissism has always been part of society, it could almost be considered a trend today. In the 1970s, Paul Vitz wrote a book called *Psychology as Religion*: The Cult of Self-Worship. [82] He describes how the intense emphasis psychology puts on self-image, self-actualisation and self-fulfilment resulted in a culture of people:

1   Unwilling to make any decisions that deny the self.
2   Unwilling to accept or condone a God whose thoughts are not their thoughts.
3   Who turned "Does it feel good for me?" into their fundamental norm.

4   Mired deep in a self-serving bias. Basically, "My success is due to my achievement, but someone else is to blame for my failures."

As narcissism becomes more acceptable in society, the predictions of Paul look like they are coming true in a big way. In 2 Timothy 3:2-5, he predicts people will be lovers of themselves during the end times, becoming "lovers of pleasure rather than lovers of God."

Pride is the root of all evil, according to the fathers of faith. In short, it is an attachment to self, a valuing of yourself higher than others. The real problem **PRIDE IS THE** with pride is that it is very hard to identify on **ROOT OF ALL EVIL** its own. When it isn't trying to convince you it doesn't exist, it is usually hiding behind its fruit. Some examples of the fruit of pride are jealousy, ungratefulness, an unforgiving spirit, not being teachable, scepticism, impatience and constant comparison to others.

One of the clearest indications of pride is selfish ambition. Philippians 2:3 says we must "do nothing out of selfish ambition or vain conceit." Ambition is the determination to achieve success, which is fine if done for the benefit of others, but not if it is self-centred. To serve others and consider them better than yourself is a central theme of the Bible, and Jesus spoke more than once about the first being last.

Another clear indicator of pride is irritation or anger. The more pride we have, the higher the expectations we have of others. And naturally, the higher our expectations are, the harder they are to meet, which leads to major frustration. Conversely, the lower our expectations, the less we are disappointed, and thus less frustrated. That is why the level of our frustration or anger is a good indicator of our pride. Not always, because issues like injustice against the oppressed should demand our anger. But if our anger stems from expectations not being met, it is typically rooted in pride.

Three vital spiritual disciplines combat an attachment to self: self-denial, submission and service. Not only do they combat pride, but they are also fantastic avenues to a deeper intimacy with God.

Self-denial

In his book, *The Calvary Road*, Roy Hession captures the essence of self-denial. He writes:

> "… the Lord Jesus cannot live in us fully and reveal Himself through us until the proud self within us is broken. This simply means that the hard, unyielding self, which justifies itself, wants its own way, stands up for its rights, and seeks its own glory, at last bows its head to God's will, admits that it is wrong, gives up its own way to Jesus… it is dying to self and self-attitudes." [83]

In Mark 8:36-37 (MSG), Jesus says: "Self-help is no help at all. Self-sacrifice is the way, my way, to saving yourself, your true self. What good would it do to get everything you want and lose you, the real you? What could you ever trade your soul for?"

And when John the Baptist said: "He must be more and I must be less", he set us a great example how self-denial can lead to greater intimacy with God.

Self-denial is best expressed through selfless, no-expectation, sacrificial love. 1 John 4 says that if we love like that, we are born of God, know him and live in him as he lives in us — what amazing intimacy!

(See chapters 4.3 (Humility) and 4.4 (Descending into Greatness) for elaboration on the topic of self-denial.)

Submission

Submission is arguably the most difficult thing for people to do these days. It is easy to say we submit to God. We sing, "I surrender all" with great fervour, but prove our words hollow when faced with submitting to the authority of another human being. This voluntary revolutionary subordination is the greatest discipline towards intimacy with God. As children learn to obey their parents, they are training themselves to be submissive. Practised submission opens our hearts to obedience to God. A special intimacy is the prize for obedience. (See chapter 2.7 for more on submission.)

Service
Service is the third discipline which can help us get rid of self-attachment. In true service, you care for the needs of others, forcing your attention away from yourself. Mother Teresa's greatest inspiration was to serve Christ by serving the needs of others. As we engage in true service, new avenues of intimacy open as we experience God by serving others through him.

So many people become professional self-servers. If you look at the amount of time spent on recreation or self-centred ambition, it becomes evident that "what I want" has become the domineering power of the world. So many marriages suffer, or never even get off the ground due to this self-centred bias. It was a significant revelation in my life when I realised that the self is the biggest enemy of God. In paradise, Satan did not present himself as the big enemy of God. He pushed the self-interest of the human being to the centre, saying "... when you eat from it your eyes will be opened, and *you will be like God*, knowing good and evil"(Gen 3:5, emphasis mine).

As we strive for intimacy with God, our biggest victory will be when God becomes the pivotal point of our lives. When we realise that life is about God, not us. Then we become missionaries of God, and everything we do becomes missional.

Our marriages become missional.

Our recreation becomes missional.

Even our ambition becomes a missional endeavour.

(See chapter 4.5.4 for more on service.)

2 An Attachment To Other People

While our own self-interest is the strongest lure away from God, there are many others. One of the hardest ones to balance is our relationships with others. The fundamental nature of the Kingdom is relational, and healthy relationships are a critical part of Kingdom life. However, we tend to get so occupied with people in close relationships we run out of time to spend with God and Kingdom building. Jesus confronts this tendency in Luke 14:26 (AMP):

"If anyone comes to Me, and does not hate his own father and mother and wife and children and brothers and sisters, yes, and even his own life [in the sense of indifference to or relative disregard for them in comparison with his attitude toward God] — he cannot be My disciple."

Paul also talks about minimising complications to commit more fully to God:

"I do want to point out, friends, that time is of the essence. There is no time to waste, so don't complicate your lives unnecessarily. Keep it simple — in marriage, grief, joy, whatever. Even in ordinary things — your daily routines of shopping, and so on. Deal as sparingly as possible with the things the world thrusts on you. This world as you see it is on its way out" (1 Cor 7:29-31 MSG).

Although they may not intend to, many parents make their children "gods" in their lives. They focus all their energies on the needs and wants of their children. While this seems noble, Jesus' reminder is clear: God needs to come before all others. Attention addiction is another issue that comes between us and God. We invest inordinate amounts of our time and resources into serving our relationships with people, not God. We find the idea of being separated from other people even worse than the thought of separation from God.

3 An Attachment To The World

The world can be terrible, but it can be staggeringly attractive as well! Satan was convinced that the world would tempt Jesus because he offered him the kingdoms of the world. But Jesus' answer was definite: "Away from me, Satan! For it is written: Worship the Lord your God, and serve him only" (Matt 4:10).

The embrace of the world separates us from the Lord with subtle ease. One evening, my family was having a family devotion on 1 John 2:15. The verse reads, "Do not love the world or anything in the world. If anyone loves the world, love for the Father is not in them." This is a challenging concept to accept, so my son asked me to help him understand it better. At that stage of his life, rugby completely occupied his mind, so I said:

"George, if you love rugby, you cannot love God."

The shock on his face was clear: "No Dad! Really?"

Borrowing from Bonhoeffer, I replied. "Yes, George. Our hearts only have space for one God. If God is in our lives, all other things must serve him. If rugby is in the centre of your life, you will want God to serve it."

George had to detach from rugby and to make it subservient to God before he could embrace it again. Many disciplines can help us detach from the world. Fasting, sacrificial giving and taking a proper Sabbath are three the Bible encourages us to use. We must create distance from the embrace of the world to have closeness with God.

4 Emotional Deficiencies

Peter Scazzero says it is impossible to be mature spiritually while remaining immature emotionally. [84] He then goes on to say that getting to know ourselves better will help us know God better. I have spent decades trying to help people live more intimately with God. In that time, I learned that our emotional condition has a very direct link to our spiritual condition.

Even as adults, what we experienced as children still moulds our emotional condition. A poor connection with your mother during your first few years of life limited her impartation of intimacy. This could cause you to keep emotional distance from people, and from God. If your father was absent or his love was conditional — especially when you were between 6 and 11 years old — you may well struggle with an unhealthy concept of God. Our emotional wounds often cause spiritual wounds, which can often only be removed after the emotional issues have been dealt with.

Some of us live with an ambivalent experience with God due to our emotional wounds. Os Guinness offers a brilliant analogy to explain why. If you burn your hand, then try to pick up a glass of water with that hand, it will be painful and you will probably put down the glass. You need the water, but as your hand clasps the glass, the burning sensation makes you pull away. While the effects of the burn are still present, it is impossible to hold the glass normally. Emotional wounds work the same way. The only solution is to make sure the wound heals first before you can enjoy the water.

If you are aware of a parent-related emotional wound in your life, I encourage you to get professional help. Ask a Christian counsellor or psychologist to help you work through the wounds and find healing. Emotional healing often precedes spiritual health.

5 A Lack Of Sabbath

God gave us the Sabbath for numerous reasons:
- To connect with him in an intimate way
- To celebrate our freedom (Deut 5:13-15), especially our freedom in Christ through the resurrection
- To re-orientate life around him and his mission; to realign our priorities with his
- To understand that it is not our hard work that makes the world turn around, or that we earn our worth by what we do
- To rest physically, emotionally and mentally

- To reach out to those in need
- To restore and cultivate relationships (Matt 12:12).

If we do not stop and re-adjust, our lives flow with the stream of culture, one of the strongest powers in this world. We will, if we are not careful, conform to a secular way of living where there is no place for God. We need the Sabbath to have a God-centred life!

6 The Pull Of The Flesh

When Galatians 5:18-19 says the flesh and spirit are in constant battle within us, it is not exaggerating! The battle is fierce, furious and unceasing.

As Christians, we have been transformed from people who lived by their natural desires to people who live by God's voice. However, we constantly have the "power of gravity" pulling us from flying in the Spirit. Paul phrases it this way in his letter to the Roman church:

"I want to do what is good, but I don't. I don't want to do what is wrong, but I do it anyway" (Rom 7:19 NLT).

While you are stretching towards God's purpose for your life (Phil 3:12) with one hand, the other hand should be fending off the call of the flesh. The more we do what we ought to do (or what the Spirit tells us to do) instead of what the flesh desires, the closer we live to God. The Bible calls us to do so by saying NO to evil desires and foolish arguments, and YES to righteousness, faith and love (2 Tim 2:22-23).

The Spirit is given to us to help us to live in victory. Those who live according to the Spirit set their minds on what the Spirit wants (Rom 8:5) and put to death the sinful deeds of the body. Paul says it this way:

"But if [you are living] by the [power of the Holy] Spirit, you are habitually putting to death the sinful deeds of the body, you will [really] live forever" (Rom 8:13 AMP).

This battle is fierce, but we are encouraged to persevere!

7 An Addiction To The Media

A new enemy of intimacy with God has emerged: digital media. Digital media isn't all bad — the writing of this book relied on it. However, it is frightening how rapidly digital media can become an addiction, or even an obsession. In his book, *Digital Cocaine*, Brad Huddleston describes how damaging addiction to digital media can be. For many people, the first thing they touch in the morning and the last thing they hold at night is their cellphone. With their insatiable demand on our time, priorities and energy, cellphones have taken an unnaturally high priority in our lives. In many cases, they have taken over the throne of God. Huddleston ends with this poignant lament:

"TECHNOLOGY HAS ROBBED US OF THE INTIMACY THAT GOD DESIGNED FOR US TO HAVE TOWARD HIM"

"Technology has robbed us of the intimacy that God designed for us to have toward Him." [85]

We must be intentional about combating the coup d'état of digital media on the centrality of God in our lives. This process will require us to be both proactive and reactive. Spiritual disciplines can help us get our focus on God right, but we should also put wise boundaries in place. Limiting our use of cellphones, computers and TV will help contain the space and influence digital media has in our lives.

8 Unforgiveness

While he was teaching his disciples how to pray, Jesus said, "Father, forgive us as we forgive others". This points to a direct relationship between unforgiveness and a lack of intimacy with God. Unforgiveness doesn't just infect your relationship with others. It directly poisons your intimacy with God.

Too many people justify their attitude or behaviour by how badly they have been hurt. They use phrases like: "I don't trust people anymore" or, "I am angry with God because of what happened in the church". No matter what you feel, you need to accept responsibility for your own choices and actions. Yes, someone may have hurt you, but choosing to distance yourself from God is still your choice. If we want intimacy with God, we often need to act contrary to our human nature. Forgiveness may or may not relieve the pain. Either way, it remains a prerequisite for intimacy with God. When you take the steps to forgive others unconditionally, you will experience a closer intimacy with God. God appreciates it when we value his forgiveness for our sins so much that we share the gift of grace with others.

UNFORGIVENESS DOESN'T JUST INFECT YOUR RELATIONSHIP WITH OTHERS. IT DIRECTLY POISONS YOUR INTIMACY WITH GOD

If you want to step closer to God, write off all emotional debt you hold against others in a bold step of forgiveness!

9 Disobedience

How close can we stay to God if we refuse to obey him?

John, the "disciple Jesus loved", understood the relationship between loving God and obeying God well. In his first letter, he describes those who are loving (1 John 4:7) and those who do right as children of God (1 John 2:29). He also talks about how those who keep God's commands live in him, and he in them (1 John 3:24), and summarises everything in one beautiful line:

"This is love for God: to keep His commands" (1 John 5:3).

If we walk in disobedience, we will never be close to God, because God cannot associate with sin. Many people are consciously dabbling in sin and still think they are close to God. This is impossible. Therefore, confessing of all known sin is the first step in moving closer to God.

On the other hand, God loves obedience and will reward it abundantly. Deuteronomy 6:3 says, "... be careful to obey, so that it may go well with you..." Jesus put it this way: "[My Father and I] will make our home with them [that obey]" (John 14:23).

The practice of immediate obedience is a great discipline for disciples (see chapter 6.3 on obedience). Procrastination has always been an efficient tool of Satan to get us out of our commitments. We encourage everyone to make immediate obedience part of their daily Bible study. We must read the Bible as God's instruction manual and quicken our step with the mantra: "He says, I do!"

10 Performing For God

What does it mean to be saved by grace? This is a simple yet difficult question to answer. To better understand what it means to be saved by grace, it helps to ask the question from the other side. What is the opposite of being saved by grace? When we study the Scripture on these questions, the answer becomes clearer. It is interesting to note that in the New Testament, when the author describes grace, he usually also mentions an opposite of grace. Let us look at one example:

"For it is by grace you have been saved, through faith — and this is not from yourselves, it is the gift of God — not by works, so that no one can boast" (Eph 2:8-9). See also Galatians 2:16-21, Galatians 4:4-5, 1 Timothy 1:9, Romans 3:20-28, 4:2-6, and John 1:17 for more on this.

The word "works" echoes through the Scriptures as an answer to the opposite of being saved by grace. Hoping that "works" can earn our salvation is an evidently crooked understanding of the Gospel. This fundamental biblical principle is critical, both to our understanding of salvation and to our intimacy with God. Too often we try to earn our intimacy with God. We pray with more concentration, worship with more intensity, spend more time in stillness, read more of the Bible and confess more sins in the hope of earning intimacy with the Father. We perform on the spiritual stage and try all sorts of works to convince ourselves that we can now approach God. The problem is, we are missing the point. Ironically, we might be pulling ourselves away from God by trying so hard to get closer to him.

As "works" are the opposite of grace, so performing for God seems to be the opposite of becoming intimate with God. On the theatrical stage, there is distance between the stage and the audience. In the same way, performing on the spiritual stage distances us from God. He wants to draw near to us, but can only do so when we stop performing, surrender to him and accept his grace. It is a shift from the action of performance to the intentional process of surrender and acceptance that brings intimacy with God.

But are we then supposed to stay away from spiritual disciplines? No, absolutely not! Richard Foster, in his book *Celebration of Discipline*, writes about the spiritual disciplines of prayer, fasting, worship and submission. He makes it clear at the start of the book that if the heart approach to these disciplines is wrong, we will misunderstand them. These disciplines are for the "liberation of the soul", mere vehicles that allow for greater opportunities for us to be changed. We must understand and be reminded that Christ does the changing, not us. We are merely bringing our hardened hearts to the surgery table for our great Doctor to do the changing.

If we can overcome these 10 barriers, we will have a more "open channel" with God. This enables us to have a more intimate relationship with God. To grow that relationship, we need a right understanding of God, to spend time with God, and a love-life of obedience with God. This will result in men and women after God's heart!

Discussion questions:

1   In this chapter, 10 barriers to intimacy with God were discussed.
    • Name the three barriers you battle the most with and try to explain why you find them so challenging.
    • Choose one which you think God wants you to attend to most urgently and describe how you think you should go about overcoming it.
2   Describe to each other what you think intimacy with God is all about. It will be good if you can use Scripture to support your views.

Scripture to study • 2 Timothy 2:14-3:9

Books to read• The Overcoming Life, *by Watchman Nee*
• Counterfeit Gods, *by Tim Keller*

5.3 DIVINE ADORATION

—•—

Cassie Carstens

Exclusively God's

What is the most important thing for disciples to know and focus their lives on? Jesus answers that question very clearly: "Love the Lord your God with all your heart and with all your soul and with all your mind" (Matt 22:37)! As our discipler, Jesus wants our lives to centre on God, as his life did. Paul reminds us in his letter to the Roman church: "From him and through him and for him are all things" (Rom 11:36). Our life direction should be derived from God, should be lived by his instructions and should be purposed for his glory!

That truth should frame our discipleship journey. So it makes sense then, to start it with adoration. Being led by the voice of the Father (the Word) and surrendering to his authority out of our love for him allows us to focus on his dream. As we focus on his dream we become united with his will, so that he reigns as the only God amongst us! This helps us avoid becoming too accustomed to God, and falling from awe into routine, and from routine into disregard.

The Bible warns us in 2 Timothy 3:2-4 that at the end of times, people will be lovers of themselves instead of lovers of God. To avoid this, we must help our disciples to "live Godward", and to give glory where glory belongs. Like the Jews of old, we ought to remind ourselves constantly to hold an attitude of adoration and devotion to God. The Jewish culture was full of rituals to remind them of the most central truth: "Love the Lord your God with all your heart and with all your soul and with all your strength" (Deut 6:5).

This requires an orientation of the whole self to the rule of God where life is about God alone. Where our undivided devotion is to God, and exclusively to God! Jahwe 'echad! (God alone!)

Made To Adore

Alex Ribeiro, the chaplain of the Brazilian soccer team for a time, told me the following story.

When Brazil won a soccer World Cup, the team paraded through Brazil on a bus in a victorious homecoming. As the music pounded and the announcer's voice blared, millions of people lined up in a celebratory frenzy. Looking down at the crowd, Alex noted their eyes and posture communicating complete adoration. It was as though they had lost their own consciousness in offering up praise to their heroes. They weren't just praising victorious sportsmen; they were seeking complete fusion with their newly crowned gods. People threw clothing at the bus, hoping that one of the players would catch it and rub it against their skin. When the clothing was thrown back down, the worshippers exploded in an even bigger consummation. It was a remarkable experience. The people seemed willing to sacrifice their lives in total surrender to the glory of the soccer players. As he sat on the bus, ears ringing from the crowd's euphoria, Alex realised that people are made to worship. If they don't worship God, they will find something else. Be it themselves, another person, a possession or a career; people will always find a god to worship. Then another thought struck him. If worshipping mortal beings looks like this, what should worshipping God look like?

The Westminster Confession of Faith asks: what is the chief end of man? And then responds: man's chief end is to glorify God, and to enjoy him forever.

That is what we were made for, and that is what we should pursue. We should not allow ourselves to settle for an inferior purpose in life, like worshipping ourselves or another. Since worship is one of the most pivotal elements of the Christian life, discipleship should encourage and train us towards divine adoration.

Paul Grutsch defines adoration as: "... a docile heart, an assent to God's sovereignty over our lives, a constant posture of humility before him, and gifts of love offered in homage." [86]

A Yielding Heart

In the Psalms, David describes the attitude our hearts should take when before God. He writes: "Worship the Lord and serve Him with reverence [with awe-inspired fear and submissive wonder]" (Ps 2:11 AMP).

Jesus also speaks to the attitude of the heart when he says that true worshippers will worship God in spirit and truth (John 4:23-24). We willingly submit ourselves to God, in both heart and mind. We humbly admit that God's perfection is infinite, which leads us to worship him in a manner that is reserved for him alone.

A yielding heart is an assent to God's sovereignty over our lives

We acknowledge that none but God will rule and reign over our lives. Our adoration will cultivate in us a sense of divine dependency. We are not the source of life, and we are not the source of the fruit we bear in life. As the source of our life, his Word and Spirit will direct our steps. As St. Augustine reminded us that "the essence of religion is to imitate the one whom you adore", we commit to walking as Jesus walked (1 John 2:6 ESV).

Our goal is to be conformed to Christ; to think God's thoughts after him; to desire the things he desires; to love the things he loves; to will the things he wills.

A yielding heart is a constant posture of humility before him

In his book, *The Screwtape Letters*, C.S Lewis writes about the position of the body when praying. One line in particular captures the essence of what he is saying:

"… for [humans] constantly forget… that they are animals and that whatever their bodies do affects their souls."[87]

While internal humility is the goal, we should remember that our physical actions impact our internal attitude. Gestures such as kneeling, falling prostrate (lying face down on the ground), removing shoes, and bowing are all found in the Bible. Each one is a form of adoration, and a practice of a humble inner attitude. They show a desire for humility and help mould us internally.

A yielding heart is a gift of love offered in homage
Adoration felt within will naturally seek outward expression. The Psalmist tells us we should enter the courts of God with praise. While thanksgiving acknowledges God for what he has done, praise acknowledges God for who he is. The presence of God calls for an offering appropriate to the One being adored. Whether we bring an offering of our time, talent or treasure, it should result in a life lived in sacrificial surrender to the only One who deserves it. We live this way to glorify him in everything that we do (1 Cor 10:31). So whether you eat or drink or whatever you do, do it all for the glory of God!

In this beautiful passage, William Temple encourages us to the discipline of adoration:

To worship is to quicken the conscience by the holiness of God,
to feed the mind with the truth of God,
to purge the imagination by the beauty of God,
to open the heart to the love of God,
to devote the will to the purpose of God. [88]

Silence

We cannot overlook the practice of "silence" in adoration. Mother Teresa used to say:

The fruit of silence is prayer
The fruit of prayer is faith
The fruit of faith is love
The fruit of love is service
And the fruit of service is peace. [89]

"God is a friend of silence." Sometimes we become preoccupied with our words and thoughts during adoration, instead of allowing the beauty and "awesome majesty" of our God to envelop us. It is often in reverential silence that we find ourselves entering the presence of God. We "enter" the mystery of his greatness in our silence. We do not draw God to us in adoration. Rather, he draws us to himself!

In adoration we demonstrate the saying, "A bird does not sing because it has an answer, but because it has a song."

Our song is: "For from him and through him and for him are all things. To him be the glory forever! Amen" (Rom 11:36).

Discussion questions

1   Does the phrase "exclusively God's" stir any reservation within you? If yes, why? If not, why not?
2   Do you consistently live with "awe-inspired fear and submissive wonder"? Why or why not?
3   From what you have learnt in this chapter, what do you want to apply more in your life, and how do you plan to do so?

Scripture to study • John 4:19-26 • Romans 11:33-12:1
• Job 38:1-42:6

Books to read • The Knowledge of the Holy, *by A.W. Tozer*

5.4 ASTONISHED BY GRACE

◆

Cassie Carstens

"What is the most fundamental thing I need to grasp in my relationship with Jesus, Dad?" my son asked me one day.

"My son, I am convinced that the default attitude of a follower of Christ should be a stunned reverential awe! Essentially, we should all be overwhelmed by the amazing love God has for us."

You understand grace...
At the overwhelming moment of shocked astonishment, as the realisation dawns, "Who... Me? But I don't deserve this!"

At the moment when the culprit hears the hammer hit the gavel and the voice of the judge resounds: "You're free!"

At the moment when the neglected turn in despair but hear a voice from behind saying, "I have chosen you!"

At the moment when Life Eternal says to you, "Come and enjoy it with me!"

At the moment when the nothingness of the unmerited recipient is overwhelmed by the everything-ness of the generous Giver.

That is the moment of understanding grace; the most amazing moment to savour, the moment that should stay with us forever!

This moment leads to a freedom-filled cry of joy as your deep inner thirst is quenched by the reality of being chosen, saved, liberated, crowned.

That is the perpetual astonishment that should fill every breath that we take.

So much of this has disappeared from the Christian faith and preaching. In our effort to make the Word of God "applicable", we have regressed in our "upward" attitude. Our upward gaze at the demonstration of God himself has made way for everyday concerns that dominate our minds and attitudes.

How Can We Regain Our Upward Adoration?

To regain this "astonished awe" of the grace of God, there are a few (unpopular) principles to remember.

1. An awareness of God's wrath at sin creates awe for his grace

In today's world, any concept of God's wrath upsets our self-serving modern sentiments. If we neglect the wrath of God, we dilute morality and lose our awe. J.I. Packer explains God's wrath: "God's wrath in the Bible is never the capricious, self-indulgent, irritable, morally ignoble thing that human anger so often is. It is, instead, a right and necessary reaction to objective moral evil." [90]

God's wrath is also not only an Old Testament idea. The New Testament continues with this concept:

"The wrath of God is being revealed from heaven against all the godlessness and wickedness of people, who suppress the truth by their wickedness" (Rom 1:18).

"Coming out of his mouth is a sharp sword with which to strike down the nations. 'He will rule them with an iron scepter.' He treads the winepress of the fury of the wrath of God Almighty" (Rev 19:15).

We must remember: God's wrath is his love in action against sin!

2. An awareness of our own sin makes us gasp in awe of his grace

Our pride blinds us to the "plank in our own eye" (Matt 7:3). Seldom do we see remorseful sorrow for sin at our gatherings. Our consciences are seared by an insensitivity to the voice of the Holy Spirit and an oversensitivity to the voice of our own needs (or rather, our own wants). Additionally, the lack of accountability in the church and questioning of the authority of the Word of God leads to no real remorse for sin.

We must ask God to sensitise our conscience again (2 Tim 2:25-26) because repentance leads to life (Acts 11:18).

And when we see and discuss the sins of others, we should learn to say more often, "There but for the grace of God, go I".

3. God's inner tension between his wrath and compassion leaves us in awe of his grace

We need to understand the conflict between the wrath and compassion in God's heart. Hosea gives us a glimpse of this tension:

"How can I give you up, Ephraim?
How can I hand you over, Israel?
How can I treat you like Admah?
How can I make you like Zeboyim?
My heart is changed within me;
all my compassion is aroused.
I will not carry out my fierce anger,
nor will I devastate Ephraim again.
For I am God, and not a man —
the Holy One among you.
I will not come against their cities."
(Hos 11:8-9)

Max Lucado describes this redemptive tension in the heart of God best in his book, *In The Grip of Grace*:

"Ponder the achievement of God. He doesn't condone our sin, nor does he compromise his standard. He doesn't ignore our rebellion, nor does he relax his demands. Rather... he assumes our sin and, incredibly, sentences himself. God's holiness is honored. Our sin is punished. And we are redeemed... God does what we cannot do so we can be what we dare not dream, perfect before God." [91]

How amazing that God made Jesus, who knew no sin, to be sin for us, that we might enjoy the righteousness of God through him (2 Cor 5:21). How amazing it is that grace won the battle in the heart of God! For this was surely not cheap grace! It cost the sacrifice of his most precious and only Son!

4. The astonishment: "It was done on my behalf; it was done for me personally" fills me with awe for his grace

Even after I understood that Christ died for me, I remained a spectator at the cross and not a participant. I accepted it as something that happened for me, but not by me. Only later the realisation dawned: he was wounded for our (my) transgressions, he was bruised for our (my) iniquities; the chastisement for our (my) peace was upon him, and by his stripes we are (I am) healed (Isa 53:5 NKJV). Crowder expresses this realisation well in their song, *Forgiven*:

"I'm the one who held the nail
It was cold between my fingertips
I've hidden in the garden
I've denied You with my very lips

God, I fall down to my knees
With a hammer in my hand
You look at me, arms open
Forgiven, forgiven
Child there is freedom from all of it
Say goodbye to every sin
You are forgiven

I've done things I wish I hadn't done
I've seen things I wish I hadn't seen
Just the thought of Your amazing grace
And I cry, 'Jesus, forgive me!'
God, I fall down to my knees
With a hammer in my hand
You look at me, arms open" [92]

How amazing is this love that cares and stoops and rescues. Now I too can say, "I have been crucified with Christ and I no longer live, but Christ lives in me" (Gal 2:20). Grace is for me.

5. The realisation of my freedom ignites exaltation for his grace

The most liberating thought to embrace is that Christ did all on my behalf! Romans, Galatians and Hebrews say this better than any other. We never have to earn grace. It is unconditional love! It is mercy, not merit! I am now a child of God and no longer a slave (Gal 4:7). "Christ has set us free to live a free life" (Gal 5:1 MSG). It moves us from a sense of obligation to a sense of exaltation.

But this is not only freedom from slavery, it is also freedom into a heritage. Ephesians 2:6 says that: "God raised us up with Christ and seated us with him in the heavenly realms in Christ Jesus."

We now can see things from God's perspective.

We can walk into the victory claimed by Christ.

We can rule this world with heavenly principles.

We share Christ's responsibility of authority over an unredeemed earth.

How amazing is this grace, that we are seated in a position of authority?

How Can We Demonstrate Our Upward Adoration?

1. Continued remorse demonstrates our awe for his grace

A constant consciousness of and true remorse for our sin keeps us in a continued awe of grace! This is beautifully expressed when an underdog wins a huge championship. The supporters explode with joy, but with hand on mouth as they reveal the depth of their surprise. This astonishment should never disappear!

The New Testament authors frequently spoke of repentance (Rom 8:13; 1 Cor 11:31; 1 Pet 2:1; James 4:8; 1 John 1:9). We should constantly live in this state of confession.

2. True repentance of our sin demonstrates our awe for his grace

The Greek word for repentance is *metanoia*, which literally means "to change the mind". You were thinking one way, now you think the opposite way — that's repentance. It is to shift to God's view on the matter. Ray Pritchard said it well:

> "True repentance is more than just a mental game. Repentance is a decisive change in direction. It's a change of mind that leads to a change of thinking that leads to a change of attitude that leads to a change of feeling that leads to a change of values that leads to a change in the way you live… There must be sorrow for sin because I will see my sin the way God sees it. It will grieve me the way it grieves God. And repentance implies a decision to make a break with the past and to live a life pleasing to God." [93]

3. Living in obedience demonstrates our understanding of costly grace

How can we respond to this astounding grace of Jesus? One thing we should not do is make God's grace out to be in vain; "cheap grace", as Bonhoeffer describes it in *The Cost of Discipleship*. There are two ways we do this.

The first is when we try to attain God's grace through our performance (keeping to the rules). Christ died for nothing if we try to earn God's grace or favour through performance.

"Is it not clear to you that to go back to that old rule-keeping, peer-pleasing religion would be an abandonment of everything personal and free in my relationship with God? I refuse to do that, to repudiate God's grace. If a living relationship with God could come by rule-keeping, then Christ died unnecessarily" (Gal 2:21 MSG).

If we follow our own plan and bow to our own will, we get cut off from this grace-driven life.

"I suspect you would never intend this, but this is what happens. When you attempt to live by your own religious plans and projects, you are cut off from Christ, you fall out of grace" (Gal 5:4 MSG).

The second way of making God's grace cheap is by not living a new-created life, a free life, an in-step with the Spirit life, a life free to love and serve others.

As God's grace takes deep root in our lives, we are drawn into living from love. Christ died for nothing if we are not transformed to love others sacrificially because of his sacrifice for us. If we are not living Jesus-incarnate lives, we make God's grace out to be cheap. Bonhoeffer explains it beautifully:

> "Cheap grace is the preaching of forgiveness without requiring repentance, baptism without church discipline, Communion without confession, absolution without personal confession. Cheap grace is grace without discipleship, grace without the cross, grace without Jesus Christ, living and incarnate." [94]

> "Such grace is costly because it calls us to follow, and it is grace because it calls us to follow Jesus Christ. It is costly because it costs a man his life, and it is grace because it gives a man the only true life. It is costly because it condemns sin, and grace because it justifies the sinner. Above all, it is costly because it cost God the life of his Son: 'ye were bought at a price,' and what has cost God much cannot be cheap for us. Above all, it is grace because God did not reckon his Son too dear a price to pay for our life, but delivered him up for us. Costly grace is the Incarnation of God." [95]

This grace flows into obedience. Bonhoeffer continues:

> "The road to faith passes through obedience to the call of Jesus… only he who believes is obedient, and only he who is obedient believes." [96]

"It is absolutely clear that God has called you to a free life. Just make sure that you don't use this freedom as an excuse to do whatever you want to do and destroy your freedom. Rather, use your freedom to serve one another in love; that's how freedom grows" (Gal 5:13 MSG).

Instead of trying to earn God's grace, we ought to serve others and serve Jesus from a grace-filled, abundant heart. And as we do so, our actions are love-offerings on the altar of worship. Responding to Jesus' astounding grace is to serve God and people as a way of saying "thank you". And the bigger the "thank you" we want to say, the more we will serve.

Discussion questions

1   The "hands of our hearts" are more often in a downward begging position than in an upward adoration position. Do you agree? Why is this true, or not true?
2   We mentioned five attitudes to regain awe for God's grace. Which one appeals to you most and why?
3   We mentioned three ways in which we demonstrate our awe for God's grace. Which one appeals to you most and why?

Scripture to study • Romans 3:19-26 • Ephesians 2:1-10
• Galatians 5

Books to read • What Is So Amazing About Grace, *by Philip Yancey*
• The Grace Awakening, *by Charles Swindoll* • Cost of Discipleship, *by Dietrich Bonhoeffer*

6

PRAYER AND OBEDIENCE TO THE WORD

Connected to God to hear and do what he says

Disciples (followers of Jesus) need to spend time
with God to honour him and understand his ways.
They need his direction on how to live life,
the heaven-life on earth;
and how to obey his instructions immediately.
How do we do this?

6.1 PRAYER

—•—

Cassie Carstens

Why Pray?

Prayer should become as natural to the reborn Christian as breathing; as natural as a kiss to new lovers. In that space, asking "why pray?" simply to find motivation to pray is as ridiculous as asking "why eat?" Rather, we should let the question "why pray?" guide us in the same way that a sprinter uses running; to develop capacity. The sprinter runs, not just because he must, but because he wants to grow his lung capacity, strengthen his muscles and build his endurance.

The main reasons we as disciples want to pray are well addressed by Richard Foster in his book on prayer: [97]

1   In prayer, we are moving **inward** to seek the **transformation** we need.
2   In prayer, we are moving **upward** seeking the **intimacy** we need.
3   In prayer, we are moving **outward** seeking the **ministry** we need.

In prayer, we are moving inward to seek the transformation we need.

The philosopher Søren Kierkegaard once said: "God creates everything out of nothing — and everything which God is to use he first reduces to nothing." [98] The inward prayer seeks freedom from the everlasting burden of always having to get our own way. It means the freedom to care for others, to put their needs first, to give joyfully and freely. Inward prayer is about transforming my mind and heart from chasing my will to desiring God's will.

There are three parts to the inward prayer. Inward prayer starts best with an unflinching, Holy Spirit-accompanied evaluation through the "Prayer of Examen". This is a process of immersing yourself in God's love and asking him to reveal any wickedness in your heart and thoughts to you (Ps 139:23-24).

This should lead into penthos, the "Prayer of Tears". (The Greek word penthos (πένθος) refers to the holy mourning and deep, heartfelt remorse of a broken and contrite heart.)

This prepares your heart for the last part, the "Prayers of Relinquishment", which can be uttered in the following prayers, where each prayer focuses on the death of self-interest and invites God to take control.

- The prayer of self-emptying. Pray that the same attitude of Jesus in Philippians 2 will be in you.
- The prayer of surrender. Walk with Jesus into Gethsemane and pray like him. "Not my will but yours, no matter the cost!"
- The prayer of abandon. Anything around the theme of, "Father I abandon myself into your hands; do with me what you will."
- The prayer of release. Lift your relationships, your dreams and your negative experiences in prayer to God, then leave them in his hands.
- The prayer of resurrection. You could pray: "Lord, I leave all with you. Bring back to life what will please you and advance your Kingdom."

In prayer, we are moving upward seeking the intimacy we need.
The upward move in prayer is falling down in reverence and fear of the Lord, which moves us to exalt, glorify, honour and magnify the Triune God! It is an acknowledgement of who God is, and a surrender of your life as a living sacrifice to exalt him. In essence, you are breaking open the alabaster jar of fragrance in your spirit to celebrate the beauty of God. Divine adoration comprises both thanksgiving and praise. In thanksgiving we glorify God for what

he has done for us, while in praise we acknowledge God for who he is in himself.

Foster quotes C.S. Lewis, who discussed a few obstacles to adoration:

- Inattention: getting caught up in the hustle and bustle of life.
- The wrong attention for the context: for example, analysing God instead of worshipping him (e.g. in theology we often talk about God and not to God).
- Greed: we constantly yearn for more instead of lingering to fully appreciate a specific quality.
- Conceit: being impressed with what we discover about God instead of being impressed with God.

We are supposed to be completely unselfconscious in adoration. It is all about God and nothing else. He deserves to have our consumed focus! There are many forms of adoration, but music often voices beautifully what we carry in our hearts. So let us sing unto the Lord!

WE ARE SUPPOSED TO BE COMPLETELY UNSELFCONSCIOUS IN ADORATION. IT IS ALL ABOUT GOD AND NOTHING ELSE

The upward move in prayer is about seeking the intimacy we need. Foster calls this the prayer of the heart, or the Father (Abba) prayer. It is the prayer of love and tenderness of a child to Father God. We want to talk to the One who loves us. We are children of God, and because we are loved and love our Father, our spirit cries out for communication with him (Rom 8:16). We want to hear his voice and feel his pulse because we belong to him. Thomas Kelly puts it beautifully: "We pray to acquire a gentle receptiveness to Divine breathings." You want to become, think and love like the Father. In John 5:19 Jesus says he does nothing unless his Father tells him what to do. So when John 15:4 tells us that without Jesus we can do nothing we believe it, because we find and form our character through intimacy with him. Communication with the Father is essential in the process of being conformed to Christ: to think God's thoughts after him; to desire the things he desires; to love the things he loves; to will the things he wills.

God also has an amazing desire to commune with us! There is a powerful narrative woven through the Bible describing the enormity of God's effort to reach out to, talk and live with us! It is the story of someone wanting to live in paradise with the humans he created, and paying the ultimate cost to make it possible. When Augustine says: "God thirsts to be thirsted after", we know that he loves to be adored.

In prayer, we are moving outward seeking the ministry we need.
It is critical that we do not see prayer as an abdication of responsibility for action. Our lives should be prayer in action. I experienced an enormous shift in my spiritual life when I realised that I could be the answer to many of my prayers. I learned that as I ask and listen, God often shows me how he wants to answer my prayers through me.

When Richard Foster talks about Authoritative prayer and Radical prayer, he captures the essence of prayer moving outward in ministry. In this outward prayer, we are calling forth the will of the Father on earth. We are not so much speaking to God as speaking for God. We believe things can be different, and our aim is the total transformation of persons, institutions and societies. It is a prayer to bring the resources of heaven to bear upon certain matters on earth. In holy boldness, we cover the earth with the grace and the mercy of God. However, this is not only a prophetic claiming of the victory. It is also a redemptive mediation of the intercessory priest; a suffering prayer. We take the weight of the world on our shoulders and while repenting on behalf of all sinners, we pour out their pain at the feet of God. As we are ministering redemption to many, we bless them with the grace of God.

In this prayer, we are reaching out to the world and covering the body of Christ, who do the ministry, in redemptive prayer. We are praying with and for each other until we reach maturity in the image of Christ. We must persevere in unceasing prayer. In all our waking, waiting, working and waning hours, we should be in constant conversation with God. And we should do so as a people seeing the unseen, on our knees until we enter the Promised Land.

As much as prayer should be a spontaneous and continuous conversation with God, we should also practice it in a disciplined way to deepen our relationship with God.

Other than Richard Foster's book *Prayer*, the other book that has helped us to see the width and depth of prayer is a profound little book, written by Dick Eastman, suggesting a practical prayer format called "The Hour that Changes the World". [99] We have adapted his concept slightly, but recommend that you buy the book, since our format is abbreviated. Praying an hour a day using his format should lead to an amazing enrichment in your prayer life. You don't have to follow the exact order he uses. We want to be careful to suggest steps to prayer as it risks making prayer formulaic, but we do want to make it clear that there are benefits of sequencing some spheres of prayer. For example, we believe that when Jesus taught his disciples how to pray in Matthew 6:5-14 there was a reason why he started with "Our Father in Heaven, hallowed be your name" before he went on to pray "give us today our daily bread". The idea in this chapter is simply that you use the framework as a guide to enter, explore and go deeper into the many spheres of prayer.

Praise: The Act Of Divine Adoration

When we praise God, we are adoring him for who he is and what he has done. Here are a few things you can focus on to start with (this is by no means a complete list, so add your own praise items as you see fit):

- For who he is. You can do this by focusing on the Trinity (the Father, the Son and or the Holy Spirit), or you can focus

Temple
Cleansing
Time
Ps 139:23

Word Enrich
Prayer
Jer 23:29

Silent Soul
Surrender
Ps 48:10

Develop
Holy
Alertness
Col 4:2

CONFESSION

SCRIPTURE PRAYING

WAITING

WATCHING

Recognise
God's Nature
Ps 63:3

Remember
The World
I Tim 2:1-2

PRAISE

INTERCESSION

Prayer should begin
and conclude at this
level of praise

"What, could
you not watch
with me one
hour? Watch
and pray."
Matt 26:40-41

PRAISE

PETITION

Recognise
God's Nature
Ps 52:9

Share
Personal
Needs
Matt 7:7

LISTENING

THANKSGIVING

SINGING

Receive
Spiritual
Instruction
Eccles 5:2

MEDITATION

Confess my
Blessings
I Thess 5:18

Ponder
Spiritual
Themes
Josh 1:8

Worship
In Song
Ps 100:2

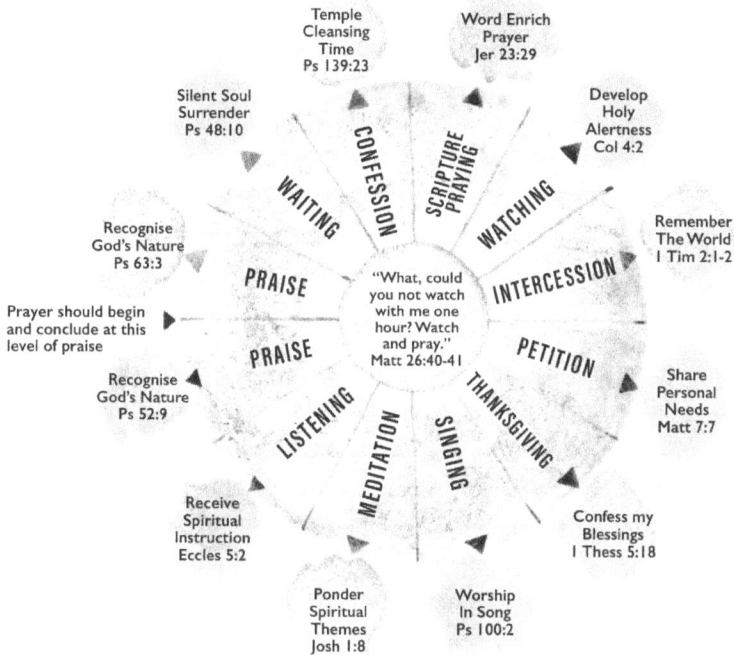

on one or more of his attributes (see chapter 5.1). Adoring
God is like staring at him, and allowing his gaze to see
through you, until you become more like him.

- For what he has created. Sometimes it is good to do this
with open eyes in nature, but it is also important that you
praise him for creating us. Genesis 1 and Psalm 8 clearly
state that humanity is the most esteemed of his creation.
- For the Bible. If it was not for his Word, how would we ever
understand his Story (see chapter 5.1)? The Bible is one of
the key ways the Spirit talks with us. It is our handbook for
life, and seed that grows into a harvest! Psalm 19 and
Psalm 119 provide a great place to adore God for his Word!
- For his plan of redemption and reconciliation. His dream
and how amazing that, by his free grace, he included us in!
Romans 1-11 helps us with this!

- For including you in his plan. How marvellous to know we are part of God's eternal plan! If we understand how small we are compared to the One that created the Universe, then we will marvel at our inclusion in his eternal plan. Ephesians 1-3 and the book of Hebrews may help us with this.

Waiting: The Act Of Silent Soul Surrender

- You are surrendering to be clay in the Potter's hand, to rest in God and allow him to mould you.
- This is a time of waiting, of sharing your love with God and allowing him to whisper into your soul that he loves you.
- In this part of the process, imagine yourself slamming a big door in the world's face for the sake of privacy with God. It brings you into a quiet attentiveness where you feel refreshed and re-orientated (centred) on God!
- You should invite the Holy Spirit to come and take control, to speak to your spirit so you can pray in the Spirit — the prayer of the heart.
- This is where we find intimate closeness with God as we draw near to him so he can draw near to us. The distance between God and us dissolves and we find joy in imparting ourselves to one another.
- This is the start of the process Mother Teresa spoke of. "The fruit of silence is prayer; the fruit of prayer is faith; the fruit of faith is love; the fruit of love is service; and the fruit of service is peace."

Confession: The Act Of Temple Cleansing Starts

- There is no escape now, and due to the knowledge of his love also no reason to hide.
- Your spirit acknowledges that God is right, good, and holy, and leads you to wonder "Is there anything in me that is right, good or holy?"

- "Peter, do you love me?" "[Your name], do you love me?" Let the painfully delivered question soak into your soul.
- Confess all your sins you know of, and even the things you aren't aware of. Don't hide behind fig leaves. Don't blame others, make excuses or hope the circumstances will change.
- Acknowledge your sins. Be specific and direct. Name them. Don't sugarcoat anything.
- Acknowledge that your sins are not just a mistake, but the result of an evil nature in you which you do not have under control.
- Face the root of all your sins, which is pride and rebellion against God!
- This is where you acknowledge that you, not Pontius Pilate, have murdered God!
- Declare yourself guilty as charged, one sin at a time!
- Here your heart cries out: "Go away from me, I am a sinful man."

Praying Scripture
- The first step here is to listen to the Word declaring you free on behalf of Christ's atonement on the cross (1 John 1:9; Rom 8:1).
- Read the Word, taking in divine nourishment as you seek to return to God's agenda.
- As you look from the perspective of God's Word, you should start seeing things differently again. The Word helps you appreciate your identity in Christ, feeds you God's way of thinking and provides you with the armour to win the battle against darkness.
- You converse with God by praying the Word, agreeing with him, strengthening your own mind and finding a new way.

Watching: The Act Of Holy (And Mental) Alertness

This alertness has more than one dimension.

- We should be alert to being steered in the right direction by God (Hab 2:1).
- We should remain prepared so that the second coming will not catch us unaware (Matt 24:24-42; 25:13).
- We should guard against the influence of the evil one and our own flesh (Matt 26:41) to maintain spiritual integrity. 1 Timothy 4:16 says: "Watch (guard) your life and doctrine closely." This is a call to faithfulness in faith and conduct. (See also 1 Peter 5:8 and the letters to the churches in Revelation 2 and 3.)
- Then there is the watchfulness against false doctrine (see 2 Peter 2).
- This alertness is also the prayer of Paul for the Ephesians (1:18), "that the eyes of your heart may be enlightened." This is to have insight into the rich inheritance God has in store for the saints.
- In this prayer we pray for discernment, guidance, discovery and focus. We pray that God will help us to know Kairos (God's opportune time for something). We pray that we will have an acute sensitivity to God's preferences.

Intercession: The Act of Earnest Appeal

In intercessory prayer, we deal with three parts of the Lord's Prayer

1 **Let your Kingdom come… on earth as it is in heaven**
   - We first get involved in God's plan for salvation. Start with intercessory prayer for Kingdom expansion worldwide, then bring it closer. Pray for your country, city, neighbourhood and, finally, individuals you know.

2 **Give us today our daily bread**
   - When you pray for the needs of people, start with the needs of others before yourself, and for their spiritual

needs before their other needs. Mediate between God and believing or unbelieving friends. Stand in the gap for them. After that you can follow with your own needs (see the section on petition below). It is essential that our prayers do not get stuck in the alley of our own needs. Our prayers should have a spirit of giving/serving before asking.

3 **Lead us not into temptation, but deliver us from evil**
   - The prayer for victory over the flesh and for protection against the evil one are spiritual battle prayers. They are part of putting on the armour (Eph 6), and they acknowledge that God the Father is the victor through his Son and his Spirit. Repenting on behalf of others (priestly prayers) should be included in this process.

Pray through these issues for specific people. When doing intercessory prayer, make sure you pray "through" something before you move on. Your spirit will tell you when the breakthrough comes.

Petition: The Act of Personal Requests

- In this prayer, we confess our helplessness. We do not deserve God's favour and cannot buy his sympathy, but we need his unmerited grace to open new outcomes for us. We should be careful to avoid falling into a "genie God" theology here though (expecting that God will give you anything you desire if you just pray hard enough). The Jabez kind of prayer (1 Chron 4:10) is appropriate here, but it is much more important that we pray for the capacity we need to maximise opportunities.
- In this prayer, the attitude of our heart should be that of a beggar's humility and a servant's carefulness. We should never pray with a demanding spirit. The attitude of the heart should be that of one who understands that we deserve absolutely nothing! On the other hand, we should

also not neglect the fact that we are children of God and not slaves. God wants to give us what is good for us. If our focus is unselfish, we can pray with the confidence of a friend.

- We should also be specific in this prayer. This will help lift our faith when God answers the prayer.

Thanksgiving: The Act Of Appreciation

- We are children of the living God. Regardless of our circumstances, that knowledge should help us live with an abundance mentality. We must fight against adopting a scarcity or entitlement mentality (assuming we will never have enough, or that life owes us something) or victim mentality (being unwilling to take responsibility for our current behaviours and attitudes due to past traumas).
- Thanksgiving is the theme song of the Christian. As Izaak Walton puts it, "God has two dwelling places: one in heaven and the other in a thankful heart." We should stay aware of the blessings we have.
- Humility is the root from which contentment grows, which leads to an attitude of deep gratitude!
- Repeatedly asking without thanking God for what he has given is like the nine lepers in Luke 17:11-19 who were healed but never returned to thank Jesus. That displays a despicable consumer mentality, which we must avoid at all costs. A thankful heart is the parent of all the other virtues.
- When we thank God in prayer, we should consider all he has done for us regarding our salvation and sanctification first. Then we can spend time on answered prayers and all our other blessings.
- We should never neglect to thank God for hard times which teach us so much! The benefits of pain and suffering are many.

Singing: The Act Of Melodic Worship

- 41 Psalms mention "singing praises". Here we can use recorded praise and worship music or hum our own songs to God.
- Themes for praise: all the aspects mentioned in sector one under the theme of praise.
- As we sing, we should remember the centrality of praise and worship in battles in the Old Testament (e.g. 2 Chron 20). This is to proclaim that the battle is not ours, but the Lord's.

Meditation: The Act Of Spiritual Evaluation

- This is the process of creating the "emotional and spiritual space which allows Christ to construct an inner sanctuary in the heart." [100] It deepens the intimacy of our relationship with God as we learn to hear and obey his voice (the primary purpose of this act.) How do we do this? We stop our "busyness" (even the "busyness" in our prayers).
- According to Foster, four practices help us find contemplative solitude:
  - Hesychia, the prayer of rest: literally, a process of finding stillness and tranquillity in mind and spirit.
  - Silencio: letting go of our desire to control and fix everything. Silence helps a great deal.
  - Recollection: considering our direction in life, particularly who we are in Christ and what our purpose for being is.
  - The prayer of ecstasy: allowing God to drop an excitement for him in our hearts.
- Sometimes our physical posture can also help us focus on God. For example, lying prostrate on the floor moves us toward submission and humility, while turning your palms to face upwards is a gesture of receptivity. Standing with your hands in the air or moving around might reflect delight or rejoicing.

- We gaze upon God in an act of supreme attention. We focus our hearts to will one thing!
- We imagine the Kingdom of God on earth from what we have learnt in the Bible.
- We ponder a spiritual theme or passage from the Bible, not as a passive observer, but as an active participant in the story.
- We can also meditate on the events of our time to understand their significance — the Bible in one hand and a newspaper in the other.
- These practices help us cultivate a harvest of fresh God-given thoughts.
- Memorising Scripture helps us "stay with God's mind" on things. In her book, *Switch On Your Brain*, Dr. Caroline Leaf states that "your mind can powerfully and unexpectedly change your brain in positive ways when you intentionally direct your attention." She adds: "When we direct our rest by introspection, self-reflection, and prayer; when we catch our thoughts; when we memorise Scripture; when we develop our mind intellectually, we accelerate the default mode network (DMN) and improve brain function as well as mind, body, and spiritual health." [101] Proverbs 4:23 confirms this, telling us to guard our hearts (in Judean tradition this means mind) above all else, for everything we do flows from it.

Listening: The Act Of Receiving Instructions

- We listen attentively, as an employee receiving their work for the day from their boss. If the instructions require a change in behaviour, we accept it and adapt accordingly.
- This act practices the law of obeying the inner voice. We pray with an attentive spirit that says: "What do you want me to do, Lord?"
- As an active participant in studying the Word, we receive guidance from the Word.

- After receiving from God, we need validation from the body of Christ. You should test what you hear from God with other believers who live by the guidance of the Holy Spirit.
- Finally, we depart with an attitude of immediate obedience to carry out the instructions we received.
- Life and prayer become interwoven and our good deeds are love offerings to God.

Praise: The Act Of Divine Magnification

- In this section, we let our praises allow the power of God to take control of our whole life.
- We are inviting God to sign his signature under all the wisdom and instructions we have received in our prayer.
- As we have learnt through Jesus' instruction on prayer, the prayer should finish with the exaltation of God. He is the Lord of his Kingdom; he is the all-powerful Master of all; he is the only One deserving the glory!

We hope that the above prayer framework motivates you to pray and opens your eyes to the rich possibilities of prayer. While focused prayer disciplines are important, prayer should become a lifestyle as we walk with God. This prayer methodology should be used to strengthen your relationship with God, not as a religious habit.

We would like to close this chapter with an encouragement to make prayer not only a scheduled event, but an ongoing event.

Foster offers four valuable steps towards a life of unceasing prayer:

1 Start with discipline. Make sure this is regular, like Daniel. Use everyday activities to remind you to pray, like mealtimes or when you are in the car.
2 Prayer (breathed longings of wonder and adoration) should settle in your subconscious like music playing in the background of your life. This will help you cope with life better.

3   Prayer moves into the heart so that sentiment and reason can act together. Our heart moves with God's heart.

4   Lastly, prayer permeates our whole personality, and like our breath and blood, moves through our entire body towards the Divine union. (Don't worry if this concept seems impossible right now. God is the one who performs this in us!)

In prayer, we live with God and he lives with us!

Discussion questions

1   How enriched are your prayer times currently?

2   What do you understand the value of prayer to be?

3   When you look at Dick Eastman's 12 disciplines in "The Hour that Changes the World", which prayer disciplines do you not apply, and what might happen if you start applying them?

4   What is the one new enriching thing you are going to do in your prayer life from now on?

Scripture to study • Matthew 6:5-18

Books to read • Prayer, *by Richard Foster* • The Hour that Changes the World, *by Dick Eastman* • Red Moon Rising, *by Pete Greig and Dave Roberts*

6.2 HEARING GOD'S VOICE

Cassie Carstens

The apostle John is clear that the way we demonstrate our love to God is through obedience (John 14:23; 1 John 5:3). Biblical obedience to God means to hear, trust, submit and surrender to God and his Word, and then act on his instructions. In other words, we must be directed by the Spirit, not by our own will. The question is, how can we make sure that our lives are not led by our own understanding (Prov 3:5), but by the Spirit of God (John 14:26)?

The Spirit vs. The Mind

From the first temptation of Adam and Eve in paradise, Satan has tried to convince us that we should follow our own will and determine right and wrong for ourselves. Ever since then we have battled to distinguish God's soft voice from the racket of our self-centred preferences which drown out all other sound.

People often trust their minds when making decisions, and not the Holy Spirit. This is why the Bible says there are things the mind has not conceived (1 Cor 2:9), things God has revealed to us by his Spirit (1 Cor 2:10) that we can only understand when we have the Spirit (1 Cor 2:12-14). Only by the Spirit do we have the mind of Christ (1 Cor 2:16). That is why many have ears but do not hear; eyes but do not see (Matt 13:15; Mark 8:18).

PEOPLE OFTEN TRUST THEIR MINDS WHEN MAKING DECISIONS, AND NOT THE HOLY SPIRIT

Our preconceived ideas can so often lead us away from hearing God's voice. We get stuck in patterns that confirm and justify our convictions, but do not allow new or deeper understanding to enter our minds. Our knowledge then leads us to self-sufficiency, self-reliance and self-righteousness (Gal 5), and we react from that basis. We follow our own reasoning and end up with man-made conclusions. Some theologians even confess that their knowledge has blocked them from a sensitive understanding of the Spirit. We have to reach a point where we do not justify our existing convictions, but where we have a soft heart to receive from the Spirit.

Purifying The Conscience

Watchman Nee has helped me to focus on listening to the Spirit and to make my mind, will and emotions subservient to the Spirit. He says:

> "[The human spirit] has three main functions: These are conscience, intuition and communion. The conscience is the discerning organ which distinguishes right and wrong... Often reasoning will justify things which our conscience judges... If man should do wrong, it will raise its voice of accusation. Intuition is the sensing organ of the human spirit. [It is very different from physical sense, coming to us] independent of any outside influence. That knowledge which comes to us without any help from the mind, emotion or volition comes intuitively. We really 'know' through our intuition; our mind merely helps us to 'understand.' The revelations of God and all the movements of the Holy Spirit are known to the believer through his intuition... Communion is worshiping God... God is not apprehended by our thoughts, feelings or intentions, for He can only be known directly in our spirits. Our worship of God and God's communications with us are directly in the spirit. They take place in 'the inner man,' not in the soul or outward man... these three elements of conscience, intuition and communion are deeply interrelated and function coordinately." [102]

We ought to discipline ourselves to purify the conscience. Our conscience, if not constantly revitalised, may grow calloused and lose sensitivity. It should function like a tuning fork for our behaviour. Calibrated to the Living Spirit, it should immediately warn us when we go off tune. To keep the conscience attuned, we should stay close to the Word (Ps 139:23-24) and the Spirit, but also constantly examine it and allow our mentors to do the same.

Purifying the conscience means to regularly ask God to reveal all sin and egocentric conduct. Ask God to show us our motives; ask our table of support to question our reasons and check our obedience. Ask God to expose us to cultures or people that broaden our culturally blinkered perspectives.

Andrew Murray wrote, "That Spirit teaches me to yield my will entirely to the will of the Father. He opens my ear to wait in great gentleness and teachableness of soul for what the Father has day by day to speak and to teach. He discloses to me how union with God's will is union with God himself; how entire surrender to God's will is the Father's claim, the Son's example, and the true blessedness of the soul." [103]

Shutting Out Wrong Voices

In his book, *Theory U*, Otto Scharmer says we will download and function from past patterns of thinking and behaviour unless we go through a transformation process to enable us to connect with God, the Source. To experience "presencing" as we connect with the Source, we need to:

- Suspend the voice of judgement to have an open mind and see with fresh eyes;
- Redirect by getting rid of the voice of cynicism to open our heart to a new discovery;
- Break through the voice of fear to have a fearless open will;
- Rediscover who we are and what our mission is;
- Then invite the new life to well up in us.

The main message from this theory is that we must get rid of the old and open up to the new. We must reconnect with God, the Source, by re-affirming our identity and purpose as a Kingdom person before we can engage in his new reality.

We are attuned to a worldly way of thinking. The Bible calls this the pattern of the world. In his book, *Hearing God's Voice* (2002), Henry Blackaby writes a profound chapter on lies and half-truths. He gives guidance on how to avoid things that have the power to distract us from God's voice, and shows how to distinguish between:

- **God's voice and Satan's voice.** Satan is happy with shallow conversions; he offers short-cuts like half-hearted obedience; he dilutes (justifies) sin; he brings division; he brings pride and he excuses the means.
- **God's will and our will.** When our will does not honour God, avoids perseverance and opposes the Bible, we should steer away from it.
- **False prophets and true prophets.** The Bible often warns against false prophets, and recent history is full of false predictions of the future and Christ's second coming.
- **God's voice and the world's voice.** Where the world focuses on strengths, God works through your weakness. Where the world urges you to claim your rights, God says you should take up your cross. Where the world pushes for values like success in performance and finances, God has other values like descending into greatness (see chapter 4.4). Where the world uses common sense, God uses divine wisdom. Where the world is out to benefit from others, Jesus as Good Shepherd sacrifices. Where the world divides, God unites.
- **The good and the best.** We often sacrifice the best by getting involved with good things. We look at opportunities offered to us instead of discovering God's timing and intention for our lives.

The world is abuzz with voices clamouring for our attention and response, so we must attune to God's voice so he can direct our lives. There are loud voices on "my rights", prosperity theology, marriage, abortion, and "don't be judgemental" as an excuse to sin. Aligning oneself to the truth of the Word of God has become more important than ever before. In most of these voices there is an omission of "cross-theology", or "sacrificial self-denial". This is exactly what 2 Timothy 3:2 says, that in the last days people will be "lovers of themselves".

Shutting yourself off from wrong voices is critical to having a mind, heart and will open to receiving God's voice. A child cannot, while licking an ice-cream, ask his dad if he can have an ice-cream, and a young girl won't discover if the guy she is kissing is right for her while kissing him. Likewise, a businessman can't decide clearly how much to give to God's kingdom work while involved in dodgy deals. We need to separate ourselves from the wrong before we can know the right. This is what sanctification means: to separate from!

How To Approach God

Before we can hear the voice of God, we should give attention to how we approach God. How we prepare our heart, attitude and approach is essential for the voice or Word of God to fall into fertile soil in our hearts.

THE MEETING WITH GOD SHOULD BE IN GOD'S HABITAT (OR HOUSE), NOT YOURS

The meeting with God should be in God's habitat (or house), not yours (Ps 26:8; 27:4). I don't know if you have also experienced how the outcome of a meeting on a contentious issue can be completely different depending on where it is held. In your own house, you have control. In another's house you are more vulnerable, and the other person has the upper hand. The rules of their house apply. We should approach God in a way that affirms he has the upper hand. We will not go for permission; we will go for instruction. We will not go for endorsement; we will go for the script. He is the speaker and we are the listeners. We go in the fear (awe-filled adoration) of God, knocking on his door.

Secondly, the meeting should be like a child sitting on their father's lap.

My first child developed the habit of sitting on my lap while I was working at my desk. I soon discovered that the purpose was not only physical closeness — that as well; but the actual reason was to imitate me. I later discovered that she held the telephone squeezed between her neck and shoulder exactly as I did… and other mannerisms followed. She was learning the ways of dad.

Psalm 103:7 says that God made his deeds known to Israel, but his ways known to Moses. There is a dramatic difference here. God's ways are his character. You do not know a person just by their deeds. Character is much more intimate than behaviour. We have to get to know God's being before we discover his doing. Our request should first be: "Lord, give me your heart, before you give me your answer."

All Aligned?

There was once a harbour which was challenging to traverse without crashing against the wall. But one old skipper had no problem, getting in and out of the tricky waters quickly and without a scratch. When others asked him how he did it, he pointed to the land beyond the harbour. "Do you see those street lights? If you position yourself by watching the lights and changing course until they align, you will sail through without a scratch every time."

It works in the same way in discovering the will of God. There are conditions that must be aligned before we should move ahead. What are these conditions?

- **Complete surrender to God so that you will accept whatever he says (Rom 12:1-2). This includes:**

- Confessing all your sin (Isa 59:1-2; 1 John 1:9),
- Counteracting your weaknesses/insecurities,
- Shunning and evading all worldly approaches,
- Availing your whole life to God and his purposes (Jer 29:11-14a) and
- Asking God for a teachable attitude (James 4:6).
- **Pray for the renewal of your mind (Rom 12:2).**
  - Present your mind to God so he can use it and fill it with anointed reason and divine vision (Prov 3:5-7).
  - Transforming the mind from the pattern of the world to a truth-based foundation may take a long time in the discipling process.
- **Looking at the issue from the general framework of the Bible, more than the particular.**
  - Continue your daily disciplined studying of the Bible while looking for the answer (2 Tim 3:16).
  - Be careful not to seek quick (or easy) answers.
- **Ask the Holy Spirit** for sanctification and guidance (John 7:37-39).
- **Pray** that the eyes of your heart might be enlightened.
- **Pray** constantly for God to give you a spirit of wisdom and revelation in the knowledge of him (Eph 1:17-18; Ps 119:18).
- **Ask yourself** if it will make you more like Christ, with selfless sacrificial love as the most evident characteristic (Rom 8:28-29).
- **Ask yourself** if there is clear evidence that this will advance the Kingdom (2 Cor 2:14,16).
- **Ask yourself** if the church family (your table of support) agree with and support it (Prov 12:15; 19:20; Eph 3:18-19).
- **Ask yourself** if it matches the Kairos (appropriate timing) of God (1 Chr 12:32; Rom 13:11).
- **Ask yourself** if peace (qualified as not a good feeling, but a sense that it is right) follows your decision (Col 3:15).

If one of the above elements are not aligned with the rest, you should wait on making a decision until all are aligned.

Corporate Guidance

The early church believed that no one could hear the whole counsel of God in isolation. The Spirit-directed body needed to find direction from God. As Richard Foster puts it, "We would be well advised to encourage groups of people to fast, pray, and worship together until they have discerned the mind of the Lord." [104]

Due to the hyper-individualised culture of today, too many people make decisions on their own. Your table of support could help a lot! They can usually see the best option because they are more objective than you. Not only does this help with decision-making, but in many cases it is the more biblical way of making a decision.

We have found that the factors most neglected in discovering God's will are the dilemmas in society and the Kairos (opportune time) of God. These factors help us "look outward" to where God is moving and move us towards where he wants to draw our energy. Instead, our focus is usually on our concerns, and we get tangled in our emotions to the point that our motives are no longer clear. Our table of support should help us carry our personal concerns so that the bulk of our decision-making energy can go to corporate searching.

Discussion questions

1 Since hearing the voice of God is not as simple as "switching on the switch", what is currently missing in your relationship with God to hear him more clearly?

2 We saw that many factors must be aligned before we can go ahead with a decision. Which of these factors do you ignore when seeking God's will, and what is the danger of ignoring them?

3 How are you currently involving others to give you a better understanding of God and his will for your life?

Scripture to study • Proverbs 3:5-7 • Romans 12:1-2
• Ephesians 3:17-19 • Luke 8:4-15

Books to read • Hearing God's Voice, *by Henry T. Blackaby and Richard Blackaby* • The Spiritual Man, *by Watchman Nee*

6.3 OBEDIENCE TO THE WORD

—•—

John Yip

"The great tragedy of modern evangelism is in calling
many to belief but few to obedience." [105]

For some, the word "obedience" evokes negative reactions: fear, revulsion, fun-spoiling. This is especially true if your experience of Christianity was strict or legalistic. However, the Bible is full of references to obedience: obey, observe, keep, adhere, follow, fulfil, hold fast, live by, submit, be faithful. Some scholars estimate there are over 2,000 verses related to obedience. Here are some key principles to help us understand "obedience" in a healthier way.

Position vs Performance

The first step to joy-based obedience is clarity about our position in Christ. What I mean by "position in Christ" is the following.

God created mankind in his image, and it was very good (Gen 1:27, 31). But sin entered the world and infected all of us (Rom 3:23), breaking our relationship with God (Isa 59:2). The price of sin is death (Rom 6:23), but God sent Jesus to die on the cross for us. Instead of staying dead he rose from the grave, conquering sin and death (John 3:16; Rom 5:8; 1 Cor 15:3-4). It is God's gift of grace through faith that saves us (Eph 2:8-9) and restores us into right relationship with him and entry into heaven (John 3:36). We must confess our sins, confess Jesus as Lord, and believe that God raised him from the dead, so that we will be saved (1 John 1:9; Rom 10:9).

If we do this, then our position/status in Christ is secure. It is faith in Christ and his grace that rescues us from eternal condemnation. It is not our obedience-based performance that saves us. Therefore, performing obedient actions is not the precondition for justification. It is by faith we are justified (Rom 5:1).

Knowing our position in Christ frees us to obey God with joy within a father-son relationship, not a chief-slave relationship. It restores us from a relationship based on fear, shame or guilt.

Obedience Is A Fruit Of Grace, Love And Gratitude

"Love is the root, obedience is the fruit." [106]

A right and sober understanding of man's sinful depravity leads to an immediate recognition that we need grace. Once we have received grace, we begin to experience God's love, which in turn leads to heartfelt gratitude. Gratitude empowers a response of obedience and service, which results in a better society.

There is an important nuance here which is worth restating. If our starting point is desiring a better society — "to bring heaven home" — then the temptation to perform good works may enslave us. But if our starting point is the Gospel of divine grace, then our works of obedient service and godly love flow from our joyful response to God's unconditional love which sets us free. A corresponding love for God and people now drives our efforts toward selfless sacrificial love, which leads to community transformation and nation-building.

IF WE REALLY UNDERSTOOD THE ROOTS OF GRACE-BASED OBEDIENCE, IT WOULD NOT BE BURDENSOME

Let's make this practical. Jesus says, "Love your enemies". Can we do it? Is this not extremely hard, almost impossible? But if we allow the knowledge that God loved us as his enemy to overwhelm us, the challenge of a loving act (e.g. forgiveness) dissolves in our over-whelmed gratitude for his grace.

If we really understood the roots of grace-based obedience, it would not be burdensome. It would be a joy to obey God. Being in an intimate awe-struck love relationship with Jesus makes it easy to obey and please our friend, confidant, lover, saviour, shepherd and king.

"In fact, this is love for God: to keep his commands. And his commands are not burdensome" (1 John 5:3).

Obedience As A Love Language To God

A study of John 14-15 is valuable for many reasons. Many people focus on the promise of the Holy Spirit in John 14, and the promise of "doing even greater things [than Jesus]" in John 14:12. The Parable of the Vine in John 15 is another firm favourite. However, more exposition on the dynamic between love and obedience is worthwhile. "If you love me, keep my commands" (John 14:15).

"'Whoever has my commands and keeps them is the one who loves me. The one who loves me will be loved by my Father, and I too will love them and show myself to them'" (John 14:21).

"Jesus replied, 'Anyone who loves me will obey my teaching. My Father will love them, and we will come to them and make our home with them. Anyone who does not love me will not obey my teaching. These words you hear are not my own; they belong to the Father who sent me'" (John 14:23-24).

"As the Father has loved me, so have I loved you. Now remain in my love. If you keep my commands, you will remain in my love, just as I have kept my Father's commands and remain in his love" (John 15:9-10).

As you read these verses, what is the starting point — is it love or obedience first? You are right! In a sense, it does not matter which is the starting point. Love and obedience can be viewed as a cycle. To love is to obey and to obey is to love.

> Grace and mercy are God's love language to mankind. We receive grace and mercy from God. We cannot show God grace and mercy, so what is our love language to God? John says that our love for each other is a result of obedience to God's commands. Our love for God is defined by our obedience. In fact it appears that God spells love o-b-e-y. [107]

If you love God, obey him! If you obey God, you love him!

Obedience And Knowledge

God speaks through the Bible, which emphasises the importance of studying it and knowing it. It's worthwhile noting that "knowing" is not the same as "obeying".

As your understanding of the Bible deepens, it should enhance your lifestyle of obedience. It is better to obey what little you know than to amass impressive Bible knowledge but not obey any of it. Beware of becoming prideful because of your knowledge (1 Cor 8:1).

It's interesting that Jesus asks his disciples to teach their disciples "to obey", instead of asking them to teach their disciples knowledge. Let's take another look at Matthew 28:19-20:

"Therefore go and make disciples... and teaching them to obey everything I have commanded you..."

Many Christians forget the words "to obey" in the above scripture. Thus, when they think about discipling others, they picture "teaching them everything" instead of teaching them how to obey.

Obedience Is Typically A Community Practice

"The call to discipleship is the call to relationship." [108]

It is easy to miss that the Scriptures were intended for public reading to a community of believers, not primarily for individual consumption (Ex 24:7; Neh 8; 13; 2 Kings 23:2; Josh 8:34-35; Col 4:16; Acts 15:21). The instructions in the Bible were given to the ones present at the time, and for subsequent generations to obey together. The instructions included promises too. See this example:

"These are the commands, decrees and laws the Lord your God directed me to teach you to observe in the land that you are crossing the Jordan to possess, so that you, your children and their children after them may fear the Lord your God as long as you live by keeping all his decrees and commands that I give you, and so that you may enjoy long life. Hear, Israel, and be careful to obey so that it may go well with you and that you may increase greatly in a land flowing with milk and honey, just as the Lord, the God of your ancestors, promised you" (Deut 6:1-3).

Another example of community practice is the Great Commission in Matthew 28, specifically in verse 19, where Jesus instructs his disciples to make disciples of "all nations".

One discouraging impact of the secular-humanistic worldview is the way we read, interpret and apply the Bible individualistically. In our discipling movement, we believe the community should listen and obey together, as demonstrated in this story in Acts 13:1-3.

"Now in the church at Antioch there were prophets and teachers: Barnabas, Simeon called Niger, Lucius of Cyrene, Manaen (who had been brought up with Herod the tetrarch) and Saul. While they were worshiping the Lord and fasting, the Holy Spirit said, 'Set apart for me Barnabas and Saul for the work to which I have called them.' So after they had fasted and prayed, they placed their hands on them and sent them off" (Acts 13:1-3).

This encourages us to listen together as a group/team/community/ church for the steps of obedience we should take together. We ask forgiveness for the body. We ask for guidance as the body. We also encourage each other to stay true to commands given to us by God.

"Though we all have to enter upon discipleship alone, we do not remain alone." [109]

Obedience Is Immediate

In our disciple-making movement, we believe obedience should be immediate. Our rule-of-thumb is to have at the most 24-48 hours to comply with what God is saying to us or the community. If we do not, the Word falls to the ground and may not bear the intended "fruit". It could take weeks or even years to implement fully (e.g. read the Bible in one year, move cross-culturally, etc.), but when God convicts, the first step of obedience should happen within 24-48 hours. Otherwise, the conviction is parked and usually forgotten. Procrastinating the commitment is disobedience most of the time.

Yes, we ought to be mindful that the 48-hour rule-of-thumb does not become a set-in-stone-rule. Immediate obedience is a principle, not a decree. That said, it is an important principle for us to practice. We want to make sure we develop a natural inclination to act on what God says without a second thought.

Immediate obedience also implies "first-time obedience". This is intuitive to any parent. Your hope is for your children to obey your instructions the first time you give them, and not to have to repeat yourself ad nauseam. Thankfully, God is gracious and sometimes offers multiple opportunities (like in the story of Jonah), but if we continue to disobey, we may lose the joy and growth opportunity of being in step with God on his mission.

A teenager started to practice the immediate obedience principle. One morning she read that we have to share the Gospel. She felt prompted by the Holy Spirit to go immediately to the nearby supermarket to obey what she read. Walking between the shelves, she saw an adult man and felt compelled to obey her earlier prompting. She walked up to him and said politely: "Sir, I just want to tell you that God loves you deeply!" The man exploded in anger: "Who are you to tell me this? You do not even know me. How dare you? You are the third person this morning to tell me this!" It would appear the obedience reaped the intended results.

God still speaks to his children today. He does this primarily through the Bible, and then through secondary means, which should always be validated by the Bible. (See the previous chapter on hearing God's voice.) When God speaks, what justification is there to disobey him? And when God speaks, is there any valid reason to delay our obedience? This is why immediate obedience is key.

We have discovered a tendency in many disciples to over-spiritualise (and therefore delay) their obedience. Here are some phrases we have picked up that illustrate when they might be falling into that trap:

"I am seeking God's will."

"I am waiting to hear from God on this matter."

"I am waiting for God to speak, direct or instruct."

"I know what God has instructed, but I am consulting with my mentors."

None of the statements above are wrong in and of themselves, but they become disobedience when they lead to procrastination. Delaying the obedience step can nullify the obedience step since it could lead to you missing the intended purpose. Be careful to use "waiting upon the Lord" as an excuse not to obey immediately.

If the action is not unbiblical, immoral or illegal, and does not contradict your primary and secondary calling, we would encourage you to act instead of delaying further. If you must ask a question, then rather ask "why should I not do it now?"

In your discipleship group, seek to establish a culture of immediate obedience. You could do this by asking your discipleship group at every gathering: "What will we/I obey from what we read in God's Word today?" Then follow up with this accountability question at the next gathering: "How did you obey God's Word since our last gathering?"

Obedience Is Costly

The USA military coined the acronym VUCA (Volatile, Uncertain, Complex, Ambiguous) to describe the modern battlefield. No one is spared from VUCA — not multinational conglomerates, global aid agencies, or even the church. In this politically correct time and with almost-instant access to information, many truths that were once held as absolute are today not as clear-cut. Allowing biblical precepts to govern our decisions on marriage, gender identity, divorce, abortion, addiction, greed and other issues can quickly lead to accusations of intolerance or discrimination.

Obedience is not an excuse for being insensitive. But being sensitive does not automatically mean the condoning and enabling of immoral living. As followers of Jesus, we must be shrewd as serpents and as innocent as doves (Matt 10:16). Persecution is the norm for anyone that earnestly follows Jesus (Matt 10:17-39). Expect obedience to lead to persecution. To stand for truth is costly.

The departure point of being obedient is total surrender (irrespective of the cost) to the will of God! "God creates out of nothing. Therefore, until a man is nothing, God can make nothing out of him." [110]

As Jesus' disciples, we embrace his worldview. We have his attitude (Phil 2:5). We carry our cross (Luke 14:27). Our old self has died (Rom 6:6). I can no longer live as my own person (Gal 2:20). Earth is not my permanent home (John 14:2-3). We become foot washers (John 13:15-16). And there are many more Kingdom counter-intuitive ideas which we hope you will discover in your adventure of becoming more like Jesus. As Dietrich Bonhoeffer says in *The Cost of Discipleship*, "When Christ calls a man, he bids him come and die." [111]

Obedience Is Holiness And A Sweet Fragrance To Seekers

"Since everything will be destroyed in this way, what kind of people ought you to be? You ought to live holy and godly lives" (2 Pet 3:11).

God is holy. Jesus consecrates us through his blood so we can stand confidently in God's presence. Obedience separates us from sin and affirms our status as those whose citizenship is in heaven.

"For the grace of God has appeared that offers salvation to all people. It teaches us to say no to ungodliness and worldly passions, and to live self-controlled, upright and godly lives in this present age, while we wait for the blessed hope — the appearing of the glory of our great God and Saviour, Jesus Christ, who gave himself for us to redeem us from all wickedness and to purify for himself a people that are his very own, eager to do what is good" (Titus 2:11-14).

The world is crying out for solutions to huge problems: economic recession, climate change, poverty, fatherlessness, abuse, crime, addiction. Jesus came to purify for himself a people (the body of Christ) who will be eager to do what is good. As we remain plugged into Jesus, our source, our true vine, we can bear much fruit (John 15:4-6). The Gospel lived out emits a sweet fragrance which is attractive to spiritual seekers who are desperate for real answers.

Conclusion

Our prayer is that your time spent in this book has compelled you to new thinking, new practices and renewed vigour towards catalysing, sustaining and multiplying a disciple-making movement undergirded by love for God and our neighbours.

Discussion questions

1 Discuss what you have learnt about obedience as an obligation and obedience as a fruit of grace.
2 Have you experienced obedience as a community practice before? If not, why not? If yes, share some of these experiences with the group.

3   Is there some "request for obedience" that you have received from God that you have not yet obeyed? How should you and the community put action to it?

Scripture to study • James 1:19-27 • James 2:14-26

Books to read • Contagious Disciple Making, *by David Watson and Paul Watson* • The Cost of Discipleship, *by Dietrich Bonhoeffer* • The School of Obedience, *by Andrew Murray*

APPENDIX

Discovery Bible Study

Discovery Bible Study is a practical method of discovering what the Bible says about God, about us and about how God wants us to build his Kingdom. Getting clarity on what the Bible wants to say is essential. However, a quick surface reading will miss the enriching complexity of Scripture completely.

The Bible is not one consistent, monolithic volume. Rather, it is:
- A collection of letters, historical annals, poems, recorded oral traditions and other types of literature,
- written by about 40 different authors,
- over the course of 1,500-odd years (the most recent of which is around 2,000 years old),
- on three different continents,
- transcribed and translated multiple times,
- with divisions, chapters and most punctuation added much later, [112]
- compiled, amended, debated about and recompiled over the course of 400 years.

Then, to add to the diversity, the authors themselves:
- Are in very different geopolitical contexts,
- with unique biases and agendas,
- in various positions of influence,
- writing to people in different social and cultural settings,
- with different goals in mind.

You might be thinking, " How can I ever understand the Bible? It seems really hard!"
Well, yes. In a way it is. [113] [114]

The Bible is not a self-help guide or novel written by a 21st-century author who looks like you, speaks your language and shares your cultural understanding, metaphors and memes. It is a rich, complex, ancient library, further filtered by our own worldviews:

- A rich white Southern Baptist man will not interpret Scripture the same way a poor woman in rural Africa will.
- A Fortune 500 CEO will have a different lens to a professor of Theology or a migrant worker from an oppressed people group.

We should expect to be challenged by the Bible. Not just by the truth revealed by the Spirit, but also by the nuanced, diverse composition of texts that reveal an oppressed people's journey through time, seeking the face of God. Especially those of us living in the comfortable "conquering superpower" [115] of Western civilisation. When we ignore the way our perspective colours how we read the text, it can lead to ungodly nonsense like Scripture being used to support Apartheid, slavery, the subjugation and domination of women, and so on.

The point of this introduction is not to scare you or put you off reading the Bible. Rather, as we dive into the practical elements of doing a DBS, allow the framework below to soften your spirit and move you to a posture of awe and humility.

Doing A DBS

The session should start with a reflection on the previous week, because the practical application of the Bible message is essential. That is why we ask questions like:

- Did what you read last week shift anything in you? How did you respond?
- What changed your life as a result of last week's discovery?
- How did you apply last week's message?
- How did it go when you shared the message with someone?

After the time of reflection, we start the DBS. We want to be sensitive to the Spirit, hungry for a deeper understanding, and willing to wrestle with new perspectives and revelations.

Start the session by framing the focus passage as well as possible. Take note of:

- **Who the author was writing to, for example:**
  - The Jewish nation?
  - The gentiles?
  - The early church?
  - A specific individual or a community?
- **The purpose and literary style of the book:**
  - Is it sharing wisdom?
  - Is it historical recollection?
  - Is it prophecy?
- **The socioeconomic and political context of the intended audience:**
  - Are they being oppressed, or are they the oppressors?
  - Is there unity or are they scattered?
  - Is the audience familiar with Jewish history and culture or not?
- **The context of the passage within the chapter and book:**
  - Is the passage an idea on its own, or is it part of a larger idea?
  - Is the author or speaker using a literary device in the passage (i.e. a parable / metaphor / quotation of Scripture etc.)?
  - Does the passage agree with the theme of the surrounding chapter/book or appear to challenge it?
  - Does the theme of the chapter, section or book influence the meaning of the passage?
- **Is there anything in the original language or culture that influenced the translation, or how we should read this passage?**

- For example, Jeremiah 29:11 was written to a group of people under extreme oppression about being delivered, but only after a further 70 years in exile. [116]

Doing this thoroughly can take a lifetime, so, choose a few key points that Bible commentaries or articles online indicate are important.

Alternatively, if this framing process is enriching the group's understanding of Scripture or stimulating valuable discussion, consider allowing the whole session to be focused on the framing and do the following steps when you next meet.

Once we understand the context of the passage better, we re-phrase the passage in our own words. For this we:

- Read through the Bible passage on our own.
- Ask someone else in the group to rephrase the passage in their own words.
- Ask the others if anything essential was left out in the retelling of the story.

Then, four main groups of questions need to be asked:

1   What does the passage say about God, such as:
     - What does this passage reveal to us about the character of God (Father, Son or Holy Spirit) through what he says, does or doesn't do?
     - What promises or claims are made about or by God?
2   What does the passage say about humanity or our new life in Christ leading to personal transformation, such as:
     - Did the author or audience struggle with anything you can relate to? What are they doing about it?
     - What does this passage teach us about humanity?
     - What should we believe or do as followers of Jesus?
     - How should we relate to our "neighbours", especially people who are different to us (race, class, gender, economic status, authority, etc.)?

3   How should we respond to this message, personally and
    corporately?
    - Are there any changes we must make in our personal lives?
    - Are there any changes we should make as a community?
    - What should we do in the next 48 hours with what we have
      learnt from the DBS?
4   What and how should we share what we learned with
    someone else to start the process of reproduction?
    - Who are you going to share the passage with before we
      meet again?
    - What do you think would be the best way of sharing the
      message?
    - Is there a need in society or of an individual that we should
      address by the message of this passage?

ENDNOTES

1   https://www.thattheworldmayknow.com/rabbi-and-talmidim
2   Dallas Willard, *The Great Omission* (HarperCollins, 2006:4), emphasis original
3   Francis Chan, *Multiply* (David C. Cook, 2012:30)
4   Dietrich Bonhoeffer, *The Cost of Discipleship* (Macmillan Paperbacks Edition, 1979:98-99)
5   David Mathis, https://www.desiringgod.org/messages/the-cost-of-disciple-making
6   Andrew Murray, *Like Christ*
7   Ibid.
8   Ray Vander Laan, https://www.thattheworldmayknow.com/define-disciple
9   Rob Bell, https://offqueue.files.wordpress.com/2009/10/dust_rabbi.pdf
10 Mark Foreman, *Wholly Jesus* (Ampelon Publishing, 2008:32)
11 Mark Foreman, *Wholly Jesus* (Ampelon Publishing, 2008:38), emphasis original
12 Landa Cope, *An Introduction To The Old Testament Template* (The Template Institute Press, 2006:150-157)
13 Mark Foreman, *Wholly Jesus* (Ampelon Publishing, 2008:39), emphasis original
14 Richard Foster, *The Challenge of the Disciplined Life: Christian Reflections on Money, Sex, and Power* (HarperCollins, 1989)
15 For more on The Navigators, visit their website, http://www.navigators.org/Home
16 For more on the original Navigators Wheel, visit https://www.navigators.org/resource/the-wheel-illustration/
17 Richard Foster, *Prayer: Finding The Heart's True Home* (Hodder & Stoughton, 2008:xii)
18 Phyllis Tickle, *The Great Emergence: How Christianity Is Changing and Why* (Baker Books, 2012)
19 Erwin McManus, *An Unstoppable Force* (David C Cook, 2013:149)
20 http://www.englishmonarchs.co.uk/bruce_16.html
21 A Dictionary of the Bible: Volume III, Ed. James Hastings (The Minerva Group, Inc., 2004:153)
22 Steven Covey, *The 8th Habit: From Effectiveness to Greatness* (Simon and Schuster, 2013:165 - 180)
23 Roy Hession, *The Calvary Road* (Roy Hession Book Trust, 1950:40, OM Books Edition)
24 Roy Hession, *The Calvary Road* (Roy Hession Book Trust, 1950:24, OM Books Edition)
25 John Churton Collins, https://www.goodreads.com/author/quotes/7282.John_Churton_Collins
26 Richard Foster, *Celebration of Discipline* (Hodder & Stoughton, 1999:140)
27 Richard Foster, *Celebration of Discipline* (Hodder & Stoughton, 1999:151)
28 Martin B. Copenhaver, *Jesus Is the Question: The 307 Questions Jesus Asked and the 3 He Answered* (Abingdon Press, 2014)
29 Cassie Carstens, *The World Needs A Father: A Trainer's Guide* (2016:142)
30 Cassie Carstens, *The World Needs A Father: A Trainer's Guide* (2016:142 - 143)
31 Cassie Carstens, *The World Needs A Father: A Trainer's Guide* (2016:143)
32 Leonard Sweet, *So Beautiful* (David C Cook, 2009:18)
33 https://www.thegospelcoalition.org/blogs/jared-c-wilson/5-reasons-you-should-probably-leave-your-attractional-church/
34 David Watson & Paul Watson, *Contagious Disciple Making* (Thomas Nelson, 2014:5)
35 Alan Cross, *When Heaven and Earth Collide* (NewSouth Books, 2014:237)
36 George Bernard Shaw, *Man and Superman* (The Floating Press, 2012:30)
37 Cassie Carstens, *The World Needs A Father: A Trainer's Guide* (2016:81, 78)
38 Garth Hewitt, *Nero*
39 Timothy Keller, *Counterfeit Gods* (Hachette UK, 2010:xiv)

40 https://bit.ly/2WMXxLh
41 Rodney Stark, *The Rise of Christianity: A Sociologist Reconsiders History* (Princeton University Press, 1996:6 - 7)
42 http://www.prayforrevival.org.uk/encourager14.html
43 Landa Cope, *An Introduction To The Old Testament Template* (The Template Institute Press, 2006:147)
44 Michael W Goheen, *Reading the Bible Missionally* (Wm. B. Eerdmans Publishing, 2016:252)
45 The Lausanne Covenant, https://www.lausanne.org/content/covenant/lausanne-covenant
46 Mark Foreman, *Wholly Jesus* (Ampelon Publishing, 2008177)
47 As quoted in Michael Mayne, *A Year Lost and Found* (Parson's Porch Books, 2011:58)
48 Landa Cope, *An Introduction To The Old Testament Template* (The Template Institute Press, 2006:144 -165)
49 Jack Dennison, *City Reaching* (Jim Herrington) (William Carey Library, 1999:106)
50 https://bit.ly/2uKbU7a
51 Landa Cope, *An Introduction To The Old Testament Template* (The Template Institute Press, 2006:144 -165)
52 https://callingeducation.org.za
53 http://www.focusonthefamily.com, https://www.theworldneedsafather.com, https://familyfoundationsafrica.com, https://www.familiesforlife.sg
54 https://www.readysetgo.ec
55 http://foundationsforfarming.org/new
56 https://www.ywam.org
57 http://www.crown.org.za
58 https://www.lausanne.org/content/media-messages-matter-christ-truth-and-the-media
59 Erwin McManus, *The Barbarian Way* (Thomas Nelson, 2005:130)
60 Ibid.
61 Richard Rohr, *Immortal Diamond: The Search for Our True Self* (Jossey-Bass, 2013:27-29, 36)
62 Erwin McManus, *The Barbarian Way* (Thomas Nelson, 2005:16 - 17)
63 Andrew Murray, *Humility and Absolute Surrender* (Hendrickson Publishers, 2005:59), emphasis original
64 Andrew Murray, *Humility and Absolute Surrender* (Hendrickson Publishers, 2005:12)
65 Andrew Murray, *Humility and Absolute Surrender* (Hendrickson Publishers, 2005:7, 5)
66 Charles Haddon Spurgeon, *Spurgeon's Sermons* Volume 01: 1855 (Lulu.com, 2017:5)
67 https://cac.org/joy-2017-06-11/
68 C.S. Lewis, *Mere Christianity* (HarperCollins, 1980:128)
69 Andrew Murray, *Like Christ*
70 Gary Thomas, *Sacred Influence* (Zondervan, 2007:26 - 27)
71 Cassie Carstens, *The World Needs A Father: A Trainer's Guide* (2016:158)
72 Cassie Carstens, *The World Needs A Father: A Trainer's Guide* (2016:158 - 159)
73 Norm Wakefield, *Equipped to Love* (Elijah Ministries, 1999:2)
74 Donald G. Bloesch, *God the Almighty: Power, Wisdom, Holiness, Love* (InterVarsity Press, 2005:145)
75 Cassie Carstens, *The World Needs A Father: A Trainer's Guide* (2016:160-161)
76 Norm Wakefield, *Equipped to Love* (Elijah Ministries, 1999:4)
77 Cassie Carstens, *The World Needs A Father: A Trainer's Guide* (2016:161)
78 Rodney Stark, *The Rise of Christianity: A Sociologist Reconsiders History* (Princeton University Press, 1996:81 - 83)
79 Norm Wakefield, *Equipped to Love* (Elijah Ministries, 1999:9)

80   https://www.crossroadsinitiative.com/saints/quotes-from-blessed-mother-teresa-of-calcutta/

81   https://www.epm.org/resources/2010/Mar/12/charles-spurgeon-subject-god/

82   Paul C. Vitz, *Psychology as Religion: The Cult of Self-Worship* (Wm. B. Eerdmans Publishing, 1994)

83   Roy Hession, *The Calvary Road* (Roy Hession Book Trust, 1950:12, OM Books Edition)

84   Peter Scazzero, *Emotionally Spiritually Healthy* (Thomas Nelson, 2011)

85   Brad Huddleston, *Digital Cocaine* (Christian Art Publishers, 2016:223)

86   https://www.catholicculture.org/culture/library/view.cfm?recnum=6558

87   C.S. Lewis, *The Screwtape Letters* (HarperCollins, 1996:16)

88   Warren W. Wiersbe, *The Wiersbe Bible Commentary: New Testament* (David C. Cook, 2007:729)

89   https://bit.ly/2uLmbzC

90   J. I. Packer, *Knowing God* (Hachette UK, 2011:151)

91   Max Lucado, *In The Grip Of Grace* (Thomas Nelson, 2011:64)

92   Crowder, *"Forgiven,"* track 8 on American Prodigal (Deluxe Edition), sixstepsrecords/Sparrow Records, 2016

93   Ray Pritchard, https://www.crosswalk.com/church/pastors-or-leadership/repent-the-forgotten-doctrine-of-salvation-1430623.html

94   Dietrich Bonhoeffer, *The Cost of Discipleship* - SCM Classics (Hymns Ancient and Modern Ltd., 2001:4)

95   Dietrich Bonhoeffer, *The Cost of Discipleship* - SCM Classics (Hymns Ancient and Modern Ltd., 2001:5, emphasis original)

96   Dietrich Bonhoeffer, *The Cost of Discipleship* - SCM Classics (Hymns Ancient and Modern Ltd., 2001:20,21, emphasis original)

97   Richard Foster, *Prayer: Finding the Heart's True Home* (Hachette UK, 2012)

98   Søren Kierkegaard, *The Journals of Søren Kierkegaard* (Oxford University Press, 1959:522)

99   Dick Eastman, *The Hour That Changes the World* (Baker Books, 2002)

100 Richard Foster, *The Celebration of Discipline* (Hodder & Stoughton, 1999:24)

101 Dr. Caroline Leaf, *Switch on the Brain* (Baker Books, 2013:92)

102 Watchman Nee, *The Spiritual Man* (Christian Fellowship Publishers, 1977:35-36), emphasis original

103 Andrew Murray, *With Christ in the School of Prayer* (Hendrickson Publishers, 2007:180)

104 Richard Foster, *Celebration of Discipline* (Hodder & Stoughton, 1999:224)

105 Jim Wallis, *Agenda for Biblical People* (Harper & Row, 1976:23)

106 Matthew Henry, *Exposition of the Old and New Testament* (Barrington & Haswell, 1828:646)

107 David Watson & Paul Watson, *Contagious Disciple-Making* (Thomas Nelson, 2014:45)

108 Peter Maiden, *Discipleship* (Colorado Springs: Authentic, 2007:15), emphasis original

109 Dietrich Bonhoeffer, *The Cost of Discipleship* (Macmillan Paperbacks Edition, 1979:113)

110 Martin Luther, *The Early Years*, Christian History

111 Dietrich Bonhoeffer, *The Cost of Discipleship* (Macmillan Paperbacks Edition, 1979:99)

112 https://rsc.byu.edu/archived/king-james-bible-and-restoration/7-chapters-verses-punctuation-spelling-and-italics

113 The following articles give a great summary on the importance of biblical interpretation: https://bible.org/seriespage/lesson-6-principles-biblical-interpretation

114 https://biologos.org/common-questions/how-should-we-interpret-the-bible/

115 Brian Zahnd talks more about this in his excellent piece, https://brianzahnd.com/2014/02/problem-bible/.

116 https://relevantmagazine.com/god/stop-taking-jeremiah-2911-out-context/

NOTES

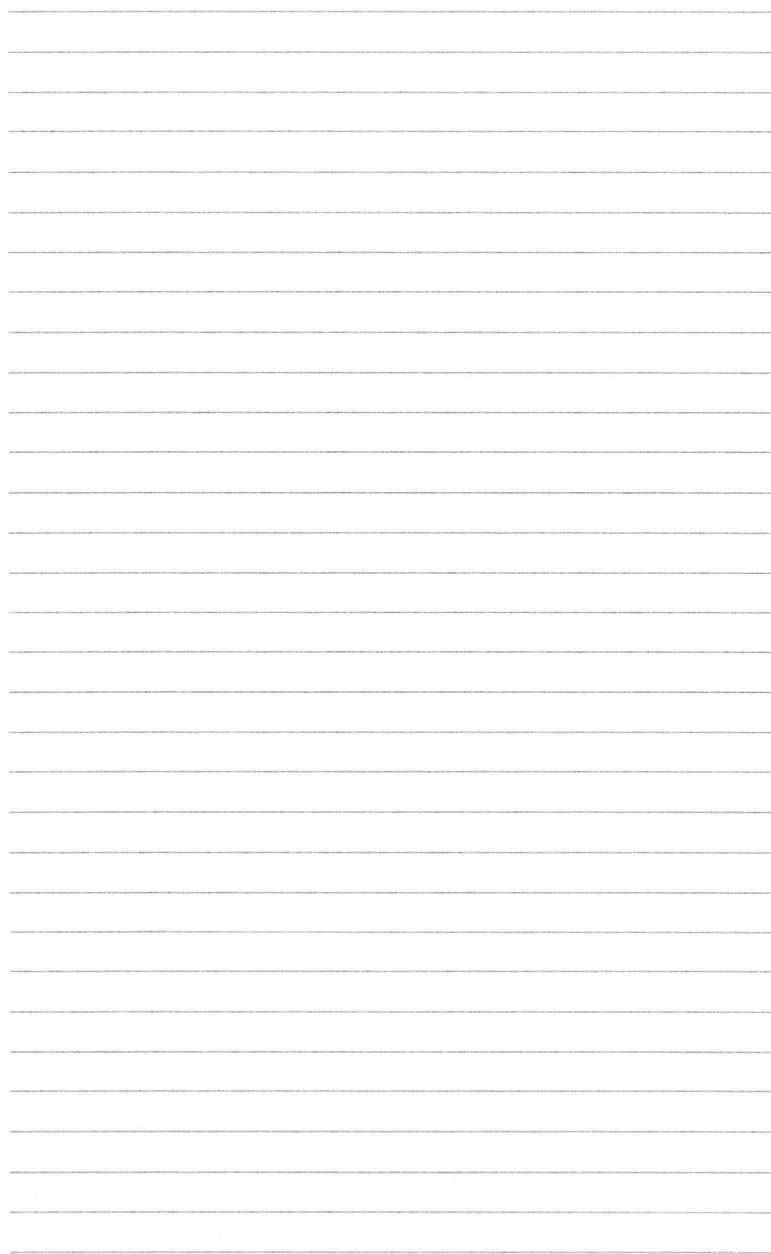

www.ingramcontent.com/pod-product-compliance
Lightning Source LLC
LaVergne TN
LVHW052013080426
835513LV00018B/2023